RAF SOUTHEND
1940–1944

PETER C. BROWN

To my wife Karen for her devotion and patience

Front cover photograph: 137 Squadron, 5 March 1943. (Rob Bowater)

First published 2012 by
Spellmount, an imprint of
The History Press
The Mill, Brimscombe Port
Stroud, Gloucestershire, GL5 2QG
www.thehistorypress.co.uk

British Library Cataloguing in Publication Data.
A catalogue record for this book is available from the British Library.

ISBN 978 0 7524 7003 0

Typesetting and origination by The History Press
Printed in Great Britain

CONTENTS

FOREWORD

War not only brings out the worst in us – it also encourages our better qualities. We never really know what is in us until tested; sometimes literally to destruction. Such was the Battle of Britain, in which RAF Southend helped to defend one of our most crucial sectors.

When I listened to Neville Chamberlain make his historic broadcast at 11 a.m. on 3 September 1939, I was a child of 10; perhaps a little precocious. We had all been expecting the worst. I received my own gas mask the previous year, read about Guernica, was warned that 'the bomber would always get through' and the need to create a refuge room. We had already floored out wet cellar as an air-raid shelter and made a pathetic attempt to camouflage the roof, due to our proximity to the aerodrome.

After the autumn and winter calm of the Phoney War while Hitler was getting his forces into position, the spring of 1940 brought a dramatic and disastrous change. First the loss of Norway, then the Blitzkrieg through the Low Countries and France, when Hitler made, in less than four weeks, conquests that had taken the Allies over four long years in the First World War.

We had not been wholly idle locally. There was a new searchlight in the field opposite our entrance, with a sandbag-encircled Lewis gun – the workings of which were explained to me. Just to our north at Canewdon, I used to cycle around some strange high wooden towers, subsequently joined by metal grid-like pylons. No one had yet told us about radar.

Our tranquil home was rapidly transformed as Southend Aerodrome became much closer to the enemy in flying time. Previously the aerodrome had been occupied by a few enthusiastic amateur pilots. There was also an Air Ferry with a twenty-minute flight across the Thames to Rochester. Suddenly we had become a front-line fighter station, the tip of the Hornchurch sword.

Our peace was shattered. Wing Commander Basil Embry, having just escaped from captivity in France, descended upon the aerodrome to knock it back into instant shape as a fighter station.

This included the requisitioning of our home as the Officers' Mess. We were given forty-eight hours to get out (fortunately stretched to seven days) but my parents still regarded Basil Embry as a charming gentleman! We moved into our rather basic lodge, without electricity, which had just been vacated by a platoon of the Black Watch, with their Bren carriers parked outside.

The pilots and their back-up quickly moved in. Nissen and wooden army huts with ablutions were built for the support staff, the stable yard was covered with camouflage netting and defences quickly emerged nearby. A troop of four 25-pounders was emplaced at Gusted Hall, a mile to the west, with their command wires running through our ditches. Anti-glider scaffold tripods sprouted in our open field (still there), facing down the road to the aerodrome. We all felt a little more secure.

The aerodrome was also getting its act together. It included a flak tower along the Eastwoodbury Lane with Bofors, more guns on the airfield, small boxes with rockets trailing wires in the path of attacking planes, strategically placed pillboxes around the perimeter and horseshoe-shaped revetments to protect the Spitfires on the ground.

I spent my school holidays at our lodge, in a cupboard-size bedroom, but loved every moment of it. We were guests at The Lawn for their 'Guests Nights', which were positive feasts, as the mess could fly in from far and wide food beyond our meagre rations. Understandably parties got a bit noisy later, when we discreetly departed. Our large dinner gong was used for revolver practice; a pilot was placed in the flowerbed without socks and then up-ended to walk over the ceiling, and there were the usual mess high jinks, all of which my parents philosophically tolerated. When sitting in the garden of our lodge, we used to see the dispersal trucks go down to the airfield, full of pilots. Sadly they did not all return.

Recently we received a knock on the door from an ex-pilot who had come 12,000 miles from Australia to look at his old billet. He immediately identified his old bed place. He had just returned from Holland, where his Spitfire had crashed in 1943 and recently been excavated – and he was very proud of the souvenir he was given for it.

I was fortunate enough to enjoy my first flight when Squadron Leader Valance, the CO, took me up for a twenty-minute flip in an Air Speed Oxford (a general work-horse) and had the exhilaration of taking the stick.

Looking back, one began to tolerate the war almost as a way of life. We were never actually frightened and certainly not even hungry. I think the war rations were brilliantly done and actually we were healthier on the wartime food than today. It also gave me an excuse at boarding school to come home early, where we had been sleeping in the shelter, to an even more dangerous area of our home under the blast path of the V1s and V2s.

There was little crime, except for the black market. Its proceeds were chicken feed to the spoils legitimately earned in today's financial markets. Generally we enjoyed a happier social climate, because everyone mucked in and helped each other. We also had a better social conscience and greater sense of discipline. National Service, which I thoroughly enjoyed, maintained this spirit through the 1950s.

Perhaps the heroism and self-sacrifice of the few had helped subconsciously to imbue us with a higher moral purpose.

David Keddie, 2012

INTRODUCTION

The Mass Evacuation of Southend

On 30 May 1940 the *Southend Standard* reported that the government had decided that in light of the fact that Holland and parts of Belgium and Northern France were in enemy occupation the following towns on the south-east coast were declared evacuation areas: Great Yarmouth, Lowestoft, Felixstowe, Harwich, Clacton, Frinton and Walton, Southend, Margate, Ramsgate, Broadstairs, Sandwich, Dover, Deal and Folkestone. Arrangements were made for those children whose parents wished them to be sent from these areas to safer districts in the Midlands and Wales.

On 6 June 1940 the *Southend Standard* reported that the first of Southend's 8,500 children to be evacuated were on their way to their schools and later, at half-hourly intervals from 7 a.m., long heavily laden trains steamed out of the central LMS station on route to the Midlands.

Tiny tots struggled with rucksacks or suitcases and junior boys and girls, high school and technical students in long 'crocodiles' marched from the marshalling ground in the station yard to the barriers and then along the platform as each train drew in. A ceaseless procession of Westcliff motor buses carried the children from the schools to the station where members of the Education Department, nurses, first-aid party workers and helpers shepherded them from their allotted places. The whole evacuation was a triumph for local organisation and with the railway staff carrying out their share so smartly the trains were always ready to leave at the scheduled time. With the majority of the pupils and the whole of the teaching staff away, the schools were closed.

A public poster dated 30 June 1940 was displayed:

PLEASE CONSIDER THIS: If evacuation of this town is ordered it may not be possible for you to take your pet animals in the train. Animals will be painlessly destroyed by competent persons.

This poster not only caused much alarm and distress to the owners of animals but frightened hundreds, if not thousands of people out of the town with their pets.

On 17 October 1940 the *Southend Standard* reported that there was no 'Intention of Re-Opening Southend's Schools'. It was definitely stated at the meeting of Southend Town Council that there was no intention of bringing the evacuated schoolchildren back to the borough and no possibility that any schools would be opened at Southend for the education of the children still in the town. The Probation Office had been urged to address the problem of hundreds of children running around the streets in this town with no provision whatsoever for their education.

Vulnerable Targets

THE EKCO WORKS

In August 1939 there was the usual throng of thousands of holidaymakers visiting Southend for a walk along the 1¼-mile-long pier, delighting in the amusement arcades, sampling the many public houses along the seafront, visiting the Kursaal, enjoying 'Old Leigh' and its many cockle sheds or simply relaxing on the miles of beach. In another part of the town, EKCO was busy with last-minute preparations for the annual Radiolympia exhibition where the company had high hopes for the show, especially since they were planning to exhibit along with their radios, for the first time on any scale, their full range of television sets; they hoped that a good show would provide continuity of employment for the 3,000 or so people working at the site in Priory Crescent.

Alas, during the course of the Radiolympia show, with the dark clouds of war gathering, the government announced that due to the international situation television broadcasts were being suspended with immediate effect and ten days later war was declared. This not only drove away the visitors from Southend but meant that EKCO, almost overnight, voluntarily ceased domestic radio and television work and made its entire production capability available to the government, which accepted the offer with thanks. Thus, in short order the company found itself manufacturing military Type 19 tank radios.

At the same time, the site at Southend was prepared for war with surface air-raid shelters being built at various locations around the site, including one long slit trench down the length of the site, these complementing the deep shelters, which had already been built under the buildings erected in 1938 in accordance with the Air Raid Precautions Act (1938). Very quickly the roofs of all the buildings were painted in camouflage paint and security barriers erected at all the entrances to the site.

Even during the Radiolympia show plans were made to purchase a secure site known as Cowbridge House, deep in the countryside of north Wiltshire for the top-secret work on airborne radar and VHF communications for the RAF.

Not all production moved away from Southend, however; the large plastics moulding machinery could not be moved, nor was the lamp manufacturing unit moved, which covertly had been turned over to the military valve manufacturers, whose products included the very specialised 'radar valves'. The plastics plant found itself working 24 hours a day making a wide variety of products, ranging from small Bakelite knobs to practice bombs.

At the time of Dunkirk (late May/early June 1940), with the Nazis having overrun Belgium and France (meaning that German aircraft could easily reach Southend which was only 100 miles away or less than half an hour flying time), the order was given by the Ministry of Aircraft Production (MAP) to evacuate the whole of the works and disperse the work to safer sites away from the risk of being bombed.

Canewdon Chain Home Radar Station

Radar, which was to play such a vital part in Britain's defence throughout the Second World War, but particularly during the Battle of Britain, had been developed in great secrecy during the mid-1930s at Canewdon, and was operational in 1938 as part of the country's Chain Home Station System.

'Chain Home' was a network of coastal stations which at that time was the most advanced early warning system in the world. By 1939 its coverage stretched from the Isle of Wight to the Scottish border, and it gave Fighter Command advanced warning of enemy aircraft approaching the English coast, making it possible for fighter aircraft to be guided to intercept them.

The station at Canewdon was sited in an area of 18 acres on the edge of the village off Gardeners Lane, which was acquired by the Air Ministry and was the fourth such station to be built in Britain. It comprised both a receiving and transmission site; the receivers were set in earth-covered concrete bunkers a few hundred yards north of the 360ft-tall triangular transmitter masts. It was a vulnerable target for aerial attack, and in an area of less than 1 square mile, at least twenty-one pillboxes and machine-gun emplacements were constructed to defend against an airborne assault.

Southend Aerodrome

The airfield was established as a landing ground for the Royal Flying Corps during the First World War. It was decommissioned in 1919 and the site reverted to farmland. The site reopened in 1935 as a civil airport. At the outbreak of the Second World War it was again requisitioned by the Air Ministry, and by 1940 it had become an important advance fighter station within 11 Group for RAF Hornchurch. The airfield was still grass surfaced, and was equipped with a mixture of Bellman and Blister aircraft hangars.

It was not a particularly good area to defend from enemy paratroop attack and aerial bombing. 'A' Infantry Coy covered the area surrounding the airfield from New Road to Warner's Bridge inclusive, and 'B' Infantry Coy covered from Avro Road exclusive to New Road inclusive.

The RAF Ground Defence Squadron consisted of LAA (Light Anti-Aircraft) Flight, AFV Flight, and PAC (Parachute and Cable) Detachment: the LAA troops were under the command of the anti-aircraft defence commander to engage enemy aircraft and in a secondary role to engage ground targets; the AFV Flight came under the direct command of the local defence commanders (LDCs) to engage and destroy enemy troops observed in the vicinity of the aerodrome; the PAC Detachment was prepared to fire rockets at enemy aircraft making low-level attacks on the aerodrome.

An RAF 'backers-up' squadron consisted of seven rifle flights and one Smith Gun Troop flight, which covered Warner's Bridge exclusive to Avro Road inclusive. 'F' Flight (backers-up squadron) came under command of 'A' Infantry Coy on 'Attack Alarm', and 'G' Flight (Smith Gun Troop) came under the direct command of the LDC.

Adjacent troops were the Reserve Battalion: 2 Platoon 'D' Coy (HG) and 9 Platoon 'B' Coy (HG) Essex.

Anti-aircraft defences on the aerodrome consisted of one troop of Light Anti-Aircraft (Royal Artillery) manning four Bofors guns.

Off-station, there were more than seven heavy anti-aircraft gun batteries around the area: Fisherman's Head, Ridgemarsh Farm and New Burwood on Foulness; and guns at Great Wakering and Sutton, Hawkwell and Rayleigh.

Troops under the command of the Reserve Battalion Area Command consisted of 1 Infantry Battalion, 'A' Battery of the Royal Artillery, and Rayleigh Coy, 1st Essex Battalion (HG).

Their Primary Defence Instructions on 'Stand-to' was the centre of the aerodrome. The intention was to defend it to the last, and if and when the aerodrome became in imminent danger of capture it would be destroyed and the troops would then be withdrawn under orders from the Reserve Battalion area commander.

The flying field had ten lines of pipes, five running east–west and five north–south. Each line had a number of intermittent lengths of pipes, each 60ft long, laid just below the surface and terminated at the surface at intervals of 85ft. The pipes were filled with blasting gelignite, and at each terminal point they were fixed with a short length of pipe set vertically in the ground and covered at ground level with a wooden tile painted white. A short length of waterproofed cortex with a detonator would make contact with the explosive and at the free end a paper clip was provided to connect the cortex lines. There were four igniting points (IPs), one at each corner of the flying field, and each IP had a wired electric detonator and primer, through which an electric current was introduced by exploders. The exploders would be carried into slit trenches about 100 yards away from the nearest pipe line. The cortex lines, which could not be used whilst the field was in use as it constituted an obstruction, would be run out and connected only on orders from higher authority if and when instructions were received to demolish the airfield.

Secondary to this were the areas in the south and west-north-west of the aerodrome, Rochford Hall and church, Doggets Farm, the west edge of the woods, and road junctions west and north-west of Rochford.

9 Platoon 'B' of Southend Coy (HG) Essex Regiment were posted to defend the east and south-east approaches to the aerodrome (and thus the EKCO Works) from Fleet Hall at Cuckoo Corner. At 'Action Stations' 33 Section would take up its position at Cuckoo Corner; 34 Section at New Hall; 35 Section at Temple Farm; and 36 Section at the rectory, with standing patrols in Temple Lane, the east of Sutton Road, and Sutton Hall.

Fifty pillboxes had also been constructed to protect the aerodrome, and three Picket Hamilton forts were sunk into the grass within the area of the landing strip. These were designed to be lowered to ground level while aircraft were operating, but to be raised when necessary by means of a hydraulic mechanism. The fort was manned by a crew of two with light machine guns.

The underground rooms of the Battle Headquarters, from which the defence of the airfield was coordinated, are still there today.

The two bituminous runways, 06/24 (1,605 x 37m) and 15/33 (1,131 x 27m), were laid using the method of soil stabilisation in 1955–56.

Acknowledgements

Station Logs and Squadron Operations Records Books consulted at the Public Record Office at Kew.

Bob Cossey (74 (F) Tiger Squadron Association)
Tom Dolezal (The Free Czechoslovak Air Force)
Geoff Faulkner (264 Squadron)
Aldon Ferguson (611 Squadron Association)
Major Jay S. Medves, MB, CD (Canadian Forces)
Captain Morgan Jones (402 Squadron, RCAF)

Valerie Cassbourn, Director, Histoire et Patrimoine
Bob North & Brian Rose (81 Squadron Association)
Derek Rowe (Southend Aircrew Association)
Henry Skinner (1312 ATC Squadron)
Jim Bell
Rob Bowater
Zdenek Hurt
David Keddie
Robert Ostrycharz
Chris Poole
Terry F. Smith
Robin McQueen

Special thanks to Dee Gordon for her advice and assistance.

1
1940

OCTOBER

28 OCTOBER

RAF Rochford, a satellite aerodrome of RAF Hornchurch in 11 Group, Fighter Command, was renamed as RAF Southend today, although Fighter Control remained with Hornchurch. (War Establishment No. WAR/FC/218 dated 28 October 1940.)

On formation of the Station Headquarters, Wing Commander B.E. Embry, DSO, AFC was posted to command (he had recently escaped capture after he was shot down in a Bristol Blenheim bomber over France). Flying Officer E. Dodd and Flying Officer A. Cairnie (attached from RAF Hornchurch) carried out administrative duties. Flight Lieutenant W.H.A. Monkton, MM and Pilot Officer E. Thursfield (attached from RAF Hornchurch) carried out duties of intelligence officer and ground defence officer respectively. Flying Officer R.L.G. Nobbs carried out medical duties on the station.

29 OCTOBER

264 Squadron arrived for night-flying duties; 'A' Flight flew in from RAF Martlesham Heath, and 'B' Flight from RAF Luton. They had suffered huge losses over the past months and their Boulton-Paul Defiants, which were no match for the Luftwaffe's Messerschmitt Me 109s, were withdrawn from front-line operations.

Sergeant Alexander MacGregor (109895) of 19 Squadron, from RAF Duxford, made a forced landing in Spitfire P7379.

30 OCTOBER

Personnel from various units began to arrive to complete the establishment. These airmen were accommodated in requisitioned houses in the locality. The Station Headquarters offices and station stores were situated on the aerodrome.

31 OCTOBER

The Battle of Britain is officially regarded as having come to an end on this date but it actually proved to be one of the quietest days in four months. It was ironic that the aeroplane, an offensive weapon, should win its first and greatest battle as a defender.

Throughout the day from 07.30hrs until dusk, reconnaissance and scattered bombing raids were made over East Anglia, Kent, Sussex, South Wales, Hampshire and Lancashire. Bombs were dropped on the airfields of Bassingbourne, Martlesham and Poling with further targets in the Monmouth and Newport areas also being attacked.

Without victory, the Second World War would have taken a different course; with air supremacy the German Army could have landed and the odds are that it would have succeeded as the British Army had not yet recovered after the Dunkirk evacuation. Britain could not have been the base for either the Allied air offensive against Germany or the Normandy landings that led to the liberation of Europe in 1944–45. The Battle of Britain was, therefore, not just a local, territorial success over the south of England in the summer of 1940, but one of the most significant conflicts of the Second World War and the only major, self-contained and absolutely decisive air battle in history.

The battle was over. The war was just beginning.

NOVEMBER

1 NOVEMBER
Group Captain Murlis Green, DSO, MC arrived for several days on duty in connection with Night Operations.

This station was in the process of formation. Flight Lieutenant Monkton was posted in for intelligence duties, and Pilot Officer A.D. Rutherford-Jones reported on posting for equipment duties.

2 NOVEMBER
Pilot Officer William Moore (77947) returned to 264 Squadron after a visit to Messrs Boulton & Paul and Lucas in connection with the manufacture of power-operated gun turrets.

4 NOVEMBER
Pilot Officer Gillespie joined the 264 Squadron on posting from 614 Squadron.

5 NOVEMBER
At 16.15hrs, Pilot Officer František Hradil (81889), a Czechoslovakian pilot of 19 Squadron, was shot down in flames during combat over Canterbury by a Bf 109E of I/JG26. His Spitfire (P7545) crashed into the sea close to Southend Pier. His body was found on 7 November and he was buried on 12 November in Sutton Road Cemetery (Plot R, Grave 12160), Southend-on-Sea. He was 28 years old.

6 NOVEMBER
Pilot Officers Kenwyn Sutton (36282), Eric Barwell (77454), Richard Gaskell (42832) and Peter Bowen (42481) of 264 Squadron carried out night patrols and Pilot Officer Hughes carried out a dawn patrol the next morning.

7 NOVEMBER
In the late afternoon, while on convoy protection, a Me 110 was sighted and destroyed 10 miles north-east of Rochford by a flight from 603 Squadron (operating from RAF Turnhouse).

9 NOVEMBER
One section – Pilot Officers Hugh Percy (74688) and Desmond Kay (42006), and Sergeant Arnold Lauder (48822) – of 264 Squadron carried out patrols in the morning, and Sergeant Cyril Ellery (78747) arrived to join the squadron on posting from 150 Squadron.

10 NOVEMBER

Night patrols were carried out by Squadron Leader George Garvin (34237), Flying Officer Ian Stephenson (72010), Pilot Officers Gerald Hackwood (42217), Richard Stokes (42027), Terence Welsh (42033), Flight Sergeant Edward Thorn (46957) and Sergeant Endersby of 264 Squadron.

12 NOVEMBER

Flying Officer D. Edwards arrived for engineering duties, and Flying Officer (Acting Squadron Leader) Harold 'Flash' Pleasance (37914), DFC was posted here for operations duties.

Night patrols were carried out by Squadron Leader Garvin, Flight Lieutenant Smith, Flying Officer Stephenson, Pilot Officers Robert Young (NZ40197) and Welsh, Flight Sergeant Thorn and Sergeant Endersby of 264 Squadron. Pilot Officer James Melvill (74681) carried out two night patrols.

14 NOVEMBER

Flying Officer Edwards (Engineering) was granted the acting rank of flight lieutenant. Flight Lieutenant Ernest Campbell-Colquhoun (39301) left 264 Squadron on posting. Squadron Leader Garvin carried out a test of experimental exhausts. Night patrols were carried out by Pilot Officers Melvill and Young; one patrol was carried out by Flight Lieutenant Edward Smith (90093) and Sergeant Godfrey Smith (1223091), Flying Officer Stephenson, Pilot Officers Welsh, Hackwood and Kay, and Flight Sergeant Thorn with Sergeants Endersby and Lauder.

15 NOVEMBER

Squadron Leader A.T.D. Sanders was posted in for operations duties. Flying Officers K.L.S. Nobbs and R. Cargill were posted here for medical duties, and Acting Flight Lieutenant E. Dodd was posted here from RAF Hornchurch for duty as adjutant. Pilot Officer Stokes left 264 Squadron on posting.

At 18.30hrs, Flight Lieutenant Samuel Thomas (42029), and Pilot Officers William Knocker (74333) and Bowen of 264 Squadron took off for night patrols. Knocker's aircraft, Defiant N1547, caught fire in mid-air and, after an unsuccessful attempt to land down wind before another attempt could be made, hit a tree and crashed on Rochford golf course, adjacent to the aerodrome. The wrecked aircraft burst into flames, but Knocker managed to crawl away quickly from his blazing cockpit whereupon he then passed out. His gunner, Pilot Officer Frank Albert Toombs, was trapped inside the gun turret. Two soldiers in the vicinity ran up to the crashed aircraft and reportedly could see Toombs struggling inside the gun turret as flames from the fire licked around him, but did not attempt to rescue him.

Many more minutes were to pass before the station medical officer (SMO) arrived on the scene to find the air-gunner still trapped within the gun turret, and that he was now hideously burned.

Showing commendable bravery the SMO pulled Toombs from the inferno and dispatched him with haste to hospital where medical staff worked frantically to treat his terrible burns. Sadly, Frank succumbed to his wounds and died two days later.

18 NOVEMBER

'The Lawn' in Hall Road, Rochford, was requisitioned by the RAF as the Officers' Mess.

19 NOVEMBER
Pilot Officer Rutherford-Jones was promoted to flying officer. Pilot Officer Hughes and Sergeant Lauder of 264 Squadron carried out a night patrol.

20 NOVEMBER
Flight Lieutenant Smith of 264 Squadron carried out two night patrols. Flying Officers Stephenson, Young, Welsh, Melvill and Haigh carried out one patrol, as did Flight Sergeant Thorn and Sergeant Endersby. Pilot Officer Hackwood and his gunner, Pilot Officer Alexander Storrie (43641), were killed shortly after taking off on patrol when their Defiant (N1626) crashed east of Blatches Farm, Rochford.

21 NOVEMBER
Flight Lieutenant Smith, Flying Officer Stephenson, Pilot Officers Young, Welsh, Haigh, Melvill, Flight Sergeant Thorn and Sergeant Endersby of 264 Squadron carried out night patrols.

22 NOVEMBER
Pilot Officer C.H.B. Bassett was posted here for accounting duties.

23 NOVEMBER
Acting Pilot Officer H.M. Friend was posted here for equipment duties. The Station Headquarters moved to the offices in 'Greenways' in Hall Road, Rochford.

Squadron Leader Phillip Sanders (36057) arrived to assume command of 264 Squadron.

Flying Officer Sutton and Pilot Officers Gaskell, Frederick Hughes (74706), Percy, Barwell and Curtis of 264 Squadron carried out night patrols. Pilot Officer Hughes observed a searchlight intersection in the vicinity of Braintree and climbed to 7,000ft to investigate. When approaching he noticed at the exact height but 50 yards ahead of the intersection the exhaust flames of a Heinkel III. He engaged it at once as the enemy aircraft was travelling at a much greater speed than his Defiant, and a two-second burst by his gunner Sergeant Fred Gash (146840) destroyed one engine, but unfortunately the turret jammed and at that moment the Defiant was illuminated by three searchlights. At a range of 50 yards from the enemy aircraft Hughes instructed Sergeant Gash to press the trigger while he attempted to manoeuvre the machine so that incendiary bullets struck the Heinkel. In this manoeuvre the aircraft almost collided. The enemy aircraft was again engaged as it crossed the coast and was seen to be losing height rapidly.

24 NOVEMBER
Pilot Officer Gillespie left 264 Squadron on posting and was replaced by Pilot Officer Hallet.

25 NOVEMBER
Pilot Officer J.S. Wood was posted in for code and cypher duties.

26 NOVEMBER
Flight Lieutenant Smith of 264 Squadron carried out two night patrols; Flying Officer Stephenson, Pilot Officers Young, Haigh, Melvill, Curtis, Flight Sergeant Thorn and Sergeant Endersby carried out one patrol.

27 NOVEMBER
264 Squadron left for RAF Debden, continuing their night patrols.

28 NOVEMBER
Pilot Officer T.F. Frost reported for account duties on posting with effect from (w.e.f.) 18 November 1940. He was granted the acting rank of flight lieutenant.

29 NOVEMBER
Acting Pilot Officer C.F. Colyer was posted here for administrative duties with R & R Section. Pilot Officers B. Hale and T.J. Moffatt arrived for defence duties.

DECEMBER

1 DECEMBER
Pilot Officer (Acting Flight Lieutenant) E. Thursfield was posted in from RAF Hornchurch. Wing Commander Embry visited RAF Castle Camps to inspect the aerodrome and accommodation.

3 DECEMBER
Acting Squadron Leader Pleasance, DFC attended a conference at Headquarters, 11 Group.

4 DECEMBER
603 (City of Edinburgh) Squadron arrived from RAF Hornchurch, with operational and flying practice starting the following day. This continued until the 13th, when the squadron was moved to RAF Drem. However, they left without Sergeant Pilots Stone and Strawson, who were admitted to Southend Hospital as a result of a motorcycle accident.

5 DECEMBER
603 Squadron carried out operational and practice flying every day until the 13th.

6 DECEMBER
Wing Commander Embry was posted to Headquarters, 12 Group, for Air Staff Night Operations. Pilot Officer A.L. Clow was posted here for duty as adjutant.

13 DECEMBER
At 20.00hrs, officers and around twenty airmen from 611 Squadron arrived by road in private vehicles from RAF Digby. Pilot Officer Clow was posted to 66 Squadron.

The main party of 603 Squadron moved out by train late in the evening to RAF Drem.

14 DECEMBER
At 01.00hrs, a special train carrying the ground party for 611 Squadron arrived at Rochford. Billeting had been organised in empty houses in varying distances up to 3 miles away from this station.

At 13.00hrs, seventeen Spitfires of 611 Squadron landed here, and transport aircraft and five 10-ton trucks arrived during the afternoon carrying more airmen and stores.

Pilot Officers William Assheton (41979), Donald Stanley (83271), and Sergeants Reginald Breeze (516456) and Dudley Gibbins (754428) reported to 611 Squadron on posting from 222 Squadron.

15 DECEMBER
A heavy mist grounded all aircraft today.

16 DECEMBER
Another misty day with no operational flying. 603 Squadron aircraft were also still weather-bound. Pilot Officer Smith re-joined 611 Squadron from sick leave and Flight Sergeant Venn and sixteen others of the rear party arrived by train from RAF Digby, completing the move of the squadron, apart from a few men still on sick leave. Squadron Leader Frederick Hopcroft reported on posting (supernumerary) from 57 OTU, Hawarden.

17 DECEMBER
A fine day today; 603 Squadron finally left for RAF Drem. Two patrols were carried out by 611 Squadron; all aircraft returned without incident.

18 DECEMBER
A misty day; no flying.

19 DECEMBER
A fair day but with a good deal of cloud. One long patrol was carried out in the afternoon by 611 Squadron, above the clouds, on which Blue Section landed at RAF Manston for fuel before returning. Spitfire X4589, recently damaged at RAF Sutton Bridge and repaired there, was collected by one of the pilots, bringing the complement to eighteen aircraft.

20 DECEMBER
An air-raid alarm sounded in the morning; gun posts were manned and opened fire on a lone Dornier which appeared below cloud at about 1,000ft for a few seconds. One aircraft from 611 Squadron went up on a short local patrol afterwards, returning with nothing to report.

Flight Lieutenant A. Cairnie left on attachment to the Officers School at RAF Loughborough.

21 DECEMBER
At 10.40hrs, 611 Squadron took off to rendezvous with 64 Squadron from RAF Hornchurch, and patrolled over the Maidstone patrol line. One section was detached to chase a Dornier over the Thames Estuary, and in fact the whole of the two squadrons intercepted and gave chase. Several pilots landed elsewhere for fuel before returning home, but not all without incident: Pilot Assheton, in Spitfire P9335, taxiing after refuelling at RAF Lympne, sank in a soft patch in a filled bomb crater, damaging the propeller. Flight Lieutenant Barrie Heath (90818) in Spitfire X4644 was about to make an emergency landing in a field near Rye with only 3 gallons showing on his fuel gauge when his engine packed up. He had to land, wheels down, in a ploughed field, but overturned after hitting a bump. The aircraft was severely damaged. Both pilots

returned to Southend by train. As if by providence, Spitfire X4662 had been delivered to the squadron the same day by a ferry pilot.

Pilot Officer J. McCubbin was posted here for defence duties.

22 DECEMBER
At 10.40hrs 611 Squadron was ordered to take off and patrol over the base at 10,000ft. On emerging from cloud at 5,000ft the port wing of P9429 (flown by Sergeant Peter Townsend) touched the rudder and tail fin of R6914 (flown by Flying Officer Pollard), cutting pieces off it. Both aircraft landed safely without further damage.

23 DECEMBER
A cold day with cloud. This change for the worse in the weather continued until the 27th. No flying was done.

Pilot Officer Moffatt was attached to the Anti-Gas School at Rollestone Camp for a course.

Earl's Hall Garage, Southend, was taken over for use as the station workshops.

27 DECEMBER
After a quiet Christmas Day, two aircraft of 611 Squadron, while on practice flights, were vectored towards a raider, and Sergeant Leigh got in a shot at it, but without apparent results. At midday, the whole squadron was sent up for an hour on patrol over the area.

Pilot Officer B.C. Sparrowe was posted here for duty as assistant adjutant, and Wing Commander J.M. Thompson, DFC was posted in to command RAF Southend.

28 DECEMBER
A hazy day meant no operational flying was done.

29 DECEMBER
A clear day; 611 Squadron carried out convoy patrols during which two of the pilots shot at and damaged a Dornier. Pilot Officer Assheton left the squadron for Central Flying School (CFS), Upavon, on posting on an instructor's course. Flight Sergeant E. Lewis (560863), who had been with the squadron since 1936, received promotion to temporary warrant officer w.e.f. 1 December 1940.

30 DECEMBER
Poor visibility; no operational flying was done.

31 DECEMBER
A few short patrols were carried out in the morning. A new War Establishment (WAR/FC/228 dated 16 December 1940) reduced the pilot establishment from twenty-six to twenty-three, and raised the ground staff from 160 to 166. The principle changes were in the Signal Section, with the introduction of electricians, radio telephony operators, and wireless mechanics, and the deletion of wireless & electrical mechanics and wireless operators. A flight sergeant equipment assistant came in and there were other minor changes.

2

1941

JANUARY

1 JANUARY

A very cold morning; one section of 611 Squadron carried out a convoy patrol at midday. A little later another section took off on an 'X' raid, followed by the rest of the squadron on a standing patrol over Gravesend, although nothing was sighted.

The New Year's Honours List contained the name of the 'old boy' of the squadron, Squadron Leader P. Salter, who had been awarded the AFC. The CO also posted a list of nicknames that had been allocated following suggestions some months ago: 'Charlie Two' Hopcroft, 'Lofty' Langley, 'Drunken Duncan' (Pilot Officer W.G.G.D. Smith), 'Tweakie' Askew, 'Singapore' Stanley, 'Tubby' Garrett, 'Mushroom' (Sergeant N.J. Smith), 'Limshilling' Limpenny, 'Tubby' Townsend, 'Dai' Williams, and 'Gubbins' Gibbins.

Acting Squadron Leader Pleasance, DFC was posted to Headquarters, 12 Group, and Flying Officer Nobbs was posted to 66 Squadron.

2 JANUARY

A cold morning with a dusting of snow over the aerodrome. Two short test flights were carried out, but no other Spitfire flying took place today. Warrant Officer Lewis left the squadron to take up a posting at the Aircraft Gun Mounting Establishment at Duxford.

3 JANUARY

Another cold day. At 08.25hrs, one aircraft of 611 Squadron carried out a lone patrol, but there was no other operational flying. Spitfire X4547 was returned to the squadron after repairs carried out at RAF Digby.

Acting Flight Lieutenant D. Edwards was posted from this station to RAF Wittering, and Flight Lieutenant J.L.W. Walls (Medical) and Flying Officer J. McIntosh (Engineering) were posted in. Flight Lieutenant Walls was granted the acting rank of squadron leader upon his arrival. Flying Officer Cargill was posted to 145 Squadron.

4 JANUARY

Snow still on the ground; one section of 611 Squadron flew a patrol in the morning, and returned with nothing to report.

Pilot Officer J. Sutton (90758) joined the squadron on attachment from RAF Digby, after a period of sickness. Flying Officer J. McIntosh was granted the acting rank of flight lieutenant.

5 JANUARY

A milder morning, but no signs of a thaw yet; some practice flying was done by aircraft of 611 Squadron. Pilot Officer T.J. Moffatt returned from attachment to Rollestone Camp.

6 JANUARY

A freeze-up again followed by more snow. Two aircraft from 611 Squadron carried out a local patrol, but visibility was too bad for them to see if anything else was flying.

7 JANUARY

The sky was overcast for much of the day and no flying was done, but at around tea time, three Lewis and three Hispano guns of Ground Defence opened fire (without success) on a lone enemy aircraft as it attacked the aerodrome. It dropped eight bombs (thought to be 50kg), three of which fell on the aerodrome. There were no casualties sustained and although the attack resulted in three craters, the aerodrome remained serviceable.

8 JANUARY

Although there were signs of a slight thaw in the afternoon, no flying was done today.

9 JANUARY

A clear and bright, if somewhat cold morning; one section of 611 Squadron carried out a local patrol and later in the morning the squadron patrolled over the Maidstone line.

10 JANUARY

At 12.00hrs, 611 Squadron took off to join other fighter squadrons escorting six Bristol Blenheims on an offensive sweep behind Calais. Light anti-aircraft fire was experienced, some of which made a hole in the tailplane of Squadron Leader Hopcroft's aircraft. 'A' Flight, led by Squadron Leader Ernest Bitmead (34139), put in some ground strafing near Wissant on the way home. The CO made an amendment to the list of nicknames he had posted on 1 January; against Hopcroft he deleted 'Charlie Two' and substituted 'Ack-Ack Charlie'.

Flight Lieutenant Cairnie returned to the base for a ten-day attachment (until the 20th) from RAF Loughborough.

11 JANUARY

A slight improvement in the weather; thaw set in overnight and most of the snow was cleared by the morning. Two short patrols were carried out by aircraft of 611 Squadron, but returned with nothing to report.

12 JANUARY

One patrol and some local flying practice were carried out by 611 Squadron.

13 JANUARY

No operational flying was done until the 16th owing to bad weather.

14 JANUARY

Squadron Leader Hopcroft, DFC left 611 Squadron on posting to RAF Hawkinge to command 91 Squadron, latterly known as 421 Flight.

16 JANUARY
With a break in the weather, some local flying practice was carried out by 611 Squadron.

17 JANUARY
Some uneventful patrols were carried out by 611 Squadron including one over a convoy of sixty-four ships in line astern. Temporary Squadron Leader Eric Michelmore (37112) reported to the squadron on posting supernumerary for flying duties from 57 OTU, Hawarden.

18 JANUARY
More snowfall overnight meant no flying was done today.

19 JANUARY
A heavy thaw overnight with some rain; during a convoy patrol in the morning by 611 Squadron, pilots caught a glimpse of an enemy aircraft, but took no action because of dense cloud. Squadron Leader Hopcroft, DFC arrived back from RAF Hawkinge on reposting to the squadron.

20 JANUARY
Rain and thaw all day; the aerodrome had become bogged and unserviceable – no flying was done. Temporary Squadron Leader Michelmore left 611 Squadron for RAF Biggin Hill, on attachment to 74 Squadron, pending posting.

21 JANUARY
A mild day with some drizzle; 611 Squadron carried out local patrols by a succession of single aircraft. Instructions were received that the squadron would be moving to RAF Hornchurch on Monday the 27th, exchanging with 64 Squadron.

22 JANUARY
A fair day; during flying practice in the morning, Pilot Officer Smith was vectored by Operations in chase of a bandit, but did not get the opportunity to engage it. Sergeant Eric Limpenny (189635) was on his take-off run in Spitfire X4620 when it sank in a filled bomb crater and nosed up, causing damage to the propeller and one oleo leg. Sergeant Limpenny was unhurt.

23 JANUARY
Mist and low cloud limited flying; one aircraft of 611 Squadron started a local patrol, but returned at once owing to severely reduced visibility.

24 JANUARY
A heavy mist and visibility reduced to no more than 200 yards meant there was no flying.

25 JANUARY
No flying again owing to heavy mist. Sergeant Limpenny went to Halston Hospital for diagnosis.

26 JANUARY
Again a very misty day; one aircraft of 611 Squadron went on patrol and returned with nothing to report.

27 JANUARY
Four thirty-two-seater coaches and four 3-ton lorries arrived last night from the Transport Pool at Cambridge, and a similar convoy went to RAF Hornchurch. At 09.00hrs the Southend vehicles loaded up with the first road party, consisting of half of each flight and section. They arrived at RAF Hornchurch at around 10.45hrs.

Meanwhile a similar half of 64 Squadron was brought here by the Hornchurch vehicles. At 13.00hrs, each convoy was reloaded for a return journey with the second halves of the squadrons. A few extra vehicles from Station Transport assisted with baggage and gear. The move proceeded with extreme smoothness, and transporting the men in this manner, both squadrons remained fully operational throughout the move.

The dispersal points at the aerodrome were manned from dawn by personnel of 611 Squadron detailed for the second road party. They were relieved about midday by the first arrivals of 64 Squadron from RAF Hornchurch where there was a similar change over. The aircraft were changed one section at a time; flying conditions were extremely difficult. By 17.00hrs the move of both squadrons was compete. The squadron strength at the end of the month was eighteen officers and 236 other ranks.

FEBRUARY

2 FEBRUARY
At 09.30hrs, eleven Spitfires of 64 Squadron took off on patrol over the English Channel but no contact with the enemy was made, and they landed back here at 11.05hrs, but without three of their aircraft which had to make forced landings through lack of fuel. Sergeant Tony Cooper in Spitfire P4690 went down 1 mile north-west of Eastchurch, Sergeant Allan in Spitfire P4448 went down near Faversham, Kent, and Pilot Officer Percival Beake (84923) in Spitfire P4626 went down at Shepherd's Well, Kent.

3 FEBRUARY
Eight Spitfires of 64 Squadron took off on patrol between 11.45hrs and 15.45hrs, but no contact with the enemy was made and all aircraft returned safely.

4 FEBRUARY
Spitfires of 64 Squadron carried out patrols in twos and threes between 13.50hrs and 17.50hrs, but all returned with nothing to report.

5 FEBRUARY
64 Squadron carried out uneventful patrols between 09.55hrs and 17.10hrs.

9 FEBRUARY
At 10.00hrs, three Spitfires of 64 Squadron took off on the first of the day's patrols. Squadron Leader James Rankin (37210) in P4502, Pilot Officer John Rowden (83249) in P4605, and Sergeant Thomas Savage (105167) in P4448 sighted and engaged a

Ju 88, shooting it down. Rowden's Spitfire was damaged by return cannon fire, being hit in the windscreen and starboard wing. Further patrols were made throughout the day until 17.05hrs but no further incidents were reported.

10 FEBRUARY
Standing patrols were carried out by 64 Squadron between 09.35hrs and 15.30hrs; all aircraft returned with nothing to report.

11 FEBRUARY
Six aircraft of 64 Squadron carried out patrols from 13.00hrs, returning at 14.40hrs with nothing to report.

13 FEBRUARY
Two patrols were carried out by 64 Squadron today, the aircraft returning with nothing to report.

14 FEBRUARY
At 11.25hrs, eleven aircraft of 64 Squadron took off on patrol. Enemy aircraft were sighted and some engagement took place, but with no confirmed damage to the enemy. Pilot Officer John Lawson-Brown (82692) made a forced landing 1 mile east of Hawkinge after combat, with bullets in the engine, starboard mainplane and fuselage. The other ten aircraft of the squadron returned safely, landing at 12.45hrs.

At 12.20hrs, one aircraft took off on a patrol and landed twenty-five minutes later with nothing to report. At 15.05hrs, nine aircraft took off on patrol and returned after about seventy minutes, again with nothing to report.

15 FEBRUARY
A patrol by two aircraft of 64 Squadron was carried out at 15.35hrs, and at 16.25hrs eleven aircraft took off on a sweep over the Channel, but returned without incident.

16 FEBRUARY
Standing patrols were carried out by 64 Squadron during daytime from today until the 22nd, but all had nothing of worth to report.

17 FEBRUARY
Wing Commander J.M. Thompson, DFC attended Buckingham Palace for Investiture by HM the King. Pilot Officer R.E. Smith was posted here for signals duties.

22 FEBRUARY
Pilot Officer J. McCubbin was attached to No. 1 GOGS Ronaldsway, for a gunnery course.

23 FEBRUARY
At 08.00hrs, three aircraft of 64 Squadron took off on a convoy patrol, but only one returned at 08.50hrs. The other two Spitfires failed to return; Pilot Officer Hawkins in Spitfire P7778 and Pilot Officer John Gilbert Pippet (86347) are believed to have collided.

25 FEBRUARY
Standing patrols were carried out during the day by 64 Squadron from today until
6 March, but had nothing worth reporting.

MARCH

1 MARCH
Acting Squadron Leader J. Walls (Medical Officer) was posted to 58 OTU,
Grangemouth.

6 MARCH
Following the second patrol of the day by 64 Squadron at 17.40hrs, Pilot Officers John
Rowden (83249) and Alfred Tidman (86345) crashed on landing back at base owing to
poor visibility. Neither pilot sustained injury; both aircraft were assessed and categorised 'B' (see Glossary).

7 MARCH
Standing patrols were carried out during the day by 64 Squadron but it was still very
quiet with nothing to report.

8 MARCH
Following the standing patrols carried out today by 64 Squadron, Flight Sergeant
Maurice Choron (30501) crashed on landing back at base, causing serious damage to
his aircraft, which was assessed and categorised 'E'.

9 MARCH
Standing patrols were carried out during the day by 64 Squadron but with nothing
to report.

10 MARCH
Twelve aircraft of 64 Squadron took off on an offensive sweep at 14.45hrs, but
returned with nothing to report. A Servicing Echelon was formed from personnel of
64 Squadron. Acting Wing Commander J.M. Thompson, DFC reverted to the rank of
squadron leader.

11 MARCH
Standing patrols were carried out during the day by 64 Squadron but with nothing
to report.

12 MARCH
Standing patrols were carried out during the day by 64 Squadron but there was nothing of note to report. Squadron Leader J.M. Thompson, DFC left this station by road
to attend a Headquarters, 11 Group Conference at RAF North Weald.

13 MARCH
Twelve aircraft of 64 Squadron took off at 14.10hrs on a sweep and were at 31,000ft over
Boulogne when they were 'jumped' by ten Me 109s diving from 35,000ft. The enemy

aircraft dived but never below the squadron. The squadron turned to engage but only Sergeant Slade got in a burst. The enemy aircraft maintained the advantage of height and the squadron could only evade the shallow dives. As soon as the enemy aircraft were attacked they rolled and dived away at great speed. When the squadron returned it was found that the leader, Squadron Leader Aeneas MacDonnell (33120), DFC was missing in Spitfire P7555. (He was shot down near Calais and had baled out, but was captured, spending the rest of the war as a prisoner of war. He was freed in April 1945.)

Pilot Officers Rowden and Watson took off at 19.05hrs on a moonlight patrol which was uneventful.

Pilot Officer Watson crashed his Spitfire (P7811) on landing back at base.

14 MARCH
At 11.40hrs, one patrol was carried out by 64 Squadron during the day but closing weather prevented any other flying.

15 MARCH
Bad weather grounded all aircraft today. Flight Lieutenant G.P. Kerr was posted here from RAF Hornchurch to command the station, replacing Squadron Leader J.M. Thompson, DFC.

18 MARCH
No flying today. Flight Lieutenant G.P. Kerr was granted the acting rank of squadron leader, and took over from Squadron Leader J.M. Thompson, DFC who was being posted to RAF Debden pending posting to RAF Castle Camps. In the two months that Squadron Leader Thompson had been at this station, he had carried out a large number of improvements and arranged for the siting of new buildings. Considerable progress had been made in the development of the land available for the cultivation of vegetables. Every section had been given a plot and prizes instituted for the best plot.

20 MARCH
Another quiet and relatively uneventful day for 64 Squadron. Squadron Leader J.M. Thompson, DFC proceeded to RAF Debden.

21 MARCH
Acting Squadron Leader Barrie Heath (90818) was posted from 611 Squadron to command 64 Squadron, replacing Squadron Leader MacDonnell, DFC.

23 MARCH
The station commander officially commended over the tannoy system the action of Corporal A. Nunn (530990) for his courage and devotion to duty during an incendiary attack on the district where he was billeted. The conduct of Corporal Nunn had been officially reported by the chief warden of Ashingdon.

25 MARCH
Standing patrols were carried out during the morning by 64 Squadron but nothing occurred worth reporting.

The AO C-in-C Air Marshal William Sholto-Douglas, CB, MC, DFC arrived by a de Havilland Flamingo, escorted by a section of Spitfires at 09.45hrs to inspect the station. He spent some time talking to pilots in the rest room and then toured the dispersal points and buildings on the camp. He left by air, escorted by one section of 64 Squadron at 11.00hrs.

At 14.05hrs, three aircraft of 64 Squadron were scrambled but no contact was made with enemy aircraft.

26 MARCH

At 13.05hrs, aircraft of 64 Squadron were scrambled but no contact was made with enemy aircraft.

Wing Commander L. Wynne-Tyson succeeded Wing Commander Harrison, Group Headquarters 'P' Staff, who visited the station. The heavy reduction in the establishment, particularly in connection with the posting of the Officer in Charge of Messing, was discussed.

28 MARCH

Standing patrols were carried out by 64 Squadron during the day but all returned with nothing to report.

29 MARCH

Wing Commander A.D. Farquhar, DFC returned to RAF Hornchurch after nearly a week's attachment to this station.

31 MARCH

A sweep which was to involve 64 Squadron was called off owing to bad weather closing in over the French coast. The squadron moved out later in the day.

54 Squadron, commanded by Squadron Leader Robert Boyd (90165), DFC and Bar arrived at this station today.

APRIL

1 APRIL

54 Squadron was released for training all day, and in the evening there was a complete release of the camp.

Pilot Officer B. Hale was posted to RAF Hunsdon.

2 APRIL

54 Squadron was released for training today, the weather becoming unsettled and producing some gales which meant very little flying was carried out.

At 14.00hrs, the Smith Gun Troop (station personnel) proceeded to the Rifle Range, Rochford, for firing practice. The troop consisted of one NCO and eight men.

Pilot Officer A.J. Terry was appointed Station Sports Officer of RAF Southend.

3 APRIL

54 Squadron was released for training, but there were still just over eighteen hours of operational flying carried out. The day was marred by an accident to Sergeant Thompson. He was one of a pair of Spitfires on a shipping patrol, and was taking off in Spitfire P7610 towards the hangar when there was a terrific crashing sound,

and it was soon discovered that he had hit the top of the hangar and had gone clean through both sides. It would have seemed impossible that there could be anything left of the machine, and it certainly appeared to be a miracle that anyone could live through it. However, everyone was glad (and amazed) to see that Thompson was alive, although seriously injured. The machine was scattered throughout the hangar, with pieces of wing, tail and guns strewn all over the place. It is a great compliment to the manufacturers of the Spitfire that the frame stood up so well to the crash, and had it not been for the protection of the engine in front, Thompson would most certainly have been killed.

Unfortunately two airmen who were working on an aircraft in the hangar were also seriously injured when the crash took place, one of whom died of his injuries later in the evening.

4 APRIL
Flying Officer F.F.W. Chitty was posted here.

5 APRIL
The clocks advanced this morning to Double-Summer Time. Readiness was now extended from 06.00hrs to 21.30hrs.

6 APRIL
The squadron adjutant (Flying Officer Petley) arrived to take up his duties once again. He was welcomed back after his long illness. In the morning, 54 Squadron was released for training and practice dog fights were carried out. In the afternoon, the squadron was at readiness, but owing to poor weather, nothing much happened apart from practice firing at Dengie Flats, where the squadron fired 36,325 rounds.

7 APRIL
A wing practice flight by 54 Squadron was carried out in the morning, followed by a standing patrol in the afternoon. This latter patrol, in 8/10ths cloud and a fairly strong wind, was a 'Westminster Patrol', as the object was to afford protection to any raid which might be coming in to bomb the Houses of Parliament, where the House was sitting to debate the Budget.

8 APRIL
Throughout the day, 54 Squadron had carried out a continuous patrol of two aircraft over convoys in the Thames Estuary and off Clacton. It was a beautiful day with blue sky and a certain amount of sunshine was enjoyed by all.

Flight Lieutenant J. McIntosh was posted away to RAF Inverness, and Pilot Officer C.F. Colyer went to RAF Ford.

9 APRIL
54 Squadron was up at 04.30hrs, and at 06.00hrs set out on the usual Barrow Deep patrols over convoys. In the afternoon various 'rhubarb' operations were carried out when Squadron Leader Robert F. Boyd and Sergeant Horace Cordell (100598) flew in a north-easterly direction over the North Sea and towards the Dutch coast. No enemy aircraft were sighted and there was no activity. But at 17.26hrs Pilot Officer Baxter and Sergeant Hall reported four aircraft approaching them from behind and to port.

Pilot Officer Baxter then saw four Me 109s about 200ft below and ahead of him, and he fired two short bursts at the leading Me 109. Hall reported that he saw the enemy aircraft crash into the sea, and so Baxter won his first victory against the enemy. It is noteworthy that he fired only 160 rounds.

10 APRIL

54 Squadron was released for training, so air-to-ground firing was carried out at Dengie Flats, the squadron firing 16,800 rounds in all. The squadron had only seventeen pilots now who could fly, and was due for reinforcements.

11 APRIL

A cold and misty day with poor visibility gave 54 Squadron little chance for flying, and indeed only four sorties of an hour's duration each were made.

12 APRIL

Again the weather was dull and cloudy. 54 Squadron was at readiness in the early morning, and later, at fifteen minutes' availability. Convoy patrols were maintained throughout the day, and at 12.30hrs there was a slight flap when two aircraft were ordered to patrol over the base, but nothing happened, and at 13.00hrs the squadron was released for training.

13 APRIL

54 Squadron carried out air-to-ground firing during the afternoon.

14 APRIL

54 Squadron carried out a convoy patrol in the morning, and was then released for training. Pilot Officer B.C. Sparrowe was posted to RAF Debden. Pilot Officer E. Thursfield was granted the war-substantive rank of flying officer.

15 APRIL

54 Squadron maintained Barrow Deep patrols, and in the afternoon a local squadron sweep over the coast was made with 64 and 611 Squadrons from RAF Hornchurch, but nothing was seen.

16 APRIL

54 Squadron was at readiness in the morning and at 14.45hrs 'B' Flight was ordered to patrol Maidstone at 15,000ft. Nothing was seen of enemy aircraft.

Acting Flight Lieutenant G. Henderson was posted here to command the station, and was granted the acting rank of squadron leader. Pilot Officer W.H. Green was posted here from RAF Gravesend, and Acting Squadron Leader G.P. Kerr was posted away to RAF Weeton.

The Station Headquarters offices were moved from 'Greenways', Hall Road, Rochford, to Earl's Hall School, Southend.

17 APRIL

At 06.54hrs, a 'Sphere' operation took place, the whole of 54 Squadron taking part, all eager for a shot at the enemy. 'A' Flight broke cloud north of Winerelix and dived out to sea near Wissant, firing their guns in a dive on apparent gun emplacements.

'B' Flight crossed the French coast at 24,000ft east of Dunkirk, then lost height and broke cloud 7 miles south-east of Calais. Flight Lieutenant Dorian Gribble (40695) fired into the landing ground Champs de L'Alma but saw no enemy aircraft. Pilot Officer H. Sewell saw a Bofors gun on the Easline Pier head, with four machine guns around it and about fifteen men, who were seen to fall as he fired.

During a dive, Spitfire P7738, flown by Pilot Officer Jack Stokoe (60512), was turned on its back by a close burst of anti-aircraft fire which smashed the Perspex hood.

Pilot Officers J. Harris and Shuckburgh were posted here to join to 54 Squadron from 58 OTU (Grangemouth).

There was further and more successful contact with the enemy during the morning. At 10.06hrs, eight aircraft left Southend for a practice flight to show the flag to convoys in the Thames Estuary. They had been warned of a raid when Red Section saw four Me 110s about 10 miles away and below cloud base, flying in pairs, stepped up 300ft behind and to starboard section.

Squadron Leader Boyd led Sergeant Cordell towards the port pair, and Flying Officer Edward 'Jack' Charles (36198) led Pilot Officer Henry 'Bill' Bailey (84947) to the starboard. Charles made a starboard quarter attack on the starboard leader. Pieces fell off. Charles gave another burst to make quite certain, and the enemy aircraft went into a slow spiral in an uncontrolled attitude. This enemy aircraft was confirmed by Group as destroyed and duly awarded to Flying Officer Charles, who, with 2,800 rounds fired, thus scored the 100th victory of 54 Squadron in the war. Squadron Leader Boyd increased this to 101 in the same battle, because he attacked No. 2 of the left-hand 'Rotte'. The enemy aircraft dived up and down, in and out of cloud, so Boyd waited for him – and the enemy duly obliged. He gave two bursts, which cut 3ft or 4ft off his starboard wing tip and stopped the starboard engine; the Me 110 turned sharply over and disappeared into cloud, but owing to the condition of the enemy aircraft this was allowed to be counted as a destroyed enemy aircraft. The day ended with a tally of forty-five sorties made.

Pilot Officer Harrison was posted to the squadron from RAF Heston, and Pilot Officer Grant-Govan joined them from RAF Hendon.

In the evening one section flew to RAF Gravesend for night fighting, but it wasn't carried out.

18 APRIL

Following the usual convoy patrols in the morning, air-to-ground firing filled the day for 54 Squadron.

19 APRIL

The usual convoy patrols were carried out by 54 Squadron, followed by air-to-ground firing. Squadron Leader Stapleton was posted to the unit as supernumerary from 58 OTU (Grangemouth).

20 APRIL

54 Squadron took off at 17.00hrs, 'A' Flight patrolling Barrow Deep 10 miles south-east of Clacton, and 'B' Flight patrolling Clacton at 15,000ft. 'A' Flight was vectored on to some enemy aircraft coming in from the east at 23,000ft, while the flight was at 26,000ft. No enemy aircraft were sighted, but Pilot Officer Christopher Colebrook

(86344), who was in Spitfire P7383 weaving at the rear, apparently got left behind and was never seen again, and 'B' Flight reported that they saw a Spitfire going down emitting glycol smoke.

Pilot Officer Baxter then saw four aircraft at twelve o'clock and identified them as Me 109s. He saw a Me 109 coming down on the tail of the flight and shouted, '109s behind!' The flight took evasive action, except for Pilot Officer Stokoe, who in Spitfire P7666 continued to fly straight and level. A Me 109 closed on his tail and fired – his aircraft went down in flames with Stokoe baling out into the sea. He was rescued by Air-Sea Rescue, and after a couple of days in hospital for treatment to slight injuries he had sustained he returned to the unit. It was later confirmed that he had taken down a Me 110 just before he was shot down. All the other pilots from this patrol returned safely.

22 APRIL
Sergeants F.M. Laing, Roy Keen, Aherne and Graeme Fenton (401378) joined 54 Squadron from 53 OTU, Heston.

23 APRIL
The usual convoy patrols off Barrow Deep were carried out by 54 Squadron, and the training of new pilots continued. The squadron now boasted twenty-five pilots, making for a formidable strength, although they were not fully operational.

24 APRIL
It was a dull, cold and cloudy day when Pilot Officer Bill Bailey of 54 Squadron took off in the early morning at 06.00hrs with Sergeant Allan to patrol Barrow Deep. At about 06.20hrs they were vectored on to an enemy aircraft at 5,000ft. Bailey then saw a Ju 88 three-quarters of a mile away to his port at 2,000ft flying north-west. He gave the 'Tally Ho!' and approached the enemy from below and astern, rapidly closing to 500 yards. He delivered an astern attack on the port engine and experienced return tracer fire, fortunately without response. He made two more attacks, the result being that black smoke began pouring from the port engine. The enemy aircraft disappeared into cloud at 4,000ft, and it was afterwards learnt that two Hurricanes had also attacked this enemy aircraft, finally destroying it.

Throughout the day the usual Barrow Deep patrols were maintained, and the squadron afforded fighter protection to several convoys.

25 APRIL
54 Squadron was at early readiness all week until the 28th, with nothing of importance to report.

28 APRIL
54 Squadron made forty-eight sorties today, accumulating fifty hours of flying time.

29 APRIL
54 Squadron carried out thirty-five practice sorties today.

30 APRIL
Convoy patrols were carried out in the morning by 54 Squadron and air-to-ground firing took place in the afternoon.

MAY

1 MAY

There was 10/10ths cloud at 12,000ft with visibility at 10 miles. Night flying at RAF Northolt was cancelled and the 54 Squadron was released at 20.07hrs, having done little flying throughout the day and no operational flying at all.

2 MAY

Convoy patrols were carried out by 54 Squadron during the morning, and dusk patrols were carried out by Flying Officer Charles and Sergeant Bersford at 20.20hrs.

3 MAY

Convoy patrol was carried out in the morning at Barrow Deep, and the squadron was at readiness at 09.10hrs. In the afternoon the squadron was released for training.

4 MAY

It was beautiful weather; no clouds, and the sun shining most of the day. Convoy patrols were carried out from early morning over Barrow Deep, Clacton and Burnham by 54 Squadron. At 10.40hrs, owing to a report of an enemy aircraft being in the vicinity, one aircraft took off on station defence but no contact was made. At 12.30hrs a 'rhubarb' operation was carried out in six pairs of aircraft. From 'A' Flight, the first pair flew on a course of 120° at 2,000ft over the North Sea and the other two pairs flew on parallel courses, but nothing was seen. 'B' Flight carried out the same operation over the same course about thirty minutes later, but once again all was quiet over the North Sea and the Dutch, Belgian and French coasts.

5 MAY

The only event of interest was a dusk patrol by Flying Officers Baxter and Sewell of 54 Squadron. They took off at 21.42hrs, and whilst flying towards Clacton, saw three enemy aircraft at 3,000ft, probably Ju 88s. They immediately opened fire on the Spitfires which were caught in a cone of fire, but by clever manoeuvring, Sewell managed to get on the tail of one of the enemy aircraft and fired several bursts. Baxter also managed to get on the tail of the enemy aircraft and got in a burst; however, no result was observed and the aircraft returned safely.

Sergeant Mason, an American pilot, was posted to the squadron today from 57 OTU, Hawarden.

6 MAY

There was an unusual amount of enemy activity today. Barrow Deep patrols were carried out throughout the day, with further excitement when Pilot Officer Stokoe and Sergeant Panter met four Me 109s south of Manston. These enemy aircraft were slightly above and behind our aircraft. Stokoe turned to attack the rear enemy aircraft, firing two long bursts dead astern. Black and white smoke poured out, and one Me 109 was claimed as 'damaged'. Pilot Officer Alan Campbell (42393) also fired at three Me 109s which he sighted off Ramsgate, but without a decisive result.

Squadron Leader Stapleton, on the same patrol at 13.12hrs, met three Me 109s and got engaged in an exciting dogfight over Dover. He fired at two enemy aircraft and saw one pouring out black and white smoke, and then dived down towards the sea.

Stapleton then discovered that the tail of his aircraft was on fire, so he lost height and crash-landed near the cliffs of Dover.

Pilot Officer T.J. Moffatt was attached to Douglas, Isle of Man.

7 MAY

Early morning readiness. At 10.40hrs, eleven aircraft of 54 Squadron took off to act as high cover to Blenheims which were to bomb shipping between Calais and Dunkirk. The squadron met the Blenheims, which were being escorted by 64 Squadron over Eastchurch. They flew south and crossed the French coast near Cap Gris Nez, changing course from north-east. Light anti-aircraft fire was encountered at Calais and along the coast. The squadron leader saw four Me 109s, but they were too far away to engage. Black Leader, Flight Lieutenant Gribble, chased one Me 109 into cloud, but thought it inadvisable to follow, and so broke off the pursuit. However, Black 2 (Sergeant Hall) followed in Spitfire P8178 into the cloud, and he was not seen again. This was 3 miles east of Dunkirk. Ten aircraft landed back at Southend at 12.00hrs.

8 MAY

Barrow Deep patrols were carried out in the morning and continued into dusk patrols.

9 MAY

54 Squadron was at readiness at 05.19hrs on this very cold morning. Barrow Deep patrols were carried out as well as air-to-ground firing. Later in the morning the squadron patrolled over Maidstone. Pilot Officer Campbell left the squadron after a long and faithful service, to join the Merchant Air Squadron – first of all going to RAF Farnborough.

10 MAY

Dusk patrol: during the night there was a big Blitz on London. 54 Squadron volunteered for night fighting and one patrol over the Thames was carried out by Squadron Leader Boyd, Pilot Officer Herbert Sewell (86667) and Pilot Officer Baxter. Nothing was seen of enemy aircraft, but reported that large fires were seen blazing in London.

11 MAY

At 21.30hrs, the aerodrome was circled and then attacked by seventeen high-flying Me 109s diving in line astern to machine-gun and bomb the aerodrome and the surrounding area. In all, seventeen bombs were dropped, but only four fell on the aerodrome. The Operations Room and ambulance garage were demolished by direct hits, damaging an ambulance and a fire tender. Casualties were sustained: one airman was killed and four were slightly injured. Ground Defence Hispano cannons shot down one enemy aircraft which crashed on the aerodrome beside Hangar 1. The pilot, Aldred Ludanig, was killed. (He was buried at Sutton Cemetery with full military honours.)

Pilot Officer Sewell, already on patrol over the estuary, chased some of the enemy aircraft over Kent, finally shooting one down off Dover, sending it crashing into the sea in flames.

In the early hours of the next morning, Sergeant Pilot Bedrich Kratkoruky (110669) of 1 Squadron intercepted a He 111 over Canvey Island. He chased it to Southend and attacked it. When last seen the enemy aircraft was at 2,000ft, losing height, with both engines smoking. Coastguards at Southend later reported that it had crashed into the sea off Shoeburyness.

12 MAY
Pilot Officer Knox arrived at this station from 58 OTU, Grangemouth, to join 54 Squadron.

13 MAY
54 Squadron made a sweep over Ostend, Dunkirk, Calais and Le Touquet. No enemy aircraft were seen and nothing to report.

14 MAY
'B' Flight of 54 Squadron, led by Squadron Leader Frederick Stapleton (36059), carried out an offensive patrol towards the Dutch coast, but nothing was seen.

15 MAY
Not much flying today apart from the usual Barrow Deep patrols.

16 MAY
Flying Officer C.A. Brockbank was attached here for medical duties, and Flying Officer F.F.W. Chitty was appointed to the acting rank of flight lieutenant.

17 MAY
'A' Flight of 54 Squadron patrolled Maidstone at 20,000ft, and 'B' Flight patrolled at 15,000ft. 'A' Flight were warned of bandits near Dungeness going north; they saw four Me 109s in two pairs, at the same height, flying north. The 109s manoeuvred round the Spitfires and the leader ordered the flight to break up and dive. New Zealand pilot Sergeant Erl Kean was last seen as the flight broke up and presently he went into a straight dive. He was not seen again and the wreckage of his Spitfire (P7833 *Portadown*) was found at Biddenden.

20 MAY
Today was dull and cloudy. Pilot Officer T.J. Moffatt returned to the base from the Isle of Man. 54 Squadron took off today for RAF Hornchurch. 611 Squadron, commanded by Flight Lieutenant Eric Hugh Thomas (39138), arrived and spent the rest of the day settling in.

21 MAY
In the morning the usual Barrow Deep patrols were carried out by 611 Squadron, and after lunch the squadron proceeded to mount guard over the Channel, while Blenheim bomber and other operations took place. Later in the day the squadron was detailed as close escort to a further bomber operation, with a rendezvous made at Hornchurch; alas, Hornchurch was as far as they got. The weather provided the necessary excuse and all smelt strangely of drink upon their arrival back at Southend three hours later.

23 MAY
The usual patrols were flown by 611 Squadron with nothing outstanding to report. The Spitfire Mk Vas were now being used for most operational sorties. In the evening, a station dance was held in the Concert Hall at the Station Headquarters.

24 MAY
A dull day today, although more flying was done by 611 Squadron than for several days.

25 MAY

Cloudy weather with rain in the afternoon. The usual patrols were flown by 611 Squadron and without incident.

26 MAY

Cloudy and showery weather. Uneventful patrols carried out by 611 Squadron. Wing Commander W. Morgan took over duties of assistant adjutant, Pilot Officer W.H. Green, MC. Major General Liardet, Inspector General Aerodrome Defences, inspected the station.

27 MAY

Cloudy with showers in the morning. An abortive Sphere was the only item of interest.

28 MAY

There was some excitement today during a Canterbury patrol when 'A' Flight of 611 Squadron went to investigate some smoke trails. Pilot Officer Wilfred Duncan-Smith (85684) dived on a Me 109 and fired a twelve-second burst at it, claiming it as a probable victory.

Early in the evening the squadron joined in a wing show over the Boulogne–Calais area. A total of thirteen Me 109s were seen and various engagements took place, during which Flight Lieutenant Stanley Meares (37683) opened fire on and set fire to a Me 109, and the CO claimed a probable second in Spitfire K7343 with the assistance of Flying Officer Philip Pollard (41462) and Sergeant Arthur Leigh (111975); Sergeant N.J. 'Mushroom' Smith (742558) attacked four Me 109s and neatly sprayed one all by himself, claiming it as probably destroyed. En route for home the CO was fired upon, the aircraft later being in need of a little putty here and there.

Flying Officer J.S. Wood was posted to 501 Squadron and Pilot Officer W.H. Green was posted to RAF Carew Cheriton.

29 MAY

A fine morning and the usual patrols were carried out by 611 Squadron. There was no excitement, and the weather deteriorated in the afternoon which released the squadron in the evening.

30 MAY

Very bad weather; one flight of 611 Squadron was at thirty-minute readiness and the other flight was released. The dreadful axe has fallen; one good, experienced pilot must be posted to Training Command, and Flight Lieutenant Douglas Watkins (90363), DFC has been recommended.

31 MAY

A dull and overcast morning; 611 Squadron was released in the afternoon.

JUNE

By June 1941, 1115 ATC Squadron had grown so large that a second squadron was formed from within 1115 and given the title 1312 (2nd Southend-on-Sea) Squadron.

Training and instruction sessions were held in the old London Road schools, the old municipal college and the Labour Hall in Boston Avenue. Both squadrons shared all facilities either on separate nights or with joint classes at advanced level. Also available in bad weather was the Police Hall, which also had a .22 rifle range (long since demolished for the Victoria Circus development).

Guidance and assistance was readily given by RAF Southend, both at the airfield and at the Station Headquarters, sited in Earl's Hall School in Carlton Avenue.

Later in the year the Southend Wing (ATC) was formed, with its headquarters in a house at 61 London Road, Southend-on-Sea, from where it controlled and administered all the ATC squadrons in the area, and there was no shortage of accommodation for them as all the local schools had been evacuated: 640 (Southend High School); 930 (Westcliff High School); 1115 (Southend-on-Sea); 1312 (2nd Southend-on-Sea); 1202 (Rochford, with a detached flight at Wakering); 1341 (Thames Estuary, with a detached flight on Canvey Island); 1474 (Billericay); and 1476 (Rayleigh).

The first and only commanding officer of the Southend Wing was Squadron Leader A.H. White. (Alec Hemsley White was the mayor of the County Borough of Southend in 1935/36 and was deputy mayor throughout the period of the Second World War. An ex-RFC pilot, he was commissioned in the RAFVR and appointed to command the first local squadron (1115). He was also a member of the War Emergency Committee.)

1 JUNE

Cloudy and dull with very little flying; 611 Squadron now had eighteen Spitfire Mk Vas.

Pilot Officer S.C. Flick (Intelligence Officer) was attached to the squadron from RAF Redhill as replacement for Pilot Officer Carpenter who had hurt his knee badly. The ground staff were further depleted by the detachment of Flight Lieutenant Sanderson to Halton for a six-day course in sanitation and hygiene, and Pilot Officer Langley to Rolls-Royce, Derby, for a seven-day course on Merlin engines.

2 JUNE

A little brighter today than recently although it was still very cold for this time of year. The usual patrols were flown by 611 Squadron with nothing to report. Spitfire R7343 was flown away by Flying Officer William 'Fishy' Salmond (40947) to RAF Hamble for repair. A local War Weapons Week was enlivened by twelve aircraft flying over the area in squadron formation led by Flight Lieutenant Watkins, DFC. The squadron then broke up and dropped pamphlets urging the locals to 'Lend to Defend the Right to be Free' etc. and a good time was had by all. The squadron had a useful formation practised and probably helped to bump the Savings movement.

3 JUNE

A dull and cloudy morning with rain by midday. Eight pairs of aircraft from 611 Squadron took off on a 'rhubarb' operation, but only one pair came back with anything of interest to report. Flying Officer Pollard had the satisfaction of sending two German officers scurrying from their car for cover in a ditch near Dunkirk; the two 'Jerries' were claimed as probable, with 1,000 rounds being fired by 'Polly'. Meanwhile, Flying Officer Salmond was 'knocking for six' (his own comment) a column of about 150 German troops he found farther south. He fired 1,200 rounds in all and with his second burst definitely registered upon the troops who were slogging away through the rain with heavy equipment slung all around their bodies.

Flight Lieutenant Theodorus Buys and Sergeant Peter Townsend experienced exceptionally bad cloud conditions and decided to return. They got back all right but the instruments on Buys' machine played tricks and there was an anxious period when he was cruising over Dungeness and Hawkinge was covered in mist. He effected a safe landing, however, at RAF Hawkinge, and flew back two hours later.

The nine o'clock news gave a colourful account of 'Polly' and 'Fishy'. The *Daily Sketch* of 4 June 1941 had the headlines 'Fighters Dive on Nazis' and 'Troops Attacked in France' for Flying Officer Salmond.

4 JUNE

Dull all morning with plenty of rain. The weather cleared up during the afternoon and in the early evening 611 Squadron was called upon to take part in a 'Circus Blot' operation over Le Touquet, Boulogne, Calais and Folkestone; one particular function being to patrol the Straits of Dover in the hope of finding a few enemy fighters. Most of the pilots returned without having anything of interest to report. Flight Lieutenant Stanley Meares (37683) in Spitfire R7254, however, was set upon by a Me 109 which, with a lucky squirt, pierced his tank. He came back with fuel pouring through the floor of the cockpit and a hole in the collar of his Mae West. His aircraft was rendered category 'B' by this action. Sergeant Limpenny returned with tailplane damage on R7304. Flight Lieutenant Buys in R7349 reported the destruction of a Me 109.

5 JUNE

Cloudy and wet most of the day; an uneventful Barrow Deep patrol was carried out in the afternoon.

Group Captain Broadhurst brought Squadron Leader Bitmead to visit the station in the evening – the former CO seemed unlikely to fly for a little while as he was still recovering from a fractured skull.

A new 'System of States' was introduced to RAF Southend where the pilots were to be at readiness one morning in three.

6 JUNE

A misty and wet day with only forty minutes' flying. Air Vice Marshal Leigh-Mallory, Air Officer Commanding 11 Group, visited with Group Captain Broadhurst at 15.45hrs and talked with pilots. He stayed for tea at the mess and proceeded to RAF Hornchurch for dinner. The squadron officers were invited en masse as guests at RAF Hornchurch for dinner and upon early release all available officers attended a very enjoyable function.

Pilot Officer Alan Johnson (86369) of 611 Squadron overshot upon landing in very bad weather conditions, and collided with a stationary aircraft of 'B' Flight. Both aircraft (R2717 and R7255) were rendered Category 'A/C', with both port main planes being damaged.

Flying Officer J.S. Wood was posted to Southend from 501 Squadron.

7 JUNE

A glorious summer's day. An offensive sweep over the Channel and French coast was carried out with 611 Squadron as part of the Hornchurch Wing but with no incidents worthy of note. The usual Barrow Deep patrols were carried out. Spitfire R7213 arrived at this station from 33 MU.

8 JUNE

A warm but cloudy day. The usual patrols were flown by 611 Squadron with nothing to report. Flight Lieutenant Watkins, DFC was posted to 57 OTU Hawarden (near Chester) for duties as flying instructor. He had been with the squadron since long before the war. Only Pilot Officers Thomas Williams (90658) and James Sutton (90758) of the original Auxiliary Air Force officers and Pilot Officer Pollard now remained to tell amusing anecdotes and lurid experiences of the early days of the war. Flight Lieutenant B. Sanderson and Pilot Officer H. Langley returned from their respective courses.

9 JUNE

A dull day again, with not much flying, although there was air-firing practice carried out by 611 Squadron at Dengie Flats. Two new aircraft arrived from 5 MU – R7306 and R7307 – bringing the squadron strength up to nineteen.

10 JUNE

A dull day again, with very little flying carried out. Flying Officer C.H.B. Bassett was posted to RAF Castle Camps.

11 JUNE

A fine day from the morning; the usual patrols were flown. A Sphere operation by twelve Spitfires from 611 Squadron took part in an offensive patrol over Dover–Calais–Boulogne–Dungeness. A few aircraft seen in the distance was their only report.

Another War Weapons Week 'pamphlet raid' was made over Rochford, Rayleigh and Hawkwell.

12 JUNE

A fine day and the usual patrols were carried out by 611 Squadron as well as defensive cover for returning bombers were flown. No incidents were reported. Pilot Officer C.S. Flick ceased to be attached to the squadron and returned to RAF Redhill.

13 JUNE

A fine morning with patrols being flown by 611 Squadron during which the CO, Squadron Leader Stapleton, was fired upon by Allied destroyers, but no harm was done.

At 17.00hrs, the whole squadron flew to RAF Debden for three fighter nights. Seventy of the ground crew left at 14.30hrs, and arrived safely at Debden at 16.10hrs, with the only difficulties encountered being in moving the equipment out. The equipment belonged to this station and naturally Station Headquarters did not want their equipment taken off the station, as there were no spares, i.e. starter trolleys. However, no night flying was carried out.

14 JUNE

A fine day turning to cloud later in the morning. Very little flying was done by 611 Squadron but none of it was operational. The adjutant and senior NCO visited RAF Hornchurch to arrange accommodation and transport for the exchange with 603 Squadron on 16 June. Squadron Leader Stapleton was promoted to wing commander w.e.f. 1 June 1941 (*London Gazette*).

15 JUNE

A fine day today. After patrols there was a little local flying by 611 Squadron and in the evening some night-flying practice was carried out.

16 JUNE

A very clear and bright day. The airmen of 611 Squadron who were detached to RAF Debden paraded at 07.00hrs to return to RAF Hornchurch, but owing to transportation problems, they did not leave until later in the day.

603 Squadron: thirteen officers, two warrant officers, three flight sergeants, five sergeants, fourteen sergeant pilots, and 108 airmen, a total of 145 with eighteen aircraft, arrived at Southend from RAF Hornchurch.

Air Marshal Sir William G.S. Mitchell KCB, CBE, DSO, MC, AFC, Inspector General, visited this station.

17 JUNE

Pilot Officer A. St C. Harrison was admitted to PMRAF Hospital, Halton. At 18.05hrs, twelve aircraft from 603 Squadron took off in the rear and above 54 and 611 Squadrons. Climbing to 21,000ft over Dungeness, they swept between Boulogne and Cap Gris Nez four times, losing height and then climbing back into the sun. No enemy aircraft were seen.

18 JUNE

At 17.45hrs, twelve aircraft of 603 Squadron in company with 54 and 611 Squadrons from RAF Hornchurch climbed to 18,000ft and crossed the coast at Dover and the French coast at Gravelines at 28,000ft. In sections, with pairs in line abreast, they turned west to Guines. They circled east of Gravelines across the Channel nearby to Dover, and then down the Channel to Cap Gris Nez, then a left-hand turn back to Dover.

19 JUNE

At 19.00hrs, twelve aircraft of 603 Squadron took off, meeting 611 Squadron at Gravesend; three Blenheims met over Detling at Angels 2 with 603 above at Dungeness, the squadron split into sections. Enemy aircraft attacked; five Me 109s dived with two of them going through onto 611 Squadron. Flying Officer Dudley Stewart-Clark fired at long range but with no result. On return to base, Pilot Officer P.J. Delorme (157939) landed heavily owing to oil on his windscreen preventing him seeing clearly. His port oleo leg broke away and he took off for another circuit, making a good landing on one wheel and one wing. The aircraft was damaged but repairable on station.

21 JUNE

Twelve aircraft of 603 Squadron left the aerodrome at noon as part of a target support wing. Sergeant Pilot Jackman destroyed one Me 109, which was seen to blow up, and damaged one other. Flight Lieutenants George Gilroy (90481) and Francis Scott-Malden (74690), together with Sergeant Pilot Neill, claimed to have damaged Me 109s.

At 15.45hrs, ten aircraft took off and swept over Cap Gris Nez, and during this operation Flying Officer William Douglas (90896) destroyed one Me 109, which was seen to be on fire. Flying Officer Dudley Stewart-Clark's (78535) aircraft was badly damaged and he was forced to crash-land in the sea on the Goodwin Sands. He had previously unfastened his belt preparatory to baling out but, not having sufficient height, he decided to remain in his machine. On impact he received a cut on the fore-head from the windscreen, and a lacerated thumb. His dinghy worked successfully and he was eventually picked up by the Rescue Service Motor Launch. Gilroy remained in the vicinity until he saw that Stewart-Clark was safe.

22 JUNE
Pilot Officer Newman left to attend the Medical Board at RAF Halton at 09.30hrs on the 23rd.

At 18.10hrs, eleven aircraft of 603 Squadron took off to join up with a Hurricane squadron over the aerodrome. Having split into sections on crossing the French coast over Hazebrouck, they sighted and climbed to attack a formation of Me 109s, but lost them. Pilot Officer Delorme saw one enemy aircraft go down in flames over the target. Sergeant Pilot Deryck Lamb (112530) saw two Me 109s and fired a three-second burst but no result was seen. On the way back he shot up an enemy gun post and a white motorboat. The squadron landed back at 18.55hrs.

23 JUNE
Flying Officer Stewart-Clark was ordered on fourteen days' sick leave by the station medical officer, RAF Hornchurch.

At 12.55hrs, ten aircraft of 603 Squadron took off and joined 54 and 611 Squadrons at Hornchurch, and then swept in on the French coast on Circus 19 at Gravelines. 54 Squadron dived into a dogfight with 603 Squadron following. Flying Officer William Douglas (90896) in Spitfire W3110 was attacked by four Me 109s from above. Sergeant Pilot Lamb received a cannon shell in the fuselage and crash-landed near Dover, unhurt. Douglas had been hit in both legs and one arm by splinters of cannon shell, but he managed to land his aircraft near Hawkinge (he was subsequently taken off operations until November, and became a 'Guinea Pig' after being in the Queen Victoria Hospital, East Grinstead).

24 JUNE
At 19.55hrs, twelve aircraft of 603 Squadron took part in Circus 21, escorting Blenheims to Choeques Aerodrome, having made rendezvous with 54 Squadron and 611 Squadron. Pilot Officer Newman destroyed one Me 109. Pilot Officer K.J. McKelvie, flying Spitfire W3121, did not return from this operation and was last seen north of the coast near Gravelines. Sergeant Pilot Lamb sustained injuries force-landing Spitfire W3364 at Walmer as a result of enemy action.

25 JUNE
The Director General of Air/Sea Rescue Services visited the station today. At 11.55hrs, nine aircraft of 603 Squadron were engaged on a large offensive sweep with 54 and 611 Squadrons, crossing the French coast at 12.29hrs. They circled Hazebrouck at 12.35hrs, leaving at 12.44hrs. No enemy aircraft were near enough to attack. The squadron aircraft saw the bombers in and followed them out. One Blenheim from 21 Squadron and two Spitfires (one from 611 Squadron and one from 222 Squadron) were damaged in the operation, but they made it back as far as Southend and crash-landed on the aerodrome. The Blenheim had been severely shot up, and on landing it crashed into a Petrol Bowser. The pilot was slightly injured but two of the crew were badly hurt.

At 15.50hrs, flying again with 54 and 611 Squadrons, seven aircraft from 603 Squadron conducted a sweep over St Omer, which was reached at 16.32hrs, and then left ten minutes later. No enemy aircraft were near enough to fire at.

26 JUNE

At 10.40hrs, ten aircraft of 603 Squadron took off from RAF Hornchurch on a sweep over the French coast. During the operation Pilot Officer Delorme damaged one Me 109 and Flying Officer Henry 'Harry' Prowse (42358) also claimed to have damaged one. Pilot Officer C.A. Newman was reported missing in Spitfire R7272, last seen over the coast of France.

At 15.10hrs, ten aircraft were sent on a standing patrol over Manston at Angels 6. Nothing was seen worth reporting.

27 JUNE

At 20.51hrs, twelve aircraft of 603 Squadron rendezvoused with 54 and 611 Squadrons, with 603 on top cover, and crossed over Deal at Angels 13. Gaining height over the Channel, they crossed the coast of France east of Gravelines. The weather conditions were misty and they reached the target at 21.38hrs. They then circled once in wing formation, afterwards splitting up into sections. No enemy aircraft were seen near enough to engage. Flak was noticed further inland than usual.

Pilot Officer Nigel Keable (60085) reported to the squadron from 41 Squadron (at Catterick), and Sergeant Pilot Wood reported in from 64 Squadron.

28 JUNE

At 07.55hrs, a target support wing operation took place, twelve aircraft of 603 Squadron taking part, together with 54 and 611 Squadrons. Contact was made over the aerodrome at Angels 13. From over North Foreland a wide sweep was made up to 24,000ft. At 08.30hrs the formation was over the coast at Gravelines. At 08.38hrs, halfway to Lille, the squadron met another wing coming from the west, joined them and went on to the target. Fires were seen in and around Lille. No enemy aircraft were encountered.

29 JUNE

Acting Flight Lieutenant Scott-Malden went on leave until 5 July.

30 JUNE

At 17.40hrs, eleven aircraft of 603 Squadron acted as part of a target support wing (Circus 22). The target was Lens, but they were attacked before reaching their objective. Flying Officer Harry Prowse destroyed one Me 109E. Sergeant Pilot L.E.S. Salt did not return from this operation and was reported missing. He was last seen over the coast north of Gravelines.

Sergeant Pilots George Tabor (754844) and W.B. Rudd reported from 152 Squadron, W.J. Archibald from 111 Squadron, A.C. Hendry from 602 Squadron, and D.J. Prytherch from 72 Squadron Acklington.

JULY

1 JULY

At 17.55hrs, twelve aircraft of 603 Squadron took off, meeting 54 and 611 Squadrons from Hornchurch over Gravesend. They met up with a bomber formation over Canterbury and circled for a time over Calais. However, they lost sight of the bombers in the heat haze, which was as high as 10,000ft. They then returned east towards Gravelines, circled, split up into sections and returned to base, crossing in over Manston.

2 JULY

Major C.A.L. Coutts, of the 5th Battalion, Oxford and Bucks Light Infantry, was attached to this station as local defence commander. Sergeant Pilot Richard Jury (748441) was posted to 41 Squadron at Catterick.

At 12.55hrs, six aircraft of 'B' Flight, 603 Squadron stood by a Lysander aircraft inland off Hawkinge during a 'circus' operation.

At 17.45hrs, accompanying 54 and 611 Squadrons, 603 carried out a fighter sweep over Gravelines and Dunkirk. They proceeded inland to St Omer, where they broke into sections at 30,000ft. At 18.35hrs, they were over Le Touquet and at 18.45hrs were over Dungeness. No enemy aircraft were seen and they returned to base, landing at 19.05hrs.

3 JULY

At 11.00hrs, twelve aircraft of 603 Squadron took off, and again at 14.00hrs to take part in supporting wing operations over Hazebrouck. Pilot Officer Delorme engaged one Me 109F, which he claimed as probably destroyed. Further victories were claimed by Sergeant Pilot Jackman, one Me 109F destroyed, and Flying Officer Prowse and Pilot Officer Falconer, who claimed one Me 109F as probably destroyed.

4 JULY

At 14.15hrs, twelve aircraft of 603 Squadron were engaged in a target support wing, with Chocques Aerodrome as their objective. Pilot Officer Delorme destroyed one Me 109. Flying Officer Prowse shot down two Me 109s over St Omer but failed to return from the operation. He was last seen by Pilot Officer Falconer diving low over St Omer Aerodrome. Falconer called him on the R/T and he replied that he was 'OK' but he was not seen again. (He had been shot down by flak and crash-landed in a field. He set his Spitfire alight with a Very pistol before being captured by the Germans – and spent the rest of the war as a prisoner of war, finally being freed on 2 May 1945.)

Flying Officer Scott-Malden was re-posted as a flight lieutenant with effect from 13 April.

5 JULY

At 12.15hrs, twelve aircraft of 603 Squadron took off as part of a target support wing for Lille, with 54 Squadron as top cover and 611 Squadron bringing up the rear. Stirling bombers were met over the Thames Estuary and headed for France over the North Foreland at Angels 19. Anti-aircraft fire was encountered about 12 miles inland. The squadrons' aircraft were shadowed by Me 109s which did not engage. 603 Squadron came out with bombers, but between Lille and the coast they were unsuccessfully attacked by groups of Me 109s in echelon, but four of the aircraft were forced to land at RAF Manston to refuel.

Squadron Leader Smith proceeded on seven days' leave to Scotland. Acting Flight Lieutenant Scott-Malden returned from leave.

6 JULY

Pilot Officer T.J. Moffatt returned from a ground defence course at Douglas, Isle of Man.

During target support wing operations escorting six Stirlings to Lille, Sergeant Pilot George Tabor (754844) of 603 Squadron damaged one Me 109F.

Squadron Leader Henderson, station commander of RAF Southend, gave a party at 'The Lawn' (Officers' Mess) for the officers of the squadron and their guests. Three pipers from the squadron pipe band, Corporals Blake and Crooks, and AC1 Wilson, were in attendance.

7 JULY

At 08.55hrs, twelve aircraft of 603 Squadron took off for a Stirling escort during which Pilot Officer Delorme claimed a Me 109E probably destroyed.

At 14.55hrs, eleven aircraft took part in a 'mopping up' sweep, with 611 Squadron above and 54 Squadron below, over the French coast at Gravelines, round Chocques and out south of Hardelot. About six Me 109s were seen travelling east and slightly below them. The enemy aircraft dived away, with no shots being fired.

Pilot Officer N.H.C. Keable left the station today on a forty-eight-hour pass. Sergeant Cairns, along with three other pipers of the squadron pipe band, arrived from Turnhouse to take part in the Southend War Weapons Week.

8 JULY

Flying Officer A. Skene was attached here for medical duties.

At 05.45hrs, 603 Squadron took off, flew over the Thames Estuary and then south to the French coast. Near Hazebrouck they saw fifteen Me 109s coming towards them slightly below. Red Section on the right turned right and dived. Flight Lieutenant Scott-Malden fired at one of a pair at 400 yards range. Glycol was seen to burst from both radiators. Sergeant Pilot Wood made a half roll and dived. His aircraft was probably hit by flak as he crossed out over Calais. He was then chased by a Me 109 over the Channel. The enemy aircraft turned and he followed it, firing a burst for 80 yards. He saw his bullets rip open the fuselage, and one wing hit the water. Wood was slightly wounded and crashed at Romford Bridge, near Canterbury. His aircraft was burnt out.

Blue Section saw three Me 109s diving in front of them and opened fire on the leader, but no results were observed. The section then climbed and turned to port on to a Me 109 heading towards them. Flight Lieutenant Gilroy fired and damaged it.

At 16.30hrs, Pilot Officer Delorme was forced to land at RAF Coltishall owing to a shortage of fuel and damaged instruments. His port wing had been holed by cannon shell. He was one of a party who left base on a 'circus' over the chemical works at Lille.

When over the target, Yellow Section was attacked by fifteen Me 109s diving in echelon. Sergeant Pilot Tabor lost his section and, finding himself alone with an enemy aircraft on his tail, he circled it. The enemy aircraft turned to starboard, and Tabor fired at him from 150 yards. He saw the enemy aircraft crash south-west of Lille. Tabor then dived and, seeing a Me 109 coming 'head-on', he fired one burst and saw the enemy aircraft crash into a tree.

Red Section was not attacked; Blue Section at Angels 19 going out over Glines was attacked by four Me 109s, but dived away and flew home at zero feet.

During the afternoon the squadron moved to RAF Hornchurch.

10 JULY

At 13.20hrs, Flying Officer James Hayter (36207) of 611 Squadron was returning to Hornchurch from a sweep during which he had shot down a Bf 109, and then after his aircraft (Spitfire W3328) was badly damaged by flak, he crash-landed near Southend and was unhurt.

12–19 JULY

This station co-operated with the Naval, Army and Civilian Authorities for Southend War Weapons Week, resulting in the sum of £511,000 being raised. A dance held by the RAF Southend resulted in the sum of £20 3s 6d being sent to the authorities at Southend towards their expenses.

15 JULY

Messrs Swaffield and Edwards, civilian representatives from the Ministry of Aircraft Production, visited the station in connection with equipment matters.

18 JULY

The sum of £26 0s 0d (the result of a dance held at the Lea Bridge Rubber Works, Ltd, Southend) was presented to the RAF Southend Benevolent Fund by one of the directors of the firm. This amount was passed on by this station to the Central RAF Benevolent Fund.

19 JULY

222 (Natal) Squadron was transferred here from RAF North Weald for operational duties.

20 JULY

222 Squadron took off to make rendezvous over Manston and act as part escort to Blenheim bombers to bomb enemy supply shipping off Le Touquet. All aircraft returned safely. In the afternoon the same operation was repeated; during a brief combat with enemy aircraft, Sergeant Ferraby shot at a Me 109, damaging the tail.

21 JULY

A similar operation to the previous day was carried out by 222 Squadron, and took off again on another escorting operation in the afternoon. After returning to base, the squadron was kept at readiness until 23.30hrs.

22 JULY

222 Squadron was on Lysander escort, and saw the rescue of two German pilots by an ASR launch. The squadron was kept at readiness for most of the day, being released at 22.15hrs.

23 JULY

After a foggy morning, 222 Squadron took part in a 'circus' as part escort to Blenheims in an attack on Mazinghem. Later in the day they acted as part escort on a raid over

Gravelines. Intense flak was experienced over St Omer, but all aircraft returned home safely and without incident.

24 JULY

A fine morning and 222 Squadron was engaged on a 'circus' escorting nine Blenheims in attacking the marshalling yards at Hazebrouck. Sergeant Sharples did not take part as his aircraft struck some uneven ground on take-off and was damaged.

25 JULY

A misty start to the morning; 222 Squadron was at thirty-minute readiness, and later released for the day.

26 JULY

222 Squadron was at readiness at 05.30hrs, but Gideon 'circus' did not materialise owing to unfavourable weather. The squadron was released for the day when heavy rain persisted over the area.

One sergeant and twenty men of the Pioneer Corps arrived here on attachment from Brentwood.

27 JULY

222 Squadron was quickly recalled after taking off to take part in a 'circus' over La Traite. After a period at readiness, they were released for the evening.

28 JULY

Poor visibility from the morning caused two 'circuses' to be cancelled and 222 Squadron was released for the rest of the day.

An amended 'Operation Order for the Defence of RAF Southend' was issued today:

The possibility of enemy parachute or airborne troops landing for the purpose of sabotage or invasion still exists. Sabotage by enemy agents may also be attempted. The probable nature of an attack would be the landing of troops one to three miles from the aerodrome. These troops will be equipped with heavy and light automatics, sub-machine guns, rifles, hand grenades and possibly mortars. Flame throwers and gas are also a strong possibility.

At the same time heavy scale bombing and machine gun attacks can be expected on the Station Defence Posts and buildings to destroy aircraft and services and create chaos.

The following will be at Battle Headquarters on 'Action Stations':

The station commander in command
Local defence commander
Intelligence officer
Anti-aircraft defence commander
Forward observation officer, Field Battery, Royal Artillery
Two M/C DRs (RAF)
One tannoy operator (RAF)
Two telephonists (RAF)
One service police (Traffic Control)

Casualty Collecting Posts will be established on 'Alert 1' as follows:

Post No. 1 – Flight Office on west side of the perimeter
Post No. 2 – Flight Office on east side of the perimeter
Post No. 3 – Medical Inspection Hut in the rear of the Pilot's Rest Room

All ammunition and grenades held by the army and RAF formations will be
distributed to Platoons and taken to localities on 'Action Stations'. Reserve ammunition will be stored in the four Nissen Huts on the base.

Four Bofors Guns were operated by one troop of the Royal Artillery for Anti-
aircraft defence.

The intention in the orders is to defend Southend Aerodrome to the last, and
if and when the aerodrome becomes in imminent danger of capture it will be
destroyed by demolition.

Warning Operation Order
In order to bring about a state of readiness sufficient to deal with enemy commando raids either airborne, seaborne or both without bringing into operation all
the extensive military and civil measures which come into force with the issue of
code words 'Stand-to' and 'Action Stations', a new set of code words will be taken
into use as follows, in 11th Corps Area, Eastern Command:

Warning of a Raid 'Bandit Alert'
Raid in Progress 'Bandit Action'
Stand Down 'Bandit Stand Down'

The following code warnings will be used on this station:

Warning when an Enemy Commando raid is likely 'Defence Alert'
Raid in progress 'Raid Alarm'
Stand Down 'Normal Defence Manning'

Air Raid Warnings
The approach of enemy aircraft within 15 miles of the station will be notified by
RAF Hornchurch, and the following warnings were broadcast:
(i)   'Guns Alert'
      Followed by details of the enemy movement, e.g. 'Look North 2,000ft, enemy
      aircraft flying north to south'.
(ii) 'Take Cover'
      Given without prejudice to aircraft operations at the discretion of the station
      commander.
      Anti-aircraft posts to be prepared for action.
      Infantry Garrison to occupy their Defended localities or any available cover
      and engage enemy aircraft if within small arms range.
(iii) 'Raiders Passed'
      Given at the discretion of the station commander after 'Guns Alert' or 'Take
      Cover'. All resume normal duties.

29 JULY

During a patrol carried out by 222 Squadron in the morning, Sergeant Christie sighted and fired at two enemy minesweeping trawlers off Dunkirk, diving from 1,000ft to mast height, and observing several strikes.

30 JULY

Several patrols were carried out at Barrow Deep by 222 Squadron, and after returning were released for the day. Pilot Officer S. Knox was attached to RAF Croydon on authority from 11 Group.

31 JULY

222 Squadron was at thirty-minute readiness until 14.00hrs, and were then all released until dawn, except for one section which remained at readiness until dusk.

AUGUST

1 AUGUST

Glider attack practice was carried out by 222 Squadron throughout the day.

2 AUGUST

Patrols over Barrow Deep were carried out by 222 Squadron from the morning. Squadron Leader R.C. Love (222 Squadron) assumed command of RAF Southend, in place of Squadron Leader G. Henderson, who was on leave.

3 AUGUST

Sergeants Rudolph Ptacek and Ferraby of 222 Squadron took off on a 'rhubarb' and shot up Samer Aerodrome, destroying one Me 109 on the ground, and Ferraby disabled a high-speed launch near the shore.

4 AUGUST

A ground haze lay about in the morning, becoming generally overcast throughout the day. One patrol of Barrow Deep was carried out aircraft of 222 Squadron.

5 AUGUST

222 Squadron flew to RAF North Weald for an operation which was subsequently cancelled, and returned to base at 20.50hrs.

6 AUGUST

At 10.35hrs, 222 Squadron took off for RAF Manston, but the operation was eventually cancelled.

7 AUGUST

Sergeant Maskery of 222 Squadron took off in a Lysander to join an air-sea rescue when he was attacked by two Me 109s. He landed safely at Minster but the aircraft was written-off.

The rest of 222 Squadron took off on a 'circus 62', acting as close escort to six Blenheims in an attack over Lille.

8 AUGUST
Heavy rain; no flying today.

9 AUGUST
222 Squadron participated in a sweep over Hazebrouck, acting as close escort to
six Blenheims.

10 AUGUST
At 11.07hrs, 222 Squadron took off to make rendezvous over Hornchurch and proceeded on an offensive fighter patrol to St Omer. No enemy aircraft were seen and
they returned to base with nothing to report.

11 AUGUST
The weather deteriorated somewhat today. At 17.00hrs, four sections of 222
Squadron took off on convoy patrols to guard a large south-bound convoy entering
the Thames Estuary.
    Squadron Leader G. Henderson resumed command of the station from Squadron
Leader R.C. Love (222 Squadron) on returning from leave.

12 AUGUST
222 Squadron took off to make rendezvous with the North Weald Wing and act as
escort for six Handley-Page Hampdens. These were attacked by Me 109Es and the
squadron engaged them, destroying two. Sergeant Christie claimed one damaged, and
Squadron Leader Love and Sergeant Ptacek claimed one each as 'probable'. Sergeant
Christie did not return from this operation. Upon landing back at Southend, Sergeant
Ferraby landed with wheels up, his aircraft having been damaged by enemy cannon
during combat. He was unhurt.
    At 18.30hrs, the squadron took off again on a sweep with the North Weald Wing
over Le Touquet, St Omer and Cap Gris Nez. Flying Officer Hall and Sergeant Ptacek
engaged Me 109Es, with Hall claiming one as probably destroyed.

13 AUGUST
A very wet day; no flying was done.

14 AUGUST
A dull morning. At 14.39hrs, 222 Squadron took off for North Weald to make rendezvous with six Blenheims. No contact was made with the bombers, and so made a
sweep over Cap Gris Nez, but they returned to base with nothing to report.

15 AUGUST
Another very wet day; no flying.

16 AUGUST
At 07.25hrs, 222 Squadron took off to make rendezvous with 71 and 111 Squadrons
over Manston and proceeded on an uneventful fighter sweep over Dunkirk and
St Omer.
    At 12.00hrs, the squadron was airborne again with the North Weald Wing, acting as
escort to six Blenheims. Light flak was experienced but no enemy aircraft were sighted.

17 AUGUST

National Savings Group No. 310/1/2609 was formed at the station, with Warrant Officer W. Morgan as honorary secretary.

At 17.00hrs, 222 Squadron took off to make rendezvous with the North Weald Wing to escort three Beauforts to torpedo an enemy ship off Le Touquet. The attack was successful.

18 AUGUST

222 Squadron moved out to RAF North Weald, together with their Servicing Echelon Party.

Squadron Leader John Arthur Gerald Gordon (36075) of 151 Squadron failed to return from a sweep when he was shot down in Hurricane P3940 during combat with Bf 109s over Rochford. Gordon baled out, badly burned, and was admitted to Rochford Hospital. His aircraft crashed and burned out at Tabrium's Farm, Battlesbridge.

19 AUGUST

402 Squadron arrived from RAF Ayr in Hawker Hurricanes, together with Servicing Echelon Party.

222 Squadron from RAF North Weald made rendezvous over Southend to act as escort to six Blenheims in an attack on Hazebrouck.

21 AUGUST

A practice Alert No. 1 was held today and all station defences were manned. The exercise proved to be satisfactory.

23 AUGUST

A practice gas alarm was sounded throughout the station at 10.30hrs. The 'All Clear' was sounded at 10.45hrs. The exercise proved to be satisfactory.

26/27 AUGUST

A practice Alert No. 1 took place at 23.00hrs, and a practice attack alarm occurred at 03.40hrs on the 27th and all station defences were manned. The practice was satisfactorily carried out.

27 AUGUST

Flight Lieutenant Thomas Burgess Little (C1117) of 402 Squadron was killed in Hurricane Z5001 when he collided with a Spitfire while flying escort over the Channel. Sergeant D.W. Jenkin (R56848) of 402 Squadron was shot down in Hurricane Z3424 on the same escort. He was captured and became a prisoner of war.

29 AUGUST

A practice gas alarm was sounded throughout the station at 10.30hrs. The 'All Clear' was sounded at 11.00hrs. The practice proved satisfactory.

30 AUGUST

The Air Officer Commanding 11 Group paid a short visit to the station.

SEPTEMBER

1 SEPTEMBER

The daily routine of 402 Squadron began today with one section at readiness from first light and the remainder at thirty-minute readiness. However, there was no operational flying carried out, and even local flying was restricted owing to unfavourable weather.

2 SEPTEMBER

402 Squadron was at routine readiness today. Again, no operational flying was carried out, but other flying was formation practice and sector reconnaissance.

Lieutenant G.E. Wilson of 1 Canadian Tunnelling Company was attached to the station. Flying Officer J. Bayliss reported his arrival here on posting for equipment duties, taking over from Flight Lieutenant A.D. Rutherford-Jones.

A district court martial assembled at Southend, in connection with the trial of AC2 K. Hackett (1017305) of 222 Squadron.

3 SEPTEMBER

402 Squadron was at routine readiness today. No operational flying was carried out, but other flying was formation practice and sector reconnaissance.

The commander-in-chief of the Home Forces visited the station on a tour of inspection.

Flight Lieutenant W. Monkton, MM assumed the duties of station adjutant Flight Lieutenant E. Dodd, who was absent on leave.

4 SEPTEMBER

402 Squadron took off at 15.35hrs, and made rendezvous over Southend with the North Weald Wing, where they proceeded to RAF Manston. There they contacted twelve Blenheims at 16.00hrs, and flew as close escort to the bombers. One aircraft developed engine trouble and had to return to Southend. Following the operation, eight aircraft landed safely at RAF West Malling at 17.38hrs, and two aircraft landed at RAF Rochester at 17.30hrs. Unfortunately one aircraft force-landed on a beacon site near RAF Detling, but was not badly damaged and the pilot was unhurt.

Pilot Officer T.J. Moffatt was posted to RAF Martlesham Heath.

5 SEPTEMBER

The aircraft of 402 Squadron that landed at Detling yesterday arrived back here at 12.30hrs; the aircraft from West Malling arrived at 13.25hrs, and the aircraft returning from Rochester arrived at 14.45hrs. One section was put at readiness, with the remainder of the squadron at thirty-minute readiness.

Flying Officer Oliver Morrough-Ryan (40970) of 41 Squadron, after combat over Hornchurch, made a forced landing in Spitfire X4318 in Kemsley's Field, Star Lane, Great Wakering.

6 SEPTEMBER

402 Squadron was at routine readiness today but there was no flying at all owing to heavy fog all day.

7 SEPTEMBER

At 07.55hrs, aircraft of 402 Squadron took off on patrol of a north-bound convoy from the Thames Estuary until 13.40hrs, operating one section at a time. Other flying carried out during the day included formation practice.

8 SEPTEMBER

At 08.20hrs, aircraft of 402 Squadron took off on patrol of a north-bound convoy from the Thames Estuary until 15.05hrs, operating one section at a time, and of a south-bound convoy from 16.00hrs until 19.30hrs.

9 SEPTEMBER

402 Squadron was at routine readiness today. There was no operational flying carried out, but other flying was formation practice and sector reconnaissance.

10 SEPTEMBER

402 Squadron was at routine readiness today. One patrol was made over the Clacton area, and four convoy patrols were carried out. Formation practice, cloud flying, circuits and landings were also flown during the day.

11 SEPTEMBER

402 Squadron was at routine readiness today. One patrol was made over Clacton, and five convoy patrols were carried out. Other flying carried out was formation practice, cloud flying, circuits and landings.

Messrs E. Schoedsack and Pennington-Richards of the Walter Wanger Film Unit visited 402 Squadron in connection with the equipping of Hurricanes with cine-cameras.

12 SEPTEMBER

402 Squadron was at routine readiness today. Three convoy patrols were carried out. Other flying carried out was formation practice, cloud flying, circuits and landings. A visit to the squadron was made by Air Commodore L.F. Stevenson, AOC, RCAF Overseas.

13 SEPTEMBER

402 Squadron was on convoy patrol from 06.10hrs until 16.30hrs, covering a large convoy proceeding north from the Thames Estuary. A total of forty-one hours' flying was accrued for the day.

Flight Lieutenant E. Dodd resumed the duties of station adjutant, taking over from Flight Lieutenant W. Monkton, MM (on return from leave).

Flight Lieutenant E.H. Jones was attached here from Headquarters, 11 Group, for medical duties. Flight Lieutenant A.D. Rutherford-Jones was posted to RAF West Malling for equipment duties.

14 SEPTEMBER

402 Squadron was at routine readiness today but flying was restricted owing to fog. However, three convoy patrols were carried out. Pilot Officer T.J. Moffatt reported his arrival here, pending re-posting from RAF Martlesham, and Flying Officer M.S. Kinmonth ceased his attachment to the station on medical duties.

15 SEPTEMBER

402 Squadron was at routine readiness today. There were no operational flights today. Other flying carried out was squadron formation practice.

16 SEPTEMBER
402 Squadron flew convoy patrols all day from 08.30hrs until 20.20hrs.

17 SEPTEMBER
Convoy patrols were carried out by 402 Squadron from 08.20hrs until 12.40hrs. At 13.40hrs the squadron took off and proceeded to Maidstone, making rendezvous there with the North Weald Wing and bombers at 14.00hrs at 12,000ft. 402 Squadron acted as close support for twelve Blenheims proceeding to Mazingarbe, France.

During combat against enemy aircraft, Flying Officer Fred W. Kelly (J2972) claimed one Me 109 destroyed, and one was shared by Flying Officer F. 'Brad' Foster (J3196), Pilot Officer Sydney Amos Graham (J3707), Sergeant O'Neill and Sergeant Ronny Emberg.

At 17.45hrs, five aircraft took off to act as escort to a Lysander in search of a pilot who was downed in the Channel off Dungeness. They returned at 19.20hrs.

18 SEPTEMBER
402 Squadron took off at 11.15hrs and landed at RAF West Hampnett at 11.55hrs. At 14.05hrs they took off again to join the North Weald Wing over Hastings at 12,000ft to act as close escort to eighteen Hampden bombers. The Wing and Hampdens were not found, but the squadron spotted and formed on eleven Blenheims as close escort and proceeded to their target 5 miles west of Rouen, France. The squadron claimed one enemy aircraft destroyed by Sergeant Pilot George McClusky (R71726), two Me 109s claimed as probable by Flight Lieutenant Robert Morrow and Sergeant Graham D. Robertson (R63899), and two more damaged by Pilot Officer Bill Pentland (J3204) and Sergeant K.B. 'Butch' Handley (R63609).

19 SEPTEMBER
402 Squadron was at routine readiness today. Uneventful convoy patrols were carried out.

20 SEPTEMBER
402 Squadron took off at 12.00hrs and landed at RAF Marston (Tangmere) at 12.40hrs. At 14.55hrs, they took off again and made rendezvous with twelve Blenheims and the Tangmere Wing at Shoreham at 15.15hrs. The squadron attached itself as close escort to a flight of six Blenheims which returned inland. In turning inland the squadron left the Blenheims and returned to base with nothing worthy of reporting.

21 SEPTEMBER
402 Squadron took off at 13.25hrs and landed at RAF Marston at 14.05hrs. At 14.25hrs they took off again, making rendezvous with the Tangmere Wing and twelve Blenheims at Rye at 14,000ft to fly as close escort. Lieutenant Colonel Drew and Wing Commander Tilley visited the station today.

22 SEPTEMBER
402 Squadron was at routine readiness. There was no operational flying carried out, and the only flying was formation practice.

23 SEPTEMBER
402 Squadron was at routine readiness. Owing to heavy rain and fog there was no flying.

24 SEPTEMBER

402 Squadron was at routine readiness. Thick fog persisted today, preventing flying.

Flight Lieutenant W.H.A. Monkton, MM assumed the duties of station adjutant, taking over from Flight Lieutenant E. Dodd (who was absent on temporary duty).

25 SEPTEMBER

402 Squadron was at routine readiness today. Thick fog – no flying again.

26 SEPTEMBER

Convoy patrols were carried out by 402 Squadron at 08.40hrs and 14.40hrs. Other flying taking place was squadron formation practice. Flight Lieutenant E. Dodd resumed duties of station adjutant, replacing Flight Lieutenant W.H.A. Monkton, MM.

27 SEPTEMBER

402 Squadron was at routine readiness today. Squadron formation practice was carried out between 10.00hrs and 11.00hrs.

At 13.25hrs, the squadron took off and made rendezvous at 5,000ft with Hornchurch Wing at 13.48hrs. They proceeded to Manston to rendezvous with twelve Blenheims at 12,000ft at 14.12hrs. The target was Mazingarbe. The squadron returned to base at 16.45hrs, but on the way back it was discovered that Pilot Officer Graham was missing.

On questioning of all pilots later no information could be obtained as to when Pilot Officer Graham disappeared from the formation. No one had seen his aircraft (Hurricane Z5005) shot down. From what information was obtained it is believed that he must have been shot down by anti-aircraft fire prior to arriving over the target.

One Me 109 was claimed on this operation as destroyed by Squadron Leader Vaughan Corbett (C299) and Sergeant Pilot McClusky. Two Me 109s were claimed damaged by Flying Officer Kelly and Sergeant Pilot McClusky, and one shared by Flight Lieutenant Harry S. Crease (J3194) and Flying Officer Leslie 'Syd' Ford (J3712).

During the afternoon, twelve members of the Canadian Press, representing newspapers from Canada, visited the squadron. They had been disappointed earlier in the week when operations at a bomber station they visited were cancelled due to bad weather, but spent an interesting afternoon with the fighter pilots. The party, conducted by Mr A. Saward, was fortunate to be on hand at the time of the squadron returning from the above operation, and they were able to appreciate first hand the reactions of those pilots of these operations. The party departed Southend for London at 18.00hrs.

28 SEPTEMBER

402 Squadron was at routine readiness today. Convoy patrols were carried out between 08.00hrs and 11.30hrs. During these patrols a burning tanker of approximately 8,000 tons was seen about 8 miles north of Clacton. Other flying consisted of cine-camera gun, formation, and sector reconnaissance.

29 SEPTEMBER

402 Squadron was at routine readiness today. Flight Lieutenant R.E. Morrow (C1238) and Pilot Officer W.H. Bretz (J2975) were ordered at 12.15hrs to search for a pilot in the sea 28 miles east of Manston. The weather conditions were very poor, the ceiling heavy and visibility limited to a few hundred yards. The patrol was, however, successful in finding the pilot in his dinghy. They orbited the spot, getting a fix on the position

and stayed until the pilot was picked up by a rescue boat. Flight Lieutenant Morrow's radio went dead, but he was able to find his way back to RAF Manston. The section returned to Southend after the weather cleared, landing at 14.20hrs.

30 SEPTEMBER
Convoy patrols were carried out by 402 Squadron from 10.20hrs until 19.30hrs; a total of forty-two hours being flown on these patrols for the day.

HRH the Duke of Kent arrived here at 15.00hrs and met and talked to all officers and pilots. He later inspected the maintenance hangar, and the Airmen's Mess and quarters. Following tea in the Officers' Mess, he departed at 17.00hrs. The squadron strength on this day was nineteen officers, 211 airmen, and five personnel other than RCAF.

OCTOBER

1 OCTOBER
402 Squadron carried out convoy patrols in the morning. Lieutenant Colonel J.S. Gullet, US Army Corps, visited the station for the purpose of meeting the personnel of 402 Squadron RCAF, and for studying RCAF activity in this country.

2 OCTOBER
One section of 402 Squadron was at readiness in the morning. Convoy patrols were also carried out. Other flying consisted of formation practice and low-level flying. Squadron Leader Corbett, Flying Officer Brad Foster and Pilot Officer James A. Thompson (J2970) did the first squadron practice bombing with practice bombs at Dengie Flats.

3 OCTOBER
402 Squadron carried out convoy patrols in the morning. Other flying was formation practice, and bombing practice at Dengie Flats. At 16.50hrs, the squadron took off for RAF Manston to stand by for night fighting during moon period.

4 OCTOBER
402 Squadron was at readiness at RAF Manston. The usual convoy patrols were carried out, and although there was no operational flying, the squadron carried out night cross-country patrols. On 5, 6, 7 and 8 October heavy fog and rain restricted flying, other than the morning patrols.

6 OCTOBER
Squadron Leader W.L. Bateman reported here on posting from RAF Castle Camps. He assumed command of the station, replacing Squadron Leader G. Henderson, on 8 October.

9 OCTOBER
On their last day at RAF Manston, 402 Squadron carried out convoy patrols before returning to Southend, landing at 14.35hrs. Squadron Leader G. Henderson proceeded on his posting to RAF Castle Camps.

10 OCTOBER

One section of 402 Squadron was at readiness. convoy patrols were flown; other flying was formation practice, cloud flying and local flying. Bombing practice was carried out at Dengie Flats.

11 OCTOBER

402 Squadron was at readiness from the morning, although no operational flights were carried out. Other flying was formation practice, cloud flying and bombing practice at Dengie Flats.

12 OCTOBER

Following convoy patrols, six pilots from 402 Squadron proceeded to Sutton Bridge for air firing. The remainder of the squadron took off at 11.30hrs to make rendezvous with the wing at Hornchurch at 11.30hrs, and then to make contact with and act as close escort to twenty-four Blenheims over Rye at 12.05hrs. The target was Boulogne, which was reached at 12.20hrs and bombs were dropped. The squadron returned at 12.50hrs without incident. In the afternoon, formation practice and practice bombing was carried out.

Major C.A.L. Coutts (local defence commander) was transferred to RAF Hornchurch, on appointment to a lieutenant colonel post, and was replaced by Major K.W. Brown, TD, who reported here from RAF Hornchurch.

13 OCTOBER

After convoy patrols in the morning and bombing practice at Dengie Flats, 402 Squadron took off at 13.25hrs to make rendezvous with the North Weald Wing at 13.37hrs and then rendezvoused with eighteen Blenheims at Manston at 13.50hrs. The squadron acted as close escort to the bombers as they proceeded to their target of Mazingarbe, France. About five minutes after reaching the target Flight Lieutenant Crease was hit by flak right under the engine. The aircraft was seen to shake and go into a shallow dive, emitting streams of glycol. Flying Officer Blair Russel (C/1319) followed the aircraft down about 1,600ft, but when he flew alongside he observed that the cockpit hood was open and the cockpit was apparently empty.

Lieutenant H.O. Fergusson, Royal Engineers, was attached to the station today in connection with pipe-laying duties.

14 OCTOBER

Convoy patrols were carried out by 402 Squadron in the morning followed by practice bombing.

15 OCTOBER

402 Squadron carried out convoy patrols in the morning. Other flying consisted of practice bombing, formation practice, and circuits and landings with 250lb bombs, which had arrived and been fitted to the Hurricanes the day before.

Flying Officer J.S. McCubbin was posted to Headquarters, Fighter Command, for defence duties.

16 OCTOBER

One section of 402 Squadron was at readiness in the morning. Other flying consisted of practice bombing, formation practice, and circuits and landings with 250lb bombs.

Before a district court martial, Corporal J.J. Holland was charged with and found guilty of 'When on Active Service using violence to a Non-Commissioned Officer being in the execution of his office'. He was sentenced and reduced to the ranks. LAC J.H.J. Minifie was charged with and found guilty of 'When on Active Service using violence to a Non-Commissioned Officer being in the execution of his office'. He was sentenced to undergo detention for twenty-eight days. LAC A.H. Johnson was charged with and found guilty of 'When on Active Service resisting the Royal Air Force Police whose duty it was to apprehend him'. He was sentenced to undergo detention for twenty-eight days.

17 OCTOBER
The usual convoy patrols were carried out by 402 Squadron; other flying was bombing practice, circuits with 250lb bombs, and also target towing.

18 OCTOBER
Owing to high wind, all flying was restricted today, and there were no operational flights. Captain Donald E. McNabb, of the Canadian Dental Corps, who was attached to 402 Squadron, and Sergeant Pilot McClusky died of injuries following a crash in the Squadron Miles Magister at RAF Friston.

19 OCTOBER
One section of 402 Squadron was at readiness; there was no operational flying, and other flying was restricted owing to bad weather.

20 OCTOBER
One section 402 Squadron was at readiness but again there was no operational flying. Other flying consisted of bombing practice, circuits and landings with heavy bombs. At 18.30hrs a telephone message was received that the name and number of Flight Lieutenant Crease had been announced over the German radio as a prisoner of war.

Sergeant J.C. Gilkerson (743545) was posted to No. 1 RAF Depot, Uxbridge, on commissioning as acting pilot officer.

21 OCTOBER
Convoy patrols were carried out by 402 Squadron; other flying consisted of bombing practice, circuits and landings with heavy bombs. The coroner's inquest into the deaths of Captain D. McNabb and Sergeant Pilot McClusky was held at Eastbourne, Sussex, and the verdict reached was accidental death.

22 OCTOBER
One section of 402 Squadron was at readiness; other flying consisted of bombing and formation practice.

23 OCTOBER
One section of 402 Squadron was at readiness; other flying was high-level bombing practice and circuits and landings with heavy bombs.

The funeral of Sergeant Pilot McClusky, who was buried in Sutton Road Cemetery, Southend (Plot R, Grave 12136), took place at 14.30hrs. Squadron Leader E.W. Cockran conducted the service. Captain McNabb was buried at Brockwood Cemetery at 15.00hrs.

24 OCTOBER

One section of 402 Squadron was at readiness; there was no operational flying. Other flying was high-level bombing practice, formation practice and cloud flying.

Flight Lieutenant W.H.A. Monkton, MM, intelligence officer, Southend, gave a lecture on 'Recognition of Aircraft' in the lecture room, Earl's Hall School, to the following personnel: twelve NCOs of Army Intelligence, fifty other ranks of the Army APM Division, and fifty of the RASC.

25 OCTOBER

One section of 402 Squadron was at readiness; there was no operational flying. Other flying was bombing practice, low-level bombing attacks over the sea, army co-operation, and circuits and landings with heavy bombs.

26 OCTOBER

One section of 402 Squadron was at readiness; there was no operational flying. Other flying was bombing practice. Pilot Officer J.C. Crouch, catering officer, ceased his attachment to the station on posting to RAF Filton.

27 OCTOBER

One section of 402 Squadron was at readiness; there was no operational flying. Other flying was bombing practice, circuits and landings with heavy bombs, low-level bombing attacks over the sea, and formation practice.

28 OCTOBER

One section of 402 Squadron was at readiness; there was no operational flying. Other flying was low-level bombing attacks on ships and dive bombing. Flight Lieutenant Monkton, MM gave a second (and continual) lecture on the 'Recognition of Aircraft' in the lecture rooms, Earl's Hall School, Prittlewell.

29 OCTOBER

One section of 402 Squadron was at readiness; there was no operational flying. Other flying was low-level bombing attacks over the sea.

General courts martial on Flying Officer E. Thursfield and Pilot Officer A. St C. Harrison were held at Southend, by order of the Air Officer Commanding, 11 Group.

30 OCTOBER

One section of 402 Squadron was at readiness; there was no operational flying. Other flying was low-level bombing attacks over the sea.

31 OCTOBER

One section of 402 Squadron was at readiness; there was no operational flying. Other flying was bombing practice and cloud flying. The station warrant officer, J.D. Allan (345707), was tried by general court martial at Southend, by order of the Air Officer Commanding, 11 Group.

NOVEMBER

1 NOVEMBER
One section of 402 Squadron was at readiness; convoy patrols were carried out. Eight Hurri-bombers took off at 11.40hrs, each carrying two 250lb eleven-second delay bombs for the first low-level bombing attack over France by this squadron. The target was Merck-sur-Mer Aerodrome.

2 NOVEMBER
One section of 402 Squadron was at readiness; no operational flying. Other flying included circuits and landings carrying heavy bombs, and cloud flying.

3 NOVEMBER
One section of 402 Squadron was at readiness; no operational flying, and the squadron practised low-level bombing attacks.

Flight Lieutenant E. Dodd proceeded to RAF Stannington for a senior officers' administration course.

4 NOVEMBER
402 Squadron carried out convoy patrols in the morning. At 12.50hrs, eight Hurri-bombers took off for another low-level attack on Merck-sur-Mer Aerodrome.

5 NOVEMBER
One section of 402 Squadron was at readiness. Convoy patrols were carried out as well as a patrol of Barrow Deep.

6 NOVEMBER
402 Squadron, complete with their Servicing Echelon, left for RAF Warmwell, Dorset.

8 NOVEMBER
Acting Pilot Officer R. Foulsham reported his arrival on posting from the School of Cookery, Halton, for catering duties.

10 NOVEMBER
During a speech at the Mansion House, Prime Minister Winston Churchill stated that 'We now have an Air Force which is at least equal in size and number, not to mention quality, to the German Air Force'.

12 NOVEMBER
Flight Lieutenant F.F.W. Chitty assumed the duties of Honorary Secretary of the National Savings Association, Southend, taking over from Warrant Officer W. Morgan.

A practice manning of aerodrome defences was held between 16.30hrs and 17.30hrs by all ranks.

14 NOVEMBER
An exercise took place between 17.30hrs and 18.30hrs on station manning defences. The exercise was held to test the administrative arrangements when all RAF personnel are brought into the camp for accommodation and feeding, combined with a

'Stand-to' of the whole garrison. Valuable lessons were learned which went to show that the administrative details must be organised. Modifications were necessary should a state of siege exist over a prolonged period.

15 NOVEMBER
Squadron Leader Bennett, the Command catering advisor, visited the station in connection with catering matters.

18 NOVEMBER
Group Captain T.B. Prickman, SAO 11 Group, accompanied by Squadron Leader Cull, visited the station in connection with Station Defence, and attended a conference held in Earl's Hall School at 14.15hrs for that purpose.

19 NOVEMBER
An exercise arranged by the Counter Attack Battalion of the 9th Devon Regiment was held; the object of which was (i) to practise assembly of Counter Attack Battalion at battle stations and the aerodrome garrison, (ii) the staging of a counter attack on a portion of the aerodrome and (iii) to practise communications between the Counter Attack Battalion and Southend Aerodrome by R/T and L/T. The aerodrome defence troops taking part were 'A' and 'B' Coys, 70th Essex, and the AFV Flight.

At 08.33hrs, 'Alert 2' was received from Battalion Headquarters, and the exercise finally terminated at 13.32hrs. The 134th Infantry Brigade commander was present during the exercise and was very satisfied with the information which was passed to the Counter Attack Battalion from the aerodrome.

23 NOVEMBER
Flight Lieutenant E. Dodd returned from a senior officers' administrative course at RAF Stannington. As a result of enemy action, a blast caused considerable damage to windows, doors etc. in the Station Headquarters at Earl's Hall School. Several airmen received superficial injuries; two small landmines were dropped.

26 NOVEMBER
Flight Lieutenant E. Dodd resumed the duties of station adjutant, taking over from Flight Lieutenant W. Monkton, MM.

29 NOVEMBER
Pilot Officer G.J. Jackson reported here from RAF Depot, Uxbridge, for duty as educational officer.

DECEMBER

5 DECEMBER
Acting Pilot Officer J.D. Power reported his arrival on posting as supernumerary signals officer. Flying Officer E. Thursfield left the station on being cashiered as a result of a general court martial which assembled at RAF Southend on 29 and 30 October 1941.

7 DECEMBER

The principal US naval base in the Pacific, at Pearl Harbor, Hawaii, was attacked by Japanese carrier-borne aircraft at 07.55hrs local time (18.25hrs GMT). On the evening of 7 December, it was announced in Tokyo that Japan was at war with the USA and Britain.

Even before the American entry into the war Churchill had assiduously and successfully cultivated American support.

8 DECEMBER

Britain and the USA declared war on Japan.

11 DECEMBER

Germany and Italy declared war on the USA; the USA declared war on Germany and Italy.

An exercise was held at the aerodrome in which the following troops took part: the infantry companies, RAF Ground Defence, the station medical staff and stretcher bearers, and, in addition, the local ARP, first-aid services, and the senior medical officer, 11 Group, also attended. The narrative pictured RAF Southend on 'Alert 1' since the early morning, but the enemy attack south of the River Blackwater failed. The exercise opened at 14.00hrs and, shortly after, a low-level bombing attack on the station defences was pictured as having taken place. Casualty labels were distributed as a result of this attack.

At 14.30hrs, one infantry platoon, acting as enemy paratroops, started to develop an attack on the north-east corner of the aerodrome. The AFV Flight was sent out to get information and, shortly after, reported the strength and disposition of the enemy, and that they had inflicted casualties on them. More casualty labels were issued during this action. The attack was deemed to have failed owing to the lack of mutual support. Casualties were dealt with without any serious delay, and one or two points needing correction were noted and brought up at a conference which was held on 14 December. The senior medical officer, 11 Group, complimented the station medical officer on the medical arrangements made.

13 DECEMBER

Pilot Officer C.W. Bray returned from a PAC course at Eastchurch.

19 DECEMBER

Flight Lieutenant F.F.W. Chitty assumed duties of station adjutant, taking over from Flight Lieutenant E. Dodd who was absent on leave.

20 DECEMBER

Captain A.H. Bentley, 'A' Coy, 70th Essex Regiment, assumed the duties of local defence commander at RAF Southend, replacing Major K.W. Brown, who was absent on leave.

Flight Lieutenant W.H.A. Monkton, MM was promoted to the rank of squadron leader (temp.). (Extract from *London Gazette*, 16 December 1941.)

29 DECEMBER

Major K. W. Brown resumed the duties of local defence commander (on return from leave).

30 DECEMBER

Flying Officer V.A. Lanos arrived here on posting from Headquarters, 11 Group, for duties of permanent duty pilot.

3
1942

JANUARY

1 JANUARY
Flight Lieutenant E. Dodd (44332) resumed the duties of station adjutant, replacing Flight Lieutenant F.F.W. Chitty (on return from leave).

Acting Flight Lieutenant E. Dodd was appointed Member of the Order of the British Empire. (Extract from *London Gazette*, 1 January 1942.)

4 JANUARY
Authority was received for the promotion of Pilot Officer T.J. Moffatt (87884) to the rank of flying officer w.e.f. 8 November 1941.

6 JANUARY
Flying Officer T.A. Wiese (79019) reported here on posting from RAF Gravesend for duty as intelligence officer.

10 JANUARY
Flying Officer (Acting Flight Lieutenant) F.F.W. Chitty (44688) was posted to RAF Wrexham for engineering duties (a flight lieutenant post).

14 JANUARY
A lecture given by Count Balinski Jundzill on 'Poland and the German Occupation' was attended by the station commander, local defence commander, three other officers and five warrant officers and NCOs at Rayleigh.

15 JANUARY
Major General H. de R. Morgan DSO, Divisional Commander of the 45th Division visited this station to inspect the aerodrome defences.

18 JANUARY
A conference was held at the Station Headquarters, which was attended by the station commander and officers of Southend and officers of the local ATC squadrons to discuss ATC training and co-operation.

19 JANUARY
Squadron Leader W.L. Bateman relinquished command of Southend on posting to command RAF Hawkinge. Squadron Leader W.L. Bateman was granted the acting rank of wing commander on his posting.

Flight Lieutenant E. Dodd, MBE assumed temporary command of RAF Southend, and his previous duties were assumed by Flying Officer V. Lanos.

22 JANUARY
Major T.H.R. Riggs, DCM, MM was posted here from RAF Sawbridgeworth for duty as local defence commander by authority of Headquarters, 134th Brigade.

23 JANUARY
Major K.W. Brown was posted to RAF Sawbridgeworth for duty as local defence commander, replacing Major T.H.R. Riggs, DCM, MM.

Squadron Leader (Reverend) H.J.L. Norman reported here on posting from RAF Yatesbury for duty as chaplain, Church of England.

31 JANUARY
Acting Flight Lieutenant J.S. Wood assumed the duties of station adjutant, taking over from Flying Officer Lanos.

FEBRUARY

1 FEBRUARY
A lecture entitled 'Current Affairs' was given by Dr John Lewis in the station library. All ranks attended and afterwards a discussion about it took place.

2 FEBRUARY
There was a very heavy snow fall today.

3 FEBRUARY
All ranks participated in the clearance of snow from the aerodrome, which was unserviceable.

4 FEBRUARY
The aerodrome was still unserviceable today, but a thaw was beginning to set in.

5 FEBRUARY
The thaw continued today, and despite being soft, the grass landing strip was back in service, although there was no flying carried out.

Acting Flight Lieutenant Smith reported his arrival on posting by authority of 11 Group.

6 FEBRUARY
A detachment of 313 (Czech) Squadron, led by Squadron Leader Karel Mrazek (82561), DFC arrived from RAF Hornchurch.

Acting Flight Lieutenant Smith assumed the duties of station adjutant, taking over from Acting Flight Lieutenant J.S. Wood.

7 FEBRUARY
At 09.40hrs, thirteen Spitfires and a Magister of 313 Squadron arrived.

Acting Flight Lieutenant Smith assumed temporary command of RAF Southend, replacing Acting Flight Lieutenant E. Dodd, MBE; and Acting Flight Lieutenant J.S. Wood resumed the duties of station adjutant, taking over from Acting Flight Lieutenant Smith.

There was a light fall of snow during the day.

8 FEBRUARY
Air-firing practice was carried out by 313 Squadron in the morning. At 14.40hrs eleven Spitfires, led by Wing Commander Powell, took off for practice wing flying over Southend.

9 FEBRUARY
Fog prevented any flying today. Acting Flight Lieutenant E. Dodd, MBE left the station on posting to RAF Hawkinge (for duty at RAF Lympne).

10 FEBRUARY
Fog again prevented any flying.

Personnel of 1488 (Target Towing) (Lysander) Flight arrived on attachment from RAF Shoreham. Pilot Officer A.J. Terry reported here on attachment from RAF Hawkinge for equipment duties.

11 FEBRUARY
Two convoy patrols with four aircraft from 313 Squadron were carried out in the morning. Following these, the squadron took off to make rendezvous with 64 and 411 Squadrons of the Hornchurch Wing over Southend and then proceeded on an offensive sweep from Dunkirk to Calais. The squadron was acting as top cover, but as visibility over the target area was bad they kept a distance of 3 miles from the coast line. Sergeant Jiri Reznicek had to return to base with engine trouble. The squadron landed back at base with no incidents to report. Sergeant Otakar Kresta joined the squadron on detachment from RAF Hornchurch.

Flying Officer Karel Vykoukal, and Pilot Officers Vladimir Michalek and Vaclav Jicha proceeded to London in the afternoon to broadcast from the BBC after the Czech news bulletin. They returned the next day.

Squadron Leader C.H. Gadney assumed command of RAF Southend, replacing Acting Flight Lieutenant Smith.

12 FEBRUARY
Blue Section (Flight Lieutenant Stanislav Fejfar and Sergeant Dohnal) of 313 Squadron was scrambled at 09.10hrs and, after patrolling over the base at 12,000ft, landed thirty minutes later without making contact with the bandit. Air-to-air firing practice was continued by the squadron.

At 13.15hrs, the squadron made rendezvous with eight Hurri-bombers at 1,000ft over the base and flew towards Calais. Visibility was bad – around 1 mile – but a large and medium flak ship was seen. The Hurri-bombers dived and bombed them from 400ft, scoring a direct hit on the larger vessel, which was reported to have carried at least two multiple pom-pom batteries in addition to light AA and machine guns. The squadron attacked the second ship, reporting hits, and then escorted the Hurri-bombers back across the Channel and landed at base at 14.50hrs.

At 16.50hrs, 'B' Flight (six aircraft) of 313 Squadron took off on a defensive patrol over RAF Manston, sweeping the area at 4,000ft until 18.00hrs, and returned with nothing to report. Sergeant Otto Spacek pranged his aircraft on landing back at base with the undercarriage not fully locked down. The aircraft was categorised 'B'.

13 FEBRUARY

Air-to-air firing was carried out by 313 Squadron during the morning, and at 12.50hrs, twelve aircraft, led by Squadron Leader Karel Mrazek, took off to make rendezvous with 64 and 411 Squadrons over Southend at 500ft. At 13.00hrs they formed as escort to eighteen Hurri-bombers over Manston and set course for Gravelines, 313 Squadron acting as rear cover. The patrol line was kept up for twenty minutes between Gravelines, Nieuport, Calais and Dunkirk. No enemy aircraft were seen but only ten Hurri-bombers were seen returning home. Two large flak ships were beached near Calais. 313 Squadron landed back at base at 13.50hrs, and air-to-air firing was carried out during the afternoon.

Flight Lieutenant Vaclav Hajek and Flying Officer Karel Kasal arrived at this station on posting to 313 Squadron from RAF Hornchurch.

14 FEBRUARY

Air-to-air firing was carried out by 313 Squadron with 1488 (TT) Flight. Acting Flight Lieutenant J. Bayliss (31307) left on posting to RAF Fairwood Common.

15 FEBRUARY

Air-to-air firing continued today for aircraft of 313 Squadron and 1488 (TT) Flight. Black Section I and II (Pilot Officer Michalek and Flying Officer Kasal) took off for RAF Manston where they refuelled and took off on a 'rhubarb' over the Coxyde Aerodrome and the Dunkirk–Furnes Canal, crossing in at zero feet 1 mile east of Dunkirk at 11.21hrs. Light and medium flak was encountered and on taking evasive action they became separated. Pilot Officer Michalek, despite taking hits on the port wing, carried out the original plan, although no barges were seen, nor any aircraft at Coxyde Aerodrome, and he found only a machine-gun post to attack. Turning north at Furnes and passing on the east side of the aerodrome he shot up a water tower, and then flew home, landing at 12.05hrs. Flying Officer Kasal, after being separated, shot up a large factory 1 mile east of Dunkirk and then, being uncertain of his position, followed a railway line on which he observed a goods train. He attacked the engine, but saw no results. Turning north, he fired on a machine-gun post near the beach, and then flew home, landing at 12.20hrs.

16 FEBRUARY

Air-to-air firing practice was carried out by 313 Squadron today. They also took receipt of a Spitfire MkVb (BL769).

17 FEBRUARY

Five convoy patrols were carried out today by 313 Squadron, and practice flying continued.

18 FEBRUARY

Four convoy patrols were carried out today by 313 Squadron, and practice flying continued. The squadron was brought to readiness between 11.00hrs and 12.00hrs but did not take off.

19 FEBRUARY

Practice flying and cine-camera combat exercises were carried out by 313 Squadron.

20 FEBRUARY

A 'rhubarb' operation was carried out by Blue Section (Flight Lieutenants Fejfar and Vykoukal) from 313 Squadron. They took off and refuelled at RAF Hawkinge. Leaving there at 10.24hrs, they proceeded via Dungeness to attack Verton distillery and Berck Aerodrome. Flying at zero feet for several minutes over the Channel, a blinding snowstorm was encountered, and the leader decided to call off the operation and the aircraft returned to base, landing at 11.05hrs. Some local flying was carried out in the afternoon.

Three Hurricanes from A&AEE (Boscombe Down) arrived at this station ahead of a secret demonstration arranged at Shoeburyness by the Minister of Aircraft Production. Accommodation was provided for the three officers and a ground party of two airmen.

21 FEBRUARY

Snowstorms prevented any flying in the morning, but the weather cleared enough for some local flying to be carried out in the afternoon by 313 Squadron.

22 FEBRUARY

One section of 313 Squadron took off on a convoy patrol, but was recalled owing to bad weather and reduced visibility. Local flying was carried out in the afternoon.

23 FEBRUARY

At 09.55hrs, four aircraft – Red Section (Flight Lieutenant František Fajtl and Sergeant Truhlar) and Yellow Section (Flight Lieutenant Vaclav Hajek and Sergeant František Bönisch) of 313 Squadron – took off to patrol over the local area, flying at between 500ft and 1,500ft. At 10.36hrs, Sergeant Bönisch in a Spitfire Mk Vb (AD391) crashed into the sea just off the Royal Artillery Experimental Station at Shoeburyness and was killed. Eyewitnesses reported that the starboard wing of the low-flying aircraft had touched the water and after bouncing twice went straight down into the water.

Captain Cordeaux, DSO, RN, the officer commanding one of the ships in the vicinity, spent some twenty minutes in the sea and recovered the body. A man of 55 years of age, Captain Cordeaux, had to be treated at hospital following the rescue.

Three other convoy patrols were carried out between 10.45hrs and 15.15hrs, returning with nothing to report.

24 FEBRUARY

Red Section (Pilot Officer Michalek and Sergeant Miroslav Zauf) of 313 Squadron took off on a 'rhubarb', refuelling at RAF Manston, and taking off again at 11.20hrs. Landfall was made 6 miles east of Dunkirk and, flying at zero feet and encountering much flak, the section turned to starboard, passing south of Dunkirk, and flew west. At Les Hattes (near Gravelines), they attacked a factory, observing several strikes. Turning again to starboard, they attacked a goods train on the Gravelines to Bourbourg line. Firing from 400 yards, both pilots saw strikes on the engine. They then returned home, landing at 12.15hrs.

Squadron Leader W.H.A. Monkton, MM was posted to the station, supernumerary for administration duties, on authority of the Air Ministry (Dept. QJ).

25 FEBRUARY
Non-operational flying today. Flying practice was carried out by 313 Squadron.

26 FEBRUARY
Another day of flying practice was carried out by 313 Squadron.

27 FEBRUARY
Pilot Officer Michalek left the squadron for a week on army liaison duty. Practice flying was carried out for most of the day by 313 Squadron.

28 FEBRUARY
Two convoy patrols of four aircraft each were operated by 313 Squadron over the Thames Estuary from 10.55hrs until 13.20hrs. At 13.40hrs, two aircraft took off to make rendezvous over Clacton and act as escort to a Blenheim bomber on a calibration test.

Night-flying practice was carried out by Squadron Leader Mrazek, Flying Officer Kasal, Flight Sergeant Vaclav Foglar and Sergeant Herak.

MARCH

6 MARCH
313 Squadron ceased attachment to RAF Southend and returned to RAF Hornchurch.

Pilot Officer J.A. Addison reported his arrival on attachment from RAF North Weald, for defence duties.

7 MARCH
Sixteen aircraft of 411 (RCAF) Squadron arrived from RAF Hornchurch, the main party arriving by rail, and several by motor car. The squadron comprised almost all RCAF personnel, the RAF pilots having remained at Hornchurch. The afternoon was spent settling in, and through the co-operation of the RAF personnel of the station, any difficulties were ironed out and minor adjustments attended to.

8 MARCH
Twelve aircraft of 411 Squadron took off on its 'first show', the pilots clocking up twenty hours on air-sea rescue patrols.

9 MARCH
411 Squadron were once again on air-sea rescue patrols today, and returned without incident. The pilots were sad to lose a good colleague, the squadron adjutant, Flight Lieutenant R. Whalley, on his posting to 407 Squadron.

10 MARCH
A foggy morning meant very little flying was done. In the afternoon it cleared sufficiently to allow 411 up on convoy patrol. All aircraft returned safely and without incident.

11 MARCH
Poor weather closed in, which meant there was no flying done.

12 MARCH
With an improvement in the weather today, 411 Squadron put in twenty-five hours of practice flying.

13 MARCH
Eleven aircraft of 411 Squadron took off on a sweep. Although they encountered no enemy aircraft, the pilots were glad to have some operational flying, chalking up some twenty-eight hours between them.

14 MARCH
Some of the aircraft of 411 Squadron took part in a display at Brighton, demonstrating some excellent flying skills. The remainder of the squadron carried out an uneventful convoy patrol.

15 MARCH
Ten aircraft of 411 Squadron took off on convoy patrol followed by a 'rodeo'. The remaining aircraft took the advantage for some practice flying.

16 MARCH
A dull morning and rain following meant there was no operational flying for 411 Squadron, but some practice flying was carried out in the afternoon. The squadron was joined by Acting Flight Lieutenant Smith on posting.

Pilot Officer C.W. Bray (68963), defence officer, was re-posted to this station for (supernumerary) administration duties.

17 MARCH
More bad weather today meant that all aircraft were grounded.

18 MARCH
Another day of rain; one more like this and the aerodrome would become unserviceable. Despite this, 411 Squadron flew thirty-four hours of practice flying today. A 'Dining In' night was planned at the Sergeants' Mess, a pleasant interlude for the pilots and an opportunity to meet the staff of the station in social circumstances.

19 MARCH
More rain today; 411 Squadron was released at 13.00hrs. Squadron Leader R. Newton decided the aerodrome was unserviceable and stood the squadron down. Two 'Alerts' were sounded in the evening, but were quickly followed by an 'All Clear' signal. A 'Guest Night' at RAF Hornchurch was attended by Squadron Leader Newton, Flight Lieutenant Weston, Flying Officer Curtis, and Pilot Officer Green (in place of Pilot Officer Ash who was detailed for duty), to represent 411 Squadron.

20 MARCH
A dry but dull day; no flying was carried out.

21 MARCH

The aerodrome was unserviceable today after heavy rain overnight. ENSA gave a show at Earl's Hall School in the afternoon.

22 MARCH

Another quiet day with no flying. A big party was held by the pilots of 411 Squadron in the evening at the Officers' Mess, to which Group Captain Broadhurst, DSO and Bar, DFC, AFC and Wing Commander Powell, DFC were invited from RAF Hornchurch, along with many other guests.

At around 21.00hrs, there was slight enemy air activity in the vicinity of Southend during which one bomb was dropped in the area.

23 MARCH

Following the steady improvement in the weather over the last two days, 411 Squadron carried out twenty-nine hours of local flying, convoy patrols and taking part in a wing formation over London.

24 MARCH

411 Squadron took off on a sweep over France as part of the Hornchurch Wing, acting as close escort for the bombers, with 411 as top cover for the wing. Yellow Section – Pilot Officer Ash (leading), Warrant Officer Gridley, and Sergeants Taylor and Sample – turned into attacking enemy aircraft, which dived away. Shortly after, the squadron was forced to 'break' with enemy aircraft attacking from the rear. Re-forming, the squadron turned to engage the enemy. During individual dogfights, Pilot Officer Sills' aircraft was hit in the glycol tank and he broke off the engagement, diving sharply away. His aircraft was believed to have gone down and it was assumed that he had made a forced landing or had baled out. Pilot Officer Ash's aircraft was hit by fire from a Focke-Wulf Fw 190, and he, Sills and Gridley failed to return.

Sergeant Randall and Pilot Officer Eakins ran out of fuel and made forced landings at South Ockendon, and Sergeant Taylor, injured with a bullet halfway through his leg, returned to Southend. Three enemy aircraft had been shot down in the combat.

25 MARCH

Sergeants Cushing and Hartley, both Canadians, reported to 411 Squadron this morning and Flight Lieutenant Duncan-Smith arrived to take over Flight Lieutenant K. Boomer's place as commander of 'A' Flight.

26 MARCH

Practice flying only was carried out by 411 Squadron. Flight Lieutenant A.R. Russell reported his arrival here for duty as station adjutant on posting from RAF Kenley.

27 MARCH

Ten aircraft from 411 Squadron took off on a sweep over France. Three minutes over the French coast, the escorted bombers were attacked by Me 109s and Fw 190s. Pilot Officer Green shot down one Me 109 and Pilot Officer Long claimed another as 'probable', as did Pilot Officer Connolly.

Flight Lieutenant Duncan-Smith, who was to take up the duties of Flight Lieutenant Boomer, was posted to Command 64 Squadron.

28 MARCH

A massive fifty-three hours of flying time was put in today by 411 Squadron through convoy work and local flying.

Flight Lieutenant A.R. Russell took over the duties of station adjutant, replacing Squadron Leader W.H.A. Monkton, MM.

Exercise 'Wolf' was commenced. All station personnel participated in this exercise in conjunction with army personnel. The exercise was completed at noon the next day, and proved to be very satisfactory.

29 MARCH

A day of practice flying, convoy patrol work, air-to-sea firing and dive-bombing in connection with a practice attack planned on the station. At 19.20hrs, word was received that the squadron would be moving to RAF Digby the next morning. Squadron Leader Gadney of RAF Southend and the headquarters personnel helped in every way to facilitate the sudden instruction to move the squadron.

30 MARCH

411 Squadron ceased attachment to the station and moved to RAF Digby, the first party leaving at 09.10hrs by rail. The advance party of 64 Squadron arrived on attachment from RAF Hornchurch.

31 MARCH

The main party of 64 Squadron arrived soon after breakfast time and 411 Squadron left for RAF Hornchurch. Flight Lieutenants Ullestad and Austeen joined 64 Squadron on posting from 332 Squadron, Pilot Officer J. Baraw and Sergeants F. Johnson and K. Rogers were posted in from 611 Squadron, and Flight Lieutenant Kingaby, DFM and two Bars joined the squadron on posting from 111 Squadron.

APRIL

1 APRIL

At 11.55hrs, eleven aircraft of 64 Squadron took off for RAF Hornchurch, and following a briefing there, took off again at 12.20hrs as Forward Support Wing in a 'circus' operation on Boulogne Harbour. No enemy aircraft were encountered but one bomber was seen to crash into the sea just off the coast of Folkestone.

The squadron made a rushed landing back here at 13.50hrs, just in front of ten aircraft of 313 (Czech) Squadron, twelve aircraft of 403 (RCAF) Squadron, twelve aircraft of 222 (Natal) Squadron and one aircraft from 121 (Eagle) Squadron – forty-six aircraft in all. Immediately after landing a terrific thunderstorm broke out with vivid lightning and deluge, but nearly everyone was under cover by then, and a giddy reunion was held in the watch hut.

2 APRIL

A fine morning followed the storms of the previous day, and 64 Squadron was airborne on convoy patrols. In the afternoon air firing was carried out at RAF Martlesham.

3 APRIL

64 Squadron carried out air firing in the morning with the Target Towing Flight. On landing, Pilot Officer R. Thomas hit a bump and pranged a wing of his aircraft on the ground. At 17.00hrs they were released off the station.

4 APRIL

At 07.00hrs, 64 Squadron took off for RAF Hornchurch, preliminary to Circus 110. After breakfast there, they took off at 09.40hrs in the company of 313 Squadron and flew at 25,000ft as Forward Support Wing for twelve Douglas Bostons that bombed St Omer. Nothing of particular note was seen until just before re-crossing the French coast at Mardyck when a Spitfire collided with that of Leon Divoy, cutting the whole of his tail off. He immediately went into a spin but was seen to bale out at about 20,000ft. The Spitfire that collided with him also spun down, the pilot baling out before it went into the sea about 5 miles off Mardyck.

Flight Lieutenant A.R. Russell, station adjutant, took over the additional duties of Officer i/c Station Signals Section, and Officer i/c Secret and Confidential Publications.

5 APRIL

At 02.00hrs, all Operations Room and Signals Office clocks on the station were advanced one hour for summer time.

6 APRIL

Mist in the morning kept all aircraft on the ground, but after lunch it cleared sufficiently for some practice flying to be done.

7 APRIL

64 Squadron carried out convoy patrols and was released for the day at 14.00hrs. At 14.00hrs, the Smith Gun Troop proceeded to the rifle range, Rochford, for firing practice. The troop consisted of one NCO and seven men.

8 APRIL

At 07.30hrs, 64 Squadron took off, making rendezvous with 313 Squadron over the base at 5,000ft and then proceeded to meet other wings on a 'rodeo', going in east of Dunkirk, Poperinghe, St Omer, Ambletuene at 20,000ft. No one saw anything to speak of until about 15 miles south of Calais, when two Fw 190s dived past on the port side and, without a word on the R/T, Pilot Officer F. Conrad led Flight Lieutenant J. Plesman around and attacked them. Plesman lost Conrad but he was heard to call on the R/T 'I am hit' and that was the last that was heard of him. After a pretty hectic time with several Me 109s and Fw 190s he came back at zero feet to re-join the squadron.

Two convoy patrols and air firing occupied the afternoon for the squadron and in the evening they were glad to welcome Squadron Leader Watkins on a visit from 611 Squadron at RAF Drem.

Flight Lieutenant P.C. Blount, Command catering officer, visited the station in connection with mess duties.

9 APRIL

At 09.00hrs, a full-scale anti-gas exercise was carried out, ceasing at 12.00hrs. During the exercise a gas warning was broadcast over the station's tannoy system, and anti-gas clothing was worn during this period by all personnel employed out of doors. De-contamination squads carried out practice and the whole exercise proved to be satisfactory.

Flight Lieutenant J.E. Garrish reported his arrival from RAF Eglington, on attachment (pending posting) for accountant duties.

One convoy patrol was carried out in the morning by 64 Squadron but dirty weather got the squadron released for the afternoon.

10 APRIL
64 Squadron took off for a conference at Hornchurch and at 16.15hrs took off with 313 Squadron on a big 'rodeo' with seven other wings. The squadron went in at Hardelot, St Omer and came out at Gravelines at 21,000ft with the Czech squadron above them at 25,000ft. 64 Squadron saw nothing but 313 Squadron was engaged in combat with enemy aircraft and destroyed one and damaged three, but lost two of their own pilots.

Flight Lieutenant A.R. Russell took over the duties of President Service Institute, replacing Flight Lieutenant J.S. Wood.

11 APRIL
One convoy patrol was carried out by aircraft of 64 Squadron in the morning, and afterwards they put in some practice flying. At 11.45hrs, six aircraft took off for RAF Hornchurch but as they arrived they were ordered to remain airborne as air-raid sirens were going. They patrolled at 30,000ft for a time and were then ordered to Cap Gris Nez. They saw three bandits in mid-Channel and chased them into France and then returned, landing at 13.15hrs.

12 APRIL
At 11.30hrs, ten aircraft of 64 Squadron left for RAF Hornchurch and took off from there at 12.35hrs on Circus 122 against the Hazebrouck marshalling yards, and were top cover in and out at 18,000ft. After leaving the target area, enemy aircraft were sighted and engaged. The CO shot down one Fw 190, and another was claimed as damaged by Sergeant Thomas. Pilot Officer J. Stewart got shot up by a Fw 190 which left bullet holes in the port wing and tail, but he made it back home.

Pilot Officer A.C. Tapsell reported for duty here on a posting to 1488 (FG) Flight (for flying duties).

13 APRIL
Two convoy patrols were carried out by aircraft of 64 Squadron in the morning, and then seven pilots flew their aircraft to RAF Hornchurch for lunch. At 13.55hrs, 64 Squadron took off again on a completely uneventful 'rodeo', patrolling Gravelines, Dunkirk and Cap Gris Nez at 21,000ft, and landing back at 15.30hrs.

Brigadier Carden-Roe, MC Officer Commanding 134 Brigade paid a visit to the station, accompanied by the relieving Brigadier Commanding 169 Brigade.

14 APRIL
Following a convoy patrol at 08.30hrs, twelve aircraft from 64 Squadron left for RAF Hornchurch, and took off from there at 11.40hrs as part of a Diversionary Wing on Circus 124 to the power station at Caen. The operation was successful and no enemy aircraft were encountered by the squadron.

At 17.45hrs, the squadron was airborne again on a 'rodeo', the rendezvous point being at 10,000ft over West Malling. They climbed to 26,000ft crossing in at Le Touquet, when about ten Fw 190s tried to intercept the squadron, but after doing a sort of Catherine Wheel, the enemy aircraft dispersed inland. 64 Squadron landed back at base at 19.00hrs.

At about 16.00hrs, Sergeant Donald E. Kingaby (112406) shot down a fugitive balloon from 5,000ft, 3 miles off Gravesend.

15 APRIL

64 Squadron carried out two convoy patrols in the morning, and then left for Hornchurch for a conference and lunch. At 14.10hrs, they took off as part of a 'ramrod' on Devres Aerodrome. Rendezvous was made with 313 Squadron over Gravesend at 10,000ft and crossed in west of Gravelines. Three wings were involved in this operation which scared off enemy aircraft seen in the distance, and everything went according to plan. 64 Squadron returned via Folkestone and Ashford and landed back at RAF Hornchurch at 15.30hrs.

At 17.20hrs, the squadron took off again to take part on Circus 125, the target being Gravelines. They made rendezvous over Eastchurch at 15,000ft and flew out over Manston as the lower squadron in escort cover to Hurri-bombers. Crossing in over Calais Marck at 19,000ft they turned right over Guines, out over St Inglevert and, after doing a couple of wide orbits over Cap Gris Nez, returned via Dover and landed at Southend at 19.40hrs. A large number of Me 109s and Fw 190s were seen but none of them attacked.

Sergeant H. Bennett arrived here to join 64 Squadron from 57 OTU, Hawarden.

16 APRIL

64 Squadron took off mid-morning for a briefing and lunch at Hornchurch. At 13.25hrs the squadron took off on a 'rodeo', being high cover to the RAF North Weald Wing and Debden Wings at 25,000ft. 64 Squadron were supposed to go in at Hardelot, but on reaching there the CO saw suspicious-looking aircraft towards Cap Gris Nez, and so ordered a patrol just off the coast from there to Hardelot and back. Nothing of any importance was noted and the squadron landed back at Hornchurch at 15.00hrs in readiness for an evening show.

At 17.35hrs, the squadron took off again on a 'rodeo', going in at Mardyck, Cassels, just north of St Omer, and out at Gravelines then three wide orbits over Cap Gris Nez and Calais and then out over the Channel.

Flying Officer T.V. B., an officer from Headquarters, 11 Group Armament Staff, visited this station in connection with an Inspection of Armament. Station personnel received instructions as 'Backers-Up' on the rifle range. Four senior NCOs and thirty-four airmen attended the training.

17 APRIL

64 Squadron was at readiness at 10.00hrs while every other squadron in 11 Group did a 'rodeo'. Two convoy patrols were carried out and at 14.50hrs the squadron made rendezvous over Hornchurch with 313 and 122 Squadrons and the group captain moved in to lead them. They then flew as bottom squadron at 20,000ft to West Malling where they picked up the North Weald and Biggin Hill Wings. They proceeded down the Channel to the Somme Estuary, and in at Le Touquet, where Pilot Officers Derrick

Colvin, Walker and Arne Austeen were hit by flak. The squadron crossed out at Sangatte, up to Dunkirk, and then back by Deal, landing at 16.30hrs. Colvin put down at RAF Manston.

Further training of 'Backers-Up' was carried out today by two senior NCOs and forty-six airmen.

18 APRIL
At 13.05hrs, 64 Squadron took off and flew at zero feet to RAF Manston for briefing. Goering was expected to be at Sesqueux in the afternoon so a party of Hurri-bombers escorted by 313 Squadron left Hawkinge at 14.30hrs. 64 Squadron was charged with 'beating-up' operations. They crossed the French coast at Toqueville and flew south of Dieppe across the Entermer Railway, turned left past Frisnay until they hit the Aumale Railway just south of Blungy, along which they flew to Camaches. Here the CO shot up some goods wagons and then a factory. Others attacked the goods yard at Camaches and then a train on the outskirts of Le Treport. The engine was hit and the flak guns were silenced by Doherty. Hannan attacked an engine at Le Treport and caused it to explode with violence, while seven barges were shot up by Sergeant Kingaby and his section in a canal at the back of Le Treport, before they flew out and home.

19 APRIL
64 Squadron carried out a practice wing formation over Dungeness from 12.30hrs to 13.30hrs. On landing, Sergeant Engelsen pranged his aircraft (Spitfire BM416) on a bump, knocking off the port leg which made a large hole in the fuselage; in skidding round at the end of the run the port wing was also rendered u/s [unserviceable]. The rest of the day was spent practice flying.

The station commander addressed all ranks in the Airmen's Mess at 13.40hrs on the station's past and forthcoming activities.

20 APRIL
No operational flying was carried out by 64 Squadron today, but there was plenty of practice flying done.

21 APRIL
At 11.30hrs, the station commander held a conference at which all officers attended. The general administration of the station was discussed, and much benefit was derived from the consultations.

The usual convoy patrols off Barrow Deep were carried out by 64 Squadron, but with 10/10ths cloud moving down to the deck during the morning, the squadron was released at 13.00hrs for the rest of the day.

22 APRIL
With bad visibility again today, only practice flying was carried out by 64 Squadron.

Flight Lieutenant B. Joy, physical fitness officer, Headquarters, 11 Group, visited the station in connection with physical fitness training.

23 APRIL
With limited visibility again today, air firing and squadron formation flying was carried out by 64 Squadron.

24 APRIL

With a slight improvement in the weather, two convoy patrols were carried out in the morning by 64 Squadron, and then at 10.40hrs eleven aircraft led by Group Captain Harry Broadhurst (24035) took off to fly as top cover on Circus 135 to Gravelines. No enemy aircraft were encountered and the squadron landed back at 18.01hrs.

25 APRIL

64 Squadron took off at 11.15hrs on Ramrod 27 to Calais, going in as top squadron over Gravelines, Guines and out at Cap Gris Nez.

At 15.35hrs, the squadron took off again on Circus 137. The Hornchurch Wing was freelance wing and 64 Squadron was top squadron at 25,000ft. A lot of enemy aircraft were seen in the Somme Estuary, but the only engagement was from 313 Squadron as the enemy withdrew. The squadron landed back at 17.20hrs.

26 APRIL

At 09.35hrs, thirteen aircraft of 64 Squadron took off on a 'circus' as close escort to twelve Bostons, returning at 11.10hrs. The rest of the day was spent on the station, and at 19.30hrs, twelve aircraft of the squadron took off on a 'circus' as escort to Hurri-bombers against the silk factory at Calais.

27 APRIL

At 09.35hrs, 64 Squadron took off on a 'circus' as escort to Hurri-bombers to St Omer, and at 15.00hrs, the squadron was airborne again as support for a raid on St Omer Aerodrome.

28 APRIL

The only operational flying today by 64 Squadron was a sweep over St Omer at 10.30hrs. The squadron was back ninety minutes later with nothing to report.

29 APRIL

At 15.00hrs, 64 Squadron took off on a sweep over France to a depth of 10 miles via Dunkirk. Nothing to report. Four aircraft, six pilots, and twenty-six airmen of 1488 (TT) Flight were detached to RAF Shoreham for target-towing duties on instructions received from Headquarters, 11 Group. Pilot Officer H.J. Cleary was in charge of this party.

30 APRIL

At 09.15hrs, 64 Squadron took off on a 'rodeo', sweeping over Ambleteuse, Guines and Calais, and returning with nothing to report. After lunch the squadron moved to RAF Hornchurch.

MAY

1 MAY

RAF Southend was transferred from Hornchurch to North Weald for operational control.

2 MAY

Non-operational 403 (RCAF) Squadron, led by Squadron Leader Alan C. Deere (40370), DFC and Bar, landed at 11.45hrs from RAF North Weald; their Servicing Echelon followed. In the afternoon, flying practice was carried out.

Squadron Leader R.J.V. Jackson of Headquarters, Fighter Command, visited the station in connection with maintenance matters.

3 MAY

403 Squadron carried out four practice formations and some local flying today.

4 MAY

Another day of practice flying for 403 Squadron. Group Captain T.G. Pike, station commander, RAF North Weald, visited the station. Practice live-grenade throwing was carried out by all ranks at the Brickfields, Eastwoodbury.

An accident wrecked two aircraft of 403 Squadron when Spitfire AB865 was hit by BL900 while parked. Another accident occurred during the morning, when Pilot Officer Maynard, in Spitfire BM237 of 122 Squadron, overshot on landing here, causing slight damage to the aircraft. The pilot was unhurt.

5 MAY

403 Squadron became operational again today with a state of readiness at thirty minutes from dawn. At 09.00hrs, the squadron was ordered to take part with the North Weald Wing in Circus 156 to Zeebrugge with six Bostons.

The boys were briefed by the commanding officer and were airborne at 10.40hrs to make rendezvous with the bombers and four Debden squadrons at Felixstowe at 1,000ft. The North Weald Wing consisted of 222, 403 and 121 Squadrons at 20,000ft, 22,000ft and 24,000ft respectively. The Debden Wing escorted the bombers at 14–19,000ft to the target (the coke ovens at Zeebrugge). Squadron Leader Deere lost two of his section when Red 3 (Warrant Officer Campbell) was forced to return to base after having trouble with his hood, and Red 4 (Pilot Officer Hurst) turned back owing to R/T failure.

Meanwhile the squadron reached the rendezvous at Maldon with the remainder of the North Weald Wing but owing to a fault in the CO's watch the rendezvous was made a minute or so late and after orbiting for three minutes and not sighting the other two squadrons, they proceeded to Felixstowe. When about halfway there, they were ordered over the R/T to proceed direct to the target. However, the operation had been carried out and the squadron was ordered to return to base. No enemy aircraft or flak was encountered.

At 13.00hrs, 'A' Flight was at readiness; 'B' Flight at fifteen minutes for aerodrome defence. During the afternoon Flying Officer Dean and representatives of the Canadian Broadcasting Company visited this station.

Squadron Leader W.H.A. Monkton, MM represented the station commander at the funeral of the late Flying Officer D.J. Renvoize (83 Squadron) at Thundersley, Essex.

Practice live-grenade throwing was carried out by all ranks at the Brickfields, Eastwoodbury.

6 MAY

'B' Flight of 403 Squadron was at readiness at 05.25hrs; 'A' Flight was at fifteen minutes.

At 08.25hrs, Red Section took off to patrol twenty-four ships that made up the Convoy 'Numeral' off Shoeburyness. They were relieved by Yellow Section. This was followed by some non-operational flying including aerobatics, testing, and a section reconnaissance.

At 11.10hrs, Operations phoned the details of Rodeo 21 to St Omer and at 11.45hrs the squadron was briefed in Dispersal and were airborne at 12.15hrs, making rendezvous with the Hornchurch Wing and the remainder of the North Weald Wing at Clacton at 12.30hrs at a height of 6,000ft. From there the squadron climbed to bomber heights and speeds in wide formation until the French coast was crossed between Gravelines and Mardyck at 12.50hrs at 19,000ft. 222 Squadron was at 17,000ft, 121 Squadron at 21,000ft, with Hornchurch below at 14/16,000ft. The Northolt Wing were above at 23/25/27,000ft. 403 Squadron then climbed to 23,000ft and swept inland to St Omer, turning right and crossing out again at Calais. A certain amount of flak was experienced here but not in great quantity. A second entry inland was then made and the formation swept inland for about 10 miles and then returned to base, landing at 13.45hrs with nothing to report. During the afternoon there was more practice flying, and then orders were received to take part in Rodeo 22 to take place at 19.30hrs.

Following the briefing 403 Squadron was airborne at 19.00hrs to rendezvous with the remainder of the North Weald Wing at Thameshaven at 19.10hrs at 3,000ft, and then set course for Hastings to rendezvous with the Tangmere Wing at 19.30hrs at 12,000ft. They crossed the French coast between Le Touquet and Berck, with the Tangmere Wing as top cover. No enemy aircraft or flak was encountered and the aircraft returned to base at 20.15hrs.

On instructions received from Headquarters, 11 Group, this station ceased to issue Daily Routine Orders and commenced to issue Station Routine Orders three times weekly, in order to preserve paper.

Practice live-grenade throwing was carried out by all ranks. Flight Lieutenant A.R. Russell assumed duties of officer i/c station personnel (i.e. for station defence).

Wing Commanders L.E.A. Healey, armament officer, 11 Group, and R.F. Boyd, Headquarters Fighter Command (Tactics), visited the station.

7 MAY

The morning was taken up with practice flying, camera gun practice, air firing and army co-operation. After lunch Brigadier General Lyme visited the squadron and was given a flip in the 'Maggie' by Pilot Officer Somers.

At 18.20hrs, 403 Squadron was briefed in Dispersal about a 'circus' to the Zeebrugge coke ovens. The squadron took off, and at 18.53hrs made rendezvous with 122 and 222 Squadrons at Bradwell, and then proceeded to make rendezvous with the Debden Wing and six Bostons at Felixstowe at 19.00hrs. Reaching the Belgian coast, 403 Squadron was at 19,000ft. While over the target area fifteen enemy aircraft appeared about 15 miles inland, flying towards the coast which they crossed making towards the English coast at 20,000ft. There was a considerable amount of flak over the target area and after turning left, the squadron sighted enemy aircraft. Four of these came down towards the squadron and then, when the squadron closed in to 1,500 yards, dived away towards the French coast. With no further action, the squadron returned home, landing by 20.20hrs.

8 MAY

The morning was taken up with formation flying, air firing and cloud flying.

At 17.30hrs, 403 Squadron was at readiness to take off at 18.00hrs for a 'circus' to Dieppe power station with six Bostons. The North Weald Wing (403, 222, 121 Squadrons) was to act as high cover for the bombers. 403 made rendezvous with 222 and 121 Squadrons at Hornchurch at 18.20hrs and ten minutes later they made rendezvous with the six Bostons at Redhill. The escort wing (Kenley) and the escort cover wing (Biggin Hill) were contacted and course was set for Beachy Head, and from there the formation climbed until over the target. At 19.02hrs the bombing operation was carried out according to plan and the formation turned out back towards Beachy Head. The Tangmere and Northolt Wings acted as target support, entering over the French coast three minutes after the bombing and swept the area at high altitude. The operation was successful and 403 Squadron landed home at 19.45hrs.

During the afternoon, Anthony Steel, Esq., of the Dominions Office of the British Council, visited this station to discuss the question of educating Canadian personnel to appreciate the English attitude to the conduct of war and to encourage the co-operation of Canadian and English elements in the RAF.

9 MAY

403 Squadron was released for training until 13.00hrs.

At 14.39hrs, Blue Section (Pilot Officer Parr and Sergeant N. Monchier) was scrambled to patrol Clacton at 20,000ft but was soon recalled as the 'bandit' had proved to be a friendly.

403 Squadron was airborne at 15.40hrs and made rendezvous with 12 Group and three squadrons of the North Weald Wing over the base. The formation swept inland in the Pas de Calais area at about 27,000ft. No enemy aircraft were encountered but there was heavy flak which was accurate for height but was behind the aircraft. The squadron landed back at base at 16.45hrs and was refuelled, and twenty minutes later was called to readiness. At 18.26hrs the squadron was released for the rest of the day.

10 MAY

At 05.18hrs, 'A' Flight was at readiness and 'B' Flight was at fifteen-minute readiness. One section was on convoy patrol over twenty-one ships with three escort ships off Clacton. This was followed at 06.11hrs by White Section and, at 06.39hrs, Yellow Section, being scrambled to vector 070°. At 07.59hrs, Black Section was scrambled to patrol Barrow Deep at 25,000ft, but like the others, had nothing to report.

More convoy patrols were carried out until 09.19hrs when Operations phoned details of a fighter sweep with the North Weald, Hornchurch and 12 Group Wings over the Pas de Calais. Rendezvous was made over the base and then climbed as it made for the French coast, crossing over Gravelines at 16,000ft. A sweep was made over Desvres and out at Hardelot. No enemy aircraft were seen but some flak was experienced coming out from the French coast, and 403 Squadron landed back home at 12.30hrs.

There was no further operational flying for the rest of the day, but the squadron practised line astern chase, cine-gun and formation flying in the afternoon, ceasing at 16.08hrs.

Squadron Leader W.H.A. Monkton, MM (75426) proceeded to RAF Tain on posting as squadron leader (admin).

11 MAY

403 Squadron was at readiness from dawn until 10.00hrs, after which it was released for the day.

Pilot Officer A.C. Tapsell (101487) proceeded from 1488 (TT) Flight (which was re-designated this month as 1488 Fighter Gunnery Flight) to RAF Friston on posting for duty as aerodrome control officer.

12 MAY

More practice flying was carried out by 403 Squadron today, and at 15.00hrs the squadron was released for the rest of the day. Squadron Leader E.J. Moule (Organisation Branch, 11 Group) visited the station.

13 MAY

One section of 403 Squadron was at readiness, two sections at fifteen minutes and one flight at thirty minutes from the morning.

Flying Officer R.W. Weir (107789) reported his arrival on posting from RAF Biggin Hill (for dental duties).

14 MAY

One section of 403 Squadron was at readiness in the morning, two sections at fifteen minutes and one flight at thirty minutes. At 11.52hrs, one section took off on convoy patrol over Bradwell Bay going north-east. During the afternoon local flying practice was carried out.

15 MAY

At 05.27hrs, 403 Squadron was at readiness, and at 09.15hrs Operations called for two sections to take off for a convoy patrol; one to take off immediately, the other to stand by on readiness. The Convoy 'Totem' was patrolled to the estuary. At 09.47hrs, the remainder of the squadron was airborne on formation practice and local flying, landing at 10.35hrs.

At 11.45hrs, Yellow Section took off for one convoy patrol, and at 12.55hrs, the squadron was released for the afternoon.

A party of seven members of the Canadian National Film Board, Canadian Broadcasting Company, Canadian Press and British United Press, accompanied by Flying Officer Basil Dean, RCAF, public relations officer, visited the station. Group Captain (the Revd) J.F. Cox, Headquarters, 11 Group, also visited the station today.

16 MAY

Air firing was carried out by 403 Squadron at Dengie Flats, and formation flying and cine-gun practice took place during the day.

17 MAY

At 05.10hrs, 403 Squadron was at thirty-minute readiness and at 10.00hrs they were briefed at Dispersal for a 'circus' to Boulogne Docks with twelve Bostons. At 10.34hrs, they took off to rendezvous with the North Weald Wing at a point just north-east of Tilbury and then made rendezvous with the bombers at Beachy Head under 500ft at 11.00hrs. The formation then climbed en route to the target, with 403 acting as close support for the bombers. Hornchurch and Northolt Wings were acting as the diversion, sweeping Hardelot, St Omer and out at Cap Gris Nez.

Very intense flak was experienced over the Boulogne area which followed the air-craft in and out. Some of the pilots reported later that it was the worst that they had experienced. The bombing was carried out from 14,000ft with excellent results. No enemy aircraft were encountered. However, two of the Bostons were hit by flak and were escorted back to the English coast. 403 Squadron landed back home at 11.52hrs.

18 MAY

'A' Flight was at readiness at 05.40hrs. At 06.04hrs, Red Section scrambled for convoy patrol off Barrow Deep. At 08.00hrs, Red Section took off again to patrol a convoy of fourteen merchant vessels escorted by a destroyer going north-east off Shoeburyness.

At 16.45hrs, the squadron left Southend to rendezvous over base at 500ft with the North Weald Wing to act as top cover slightly above and behind 222 Squadron. They crossed the Channel and were at 6,000ft, 10 miles off the French coast at Dunkirk, when the wing turned back to base. No enemy aircraft were seen.

19 MAY

After a quiet day on the station, 403 Squadron was briefed at 19.00hrs for a 'circus' to St Omer.

The squadron made rendezvous with the North Weald Wing at Eastchurch at 20.00hrs to act as escort to six Hurricanes, and were joined by the Hornchurch Wing acting as close support, and the Debden Wing as rear support. They crossed the French coast at Gravelines at 20.19hrs and proceeded to the target area at 20.27hrs. No enemy aircraft were seen and the squadron returned home, landing at 20.55hrs. Two Belgian pilots from 350 Squadron also landed their aircraft here to refuel, and stayed overnight.

Twenty-five airmen were given instruction in combatant training for defence of the aerodrome by four NCOs of the Anti-Aircraft Flight.

20 MAY

One section of 403 Squadron carried out a convoy patrol in the morning, and the rest of the squadron did formation flying and air-firing practice.

21 MAY

One section of 403 Squadron was at readiness for station defence; the rest were at thirty minutes, and all were released at 13.00hrs.

22 MAY

One section of 403 Squadron was at readiness for station defence; the rest were at thirty minutes. Following this, practice attacks were carried out along with formation and cine-gun practice.

Yellow, White and Green Sections took off to patrol a convoy of thirty-four Merchantmen and two escort vessels off Shoeburyness, entering the estuary.

23 MAY

One section of 403 Squadron was at readiness for station defence and two sections carried out formation attacks. During the afternoon the squadron released and the pilots enjoyed a quiet time storing up their batteries for the mess dance at 'The Lawns' in the evening, which was a very nice affair. The group captain and Mrs Pike from North Weald and Wing Commander Scott-Malden were also in attendance. All of the squadron pilots had partners, with Squadron Leader Deere and Flying Officer MacKay's partners being particularly admired.

Squadron Leader J.P. Mills (Organisation Branch) Headquarters, 11 Group, visited the station.

24 MAY

One section of 403 Squadron was at readiness for station defence; the rest was at thirty minutes. The squadron carried out formation and cloud flying. Flight Lieutenant Patrick O'Leary (C/977), piloting KH-F, hit a soft spot while taxiing to a bay and turned up on the nose, damaging the propeller.

25 MAY

Considerable fog was moving in towards noon. 403 Squadron carried out one sweep to Ostend at 10.45hrs, and returned at 12.10hrs with nothing to report. The squadron was released at 16.00hrs.

26 MAY

403 Squadron was at readiness from the early morning, and then carried out formation and cloud flying, and was released at 15.00hrs.

27 MAY

During the morning 403 Squadron did aerobatics and instrument flying; air firing was also carried out. At 14.18hrs, the squadron was airborne on an anti-shipping sweep. 121 Squadron was airborne with the North Weald Wing and attacked two minesweepers and the accompanying destroyer. 403 Squadron swept the Dutch coast north from Flushing and then turned south back to the coast. The wing commander reported enemy aircraft at sea level but only one Me 109F was seen after it had attacked 222 Squadron. The North Weald Wing later reported that 121 Squadron was badly damaged by fire from the minesweepers and in combat with enemy aircraft, although one Me 109 was destroyed and four more were damaged. Sergeant Armstrong was reported missing.

Flight Lieutenant (Revd) W. Province, of the Royal Canadian Air Force Headquarters, visited this station for the purpose of spiritual contact and inspection of welfare arrangements for the personnel of 403 Squadron.

During cine-gun practice carried out by 81 (F) Squadron over Southend, two of their Spitfires of 'A' Flight collided in cloud; Pilot Officer Woodhead, a Canadian pilot in BM467 'FL-T', was killed instantly when his aircraft crashed near Southend. Sergeant Bubes, a Polish pilot in BM158 'FL-Y', with almost complete loss of aileron control of his aircraft, managed to return home.

28 MAY

403 Squadron, except for one section, was at readiness until released at 12.00hrs. Most of the pilots spent the afternoon in Southend. ENSA gave entertainment in the evening at Earl's Hall School.

29 MAY

At 10.25hrs, 'A' Flight of 403 Squadron, led by Squadron Leader Deere, took off to orbit the rescue launches in mid-Channel and circled them for an hour until Motor Rescue

Launch 27 took off south-west and Launch 24 went west, evidently to base. The flight returned at 12.20hrs. Flight Lieutenant Walker led five aircraft which then took over and escorted the launches back to base. No enemy aircraft or floating dinghy was seen.

At 18.50hrs, the squadron was airborne again on a sweep with the North Weald Wing. Rendezvous was made at Chatham and the French coast was crossed at Hardelot where the squadron swept inland, making a large right-hand orbit on a feint towards home, and then turned left and climbed to 32,000ft, sweeping back in at Berck. With the weather closing, the wing turned for Calais and then split up. 403 and 121 Squadrons turned right and swept inside Cap Gris Nez, coming out at Ambleteuese and then along the coast, turning for home between Calais and Dunkirk. All aircraft returned safely despite heavy flak around Calais.

Colonel Block had a flip in the Magister piloted by Pilot Officer Marshall looking over area defence. Flight Lieutenants Edward Darling, DFC (65979) and O'Leary, at the station commander's request, beat up the aerodrome defence batteries. They put up a wonderful show of ground attacks and low-level flying. In the evening a party was held in the Sergeants' Mess which many attended.

Further combatant training was given to fourteen airmen of station personnel, in connection with the defence of the aerodrome.

30 MAY

Formation flying practice was carried out in the morning and the squadron, with the exception of one section, was released at 12.00hrs.

Squadron Leader Morrow visited the squadron from RAF North Weald and gave notice that 403 Squadron were to move back there, much to the disappointment of the boys, who liked Southend very much.

Flight Lieutenant T.J. Moffatt, Officer i/c AA Flight at Southend, was posted to RAF Heathrow for defence duties. Squadron Leader R.E.H. Gould (79794) reported arrival on posting from Headquarters, 10 Group, for duty as Officer Commanding Defence Personnel, on the occasion of the forming of 2810 and 2830 Squadrons of the RAF Regiment at Southend.

31 MAY

A very unsettled day with rain and fog during the morning. At 11.21hrs Pilot Officer Parr and Sergeants Murphy, Johnson and Anderson of 403 Squadron took off on a 'rhubarb'. They crossed the Belgian coast at Bray Dunes (which wasn't bad as their course was to Coxyde). Picking up the route, Pilot Officer Parr and Sergeant Murphy shot up a goods train, the engine of which was stopped by cannon fire and was issuing steam. Sergeant Murphy also shot up an oil tanker coming out at La Panne. The shore batteries opened up on them as they passed. Sergeants Johnson and Anderson, who had flown too far inland, turned and picked up the Furnes Canal and saw four barges. They attacked a large motor-driven one, riddling the pilot house with cannon and machine-gun fire, seriously damaging it. Sergeant Johnson went round again and raked the other three barges, and then attacked a further cluster of six barges. They experienced much flak as they crossed out over La Planne.

At 13.05hrs, the squadron was airborne on an anti-shipping sweep. Briefed at RAF Martlesham Heath, they took off at 15.05hrs, with 222 Squadron leading, followed by 121 and 331 Squadrons. Twenty miles off the Dutch coast the wing split up: 403 Squadron, led by Flight Lieutenant James Walker (40768), crossed the Belgian coast between Ostend and Blankenberge and followed the coast north, flying at 800ft. Passing Zeebrugge heavy flak was encountered, one piece hitting the tail of Walker's aircraft. Four ships were spotted anchored inside the backwater but the anti-aircraft fire was too intense to warrant attacking.

Continuing north, the squadron passed Noorderhoofd, Holland, and then turned 180° and joined up with the balance of the wing at Walcheren, and then proceeded home at 10,000ft. En route, 10 miles off the Dutch coast, two Me 109Fs appeared following the squadron out behind and above swerving from nine o'clock to three o'clock and then dived in to attack, but broke away and evidently tangled with other squadrons of the wing. The squadron landed back home at 16.35hrs.

JUNE

1 JUNE

One flight of 403 Squadron was at readiness at 04.35hrs and one flight was at fifteen minutes.

At 09.30hrs, the squadron was briefed for a sweep and at 10.30hrs they were airborne, making rendezvous with the North Weald Wing over the base to proceed to Gravelines where they would orbit at 22,000ft as withdrawal support for the Kenley Wing. The wing was met coming out but no enemy aircraft were seen. They remained over the area for five minutes and then returned to base at 11.55hrs. No flak was encountered.

At 15.05hrs, the squadron took off for RAF Martlesham Heath to refuel for an anti-shipping attack. As part of the North Weald Wing they took off as 17.50hrs as target support for twelve Bostons. Climbing to 18,000ft over Eaamstede, they then flew south and turned west, coming out over Flushing where smoke from the bombing of the docks was observed.

When north of Ostend, they saw fifteen Fw 190s flying towards them from the south at 25,000ft and another seven or eight coming in from the north. The enemy split up, attacking 331 Squadron, the rest from the south attacking 403 Squadron. The squadron kept together with the exception of Yellow 3 (Pilot Officer Somers) and Yellow 4 (Sergeant Johnson) who got a little behind and were attacked by two Fw 190s. They turned to attack and Yellow 3 got in a three-second burst at 400 yards, hitting one of the enemy aircraft quarter port astern. He then turned to attack the second aircraft head-on and got in a two-second burst, and observed pieces of the engine cowling flying off. At the same time he was hit by cannon shell in the port wing. He spiralled down to 10,000ft and headed for home, landing without any further damage. Yellow 4 got in a two-second burst at a Fw 190 which came across his sight from starboard and cine film of his attack showed good aim and deflection fire from not over 200 yards.

The squadron encountered flak accurate for height over the target area and Sergeant Johnson saw a Spitfire pilot bale out 10 miles off Ostend. He orbited over the area giving out a Mayday.

Flying Officer (Acting Squadron Leader) H.C. Jolly reported his arrival on posting from RAF Pocklington as Officer Commanding 2810 Squadron, RAF Regiment.

Pilot Officer L.W. King reported his arrival on posting from 166 OCTU for duty with the RAF Regiment.

2 JUNE

At 04.20hrs, one section of 403 Squadron was at readiness, the rest of the squadron was at fifteen minutes. At 06.35hrs, the squadron took off on a sweep. The North Weald Wing made rendezvous over Southend and set course for Gravelines via Manston. The wing climbed as the French coast was approached and patrolled between Gravelines and Dunkirk at 20–25,000ft. No enemy aircraft were seen and no flak was encountered.

At 09.30hrs, the squadron was briefed for another sweep which would prove to be the worst the squadron had experienced since its formation.

403 Squadron formed up with the North Weald Wing at Chatham and set course for Hastings. 331 Squadron led, followed by 403 and 222 Squadrons. Rendezvous was made at Hastings with the Hornchurch Wing and course was set for Cap Gris Nez at zero feet, climbing to 20–25,000ft over the French coast. Crossing at Gravelines and sweeping St Omer, they then turned right to Le Touquet. Coming out, 403 was the last squadron, flying at 24,000ft when it was attacked from above by fifteen or twenty Fw 190s who came in from the south.

The squadron turned to meet the attack when it was attacked from above and behind by a further formation of about fifteen Fw 190s. The squadron split up into pairs and were heavily engaged in dogfights. While thus engaged, they were attacked by further enemy aircraft which came in from the south making a total of forty to fifty enemy aircraft engaging 403 Squadron.

Squadron Leader Deere was heavily attacked from all sides and exhausted all cannon and machine guns in short bursts at close range, engaging the enemy head-on, astern and full deflection. He had no time to observe the results, but did see two aircraft hit the sea 10 miles west of Le Touquet, and one, definitely a Spitfire, broke in half in mid-air and the pilot baled out. He also saw another parachute in the vicinity but was unable to give a fix as he was being chased by a Fw 190 to mid-Channel which he could not engage having no ammunition.

After the enemy aircraft broke away about 20 miles south-east of Dungeness, Deere saw a pilot bale out of a Spitfire, and so orbited the area and gave a Mayday three times but received no answer. Three more Spitfires joined in the patrol and rescue boats appeared in the vicinity coming from Dungeness. Deere then left the area 15 miles south-west of Dungeness and saw another Spitfire crash into the sea, later observing a pilot in a dinghy. He orbited several times and directed two rescue boats to the downed pilot (who was later identified as Flight Sergeant Aitken).

Deere then proceeded to Southend, landing at 12.10hrs, ahead of other aircraft of the squadron who arrived in ones and twos. However, Flight Lieutenant Darling, DFC failed to return and was reported as 'missing' over the Channel in Spitfire AR389 (KH-D). Air-Sea Rescue launches rushed to the area where Deere thought he may have seen him go down, but failed to find anything.

Pilot Officer Parr was also lost, along with Pilot Officer Hurst, Pilot Officer Somers, Warrant Officer Campbell and Sergeant Hunt.

Pilot Officer Amor, the Flight Engineer, had obtained delivery of nine new Spitfires by 17.36hrs and by the ground crew working overnight had thirteen aircraft on the front line by 09.00hrs the next morning.

Pilot Officer J.A. Addison was in charge of the AA Flight when it left Southend for RAF Heathrow, on being replaced by the RAF Regiment. The Royal Air Force Regiment was a specialist Airfield Defence Corps founded by Royal Warrant on 5 February 1942. After a thirty-two-week trainee gunner course, its members were trained and equipped to prevent a successful enemy attack in the first instance; mini-mise the damage caused by a successful attack; and ensure that air operations could continue without delay in the aftermath of an attack.

The main party left Southend (LNER station) at 10.20hrs. The unexpired por-tion of the day's rations for all ranks was carried in bulk. At 07.00hrs, Flying Officer (Acting Flight Lieutenant) Apperley reported his arrival on posting from 29 EFTS to 2830 Squadron, RAF Regiment. At 15.30hrs, Pilot Officer E.G. Heavens (109709) reported his arrival from 29 EFTS (Clyffe Pypard) for duty with 2830 Squadron, RAF Regiment. At 17.35hrs, Flight Lieutenant F.G. Christopher (45932) and Flight Lieutenant F.A. Price (108119) reported their arrival at this station from RAF Melbourne, on posting to 2810 Squadron, RAF Regiment.

Four officers and 180 other ranks of 2830 Squadron, RAF Regiment arrived at this station from 29 EFTS for defence duties. Two officers, one warrant officer and 140 airmen of 2810 Squadron, RAF Regiment, reported arrival from RAF Pocklington, on posting via railway for aerodrome defence duties at Southend. The AA Flight was billeted in Wells Avenue (where there was also a decontamination centre at 'Sunnyside'); the Headquarters Flight in the Isolation Hospital in Sutton Lane; the Rifle Flight in Sutton Lane; and flights were also dispersed in houses along Rochford Road.

3 JUNE

One section of 403 Squadron was at readiness from first light; the rest at fifteen minutes. Word came through of the pending move, and Squadron Leader Deere flew to RAF North Weald to discuss affairs. At 12.00hrs the squadron was advised to move to RAF Martlesham Heath. A Handley-Page Harrow arrived and transported the men and material, and the squadron was airborne at 18.00hrs, arriving there at 18.25hrs. Pilot Officers Amor and MacKay remained overnight at Southend to clear up loose ends. 3046 Servicing Echelon did not transfer with the squadron, remaining at Southend.

At 11.33hrs, Pilot Officer A.J.R. Cartwright (121635) reported his arrival on post-ing from 166 OCTU for duty with the RAF Regiment. Pilot Officer L.E. Sharpe (109983) reported arrival on posting from 29 EFTS to 2830 Squadron, RAF Regiment for defence duties.

403 (RCAF) Squadron was replaced by 121 (F) (Eagle) Squadron – 121 Squadron was one of three squadrons whose pilots were Americans, who flew for the RAF before America entered the war.

4 JUNE

Ten aircraft of 121 Squadron took off at 14.36hrs on a 'rodeo'. The coast was crossed at North Foreland and from there they flew to Sangatte, and proceeded on to Ardelot which was reached at 14.25hrs. The Debden and Hornchurch Wings made another sweep at the same time, but not going the same route; 121 Squadron flew as part of the North Weald Wing and were top cover. They made rendezvous over Bradwell, and crossed the coast again at Dungeness. No enemy aircraft were seen and no flak of any importance was reported. The squadron returned at 15.00hrs.

At 19.00hrs, eleven aircraft took off on a 'circus' operation, made rendezvous with six Bostons and escorted them to their target at Dunkirk. Again no enemy aircraft were seen and the flak was light. The squadron landed back at 20.25hrs.

Flight Lieutenant Du Four was posted from 71 (Eagle) Squadron to take over 'B' Flight of 121 Squadron from Flight Lieutenant Thomas Allen, who had been reported as 'missing' from a previous operation.

5 JUNE
Eleven aircraft of 121 Squadron took off on a 'rodeo' at 09.15hrs. They were supposed to meet up with the North Weald Wing over Southend, but they were not contacted. The plan was to cross the coast at North Foreland, continuing on to Mardyck, and leave the French coast just east of Dunkirk. They flew at 25,000ft but the pilots, with nothing to escort, merely stooged between Calais and Dunkirk. As they were turning for home, the North Weald Wing was contacted just as they were coming away from the French coast.

At 14.49hrs, ten aircraft took off on a 'circus' operation as close escort to six Bostons who were to bomb the docks at Ostend. Again, the squadron did not contact the bombers and remained 3 miles off the coast and stooged between Calais and Dunkirk before returning to base, landing at 16.05hrs after an uneventful trip.

Quentin Reynolds Esq., of *Collier's Magazine* (USA), and a photographer visited this station for the purpose of meeting the personnel of 121 Squadron. They were accompanied by Flight Lieutenant Peate, public relations officer.

Acting Squadron Officer J.D. Savage reported her arrival at this station from RAF Kenley for duty as Officer Commanding WAAF personnel at Southend. There being no WAAF Officers' Mess, this lady was billeted out.

7 JUNE
The weather was bad today, but local flying took place. A parade of all Church of England personnel was held at Earl's Hall School, and then marched to St Mary's church, Prittlewell, for a church service conducted by the venerable Ellis N. Gowing, Archdeacon of Southend.

8 JUNE
Training flying only was carried out today.

9 JUNE
Twelve aircraft from 121 Squadron took off on a 'rodeo' to St Omer this morning. Flight Lieutenant John J. Mooney (J/15024) attacked a Fw 190 and shot it down. Immediately after this he saw another and attacked that too, and watched as it crashed in flames. During these operations Pilot Officer Jackson 'Barry' Mahon shot down two Fw 190s and the squadron returned home without loss or damage.

In the afternoon nine aircraft took off on a shipping reconnaissance off Flushing and Ostend. Two heavily armed floating fortresses were observed off Ostend, which opened fire on the squadron. Heavy flak also came from the shore. The pilots decided it was not advisable to attack, and returned home.

The command defence officer, Brigadier C. Britten, MC, and 11 Group defence officer, visited this station and inspected 2810 and 2830 Squadrons of the RAF Regiment at 15.15hrs. They were accompanied by Brigadier Carden-Roe, the local military authority. The station defences and the RAF Regiment squadrons' training were inspected at 15.45hrs.

10 JUNE

Flight Lieutenants H.W. Goodrich and A.M. McGill, Command catering advisors, visited this station in connection with the opening up of a new 'Airmen and WAAFs Dining Hall and Cookhouse' at the Medway Knitting Factory, Prince Avenue, Prittlewell.

11 JUNE

121 Squadron was joined by Sergeants Nicholas Sintetos and Leon Blanding, who were posted in from OTU.

11/12 JUNE

A night manning exercise was held involving 2810 and 2830 Squadrons of the RAF Regiment. The exercise was timed to take place shortly after dark and extended over a period from approximately 23.30hrs in the evening until 02.15hrs the next morning.

The object of the exercise was to test the ability and time required for squadrons to take up 'Action Stations' from a 'stand-to' state of preparedness and to test certain methods of communications during and after the manning of positions.

Phase One was the manning of positions on the station. Phase Two called for certain deployment of 2810 Squadron, whose striking force was moved from its rendezvous at the locality at the North Gate, and the static Rifle Flight to meet a suspected attack along the railway line from the south (note: these moves were purely and simply for exercise purpose and it is inconceivable that they would have been used in this employment in action).

The conclusion of the exercise was that the areas of deployment would be too close to an attacking force at the secured points to effect any fall-back, and it was suggested to move 2810 Squadron northwards, and 2830 Squadron southwards to a locality near to the priory. This allowed better movement for south-westerly and eastward directions on good roads whilst still allowing quick access to the perimeter of the aerodrome. Such deployment would have the added advantage of being closer to Nobles Green, which was the rendezvous for the Counter Attack Battalion from Rayleigh.

12 JUNE

Pilot Officers Herbert Nash and Frank Boyles joined 121 Squadron today, the former from OTU and the latter from 133 Squadron.

13 JUNE

Local flying was carried out by 121 Squadron today, and Sergeant Philip Fox joined them from OTU.

16 JUNE

Pilot Officer C.W. Bray proceeded to RAF Stannington for a three-week junior administrative course on authority from Headquarters, 11 Group.

14 JUNE

Eleven aircraft of 121 Squadron took off on a shipping reconnaissance at 14.25hrs, and flew to within half a mile of Ostend, where three large tankers were making their way into the harbour. Just outside Ostend was a very large fishing fleet, the biggest that the squadron had seen to date. The pilots then proceeded to the west of Walcheren Island about 4 miles from the coast, where an armed trawler was sighted outward bound. Squadron Leader Hugh Kennard (40396), DFC made two attacks on it at deck height, the vessel having opened fire on him first with machine guns in the stern, and guns in the bows. After his attack he ordered the squadron to join in. The guns were silenced on the first attack and during a second attack a big explosion was heard in the stern, and thick black smoke issued from the vessel. It was seen to list heavily to starboard, to decrease its speed, and to make for the shore. Kennard said that the last view of the vessel showed it getting lower in the water, undoubtedly sinking and unlikely to gain the shore. No enemy aircraft were encountered and visibility was very good. The squadron landed back at base at 16.10hrs.

16 JUNE

One section of 121 Squadron went on convoy patrol over Shoeburyness in the morning. At 12.20hrs, Flight Lieutenant Mooney and Flying Officer Seldon Edner (64860) took off on a 'rhubarb' operation. Landfall was made just east of Ostend, and from there they flew for half a mile in a south-westerly direction where the main Bruges–Ostend railway was seen. A freight train was observed travelling to Ostend and they attacked it from astern, Edner giving it a four-second burst, bringing the train to a standstill. Just after this attack he missed Mooney and so called him on the R/T but his set had gone u/s. Edner then circled the train twice to see if there was any sign of him, but it was in vain. He then flew due west for a quarter of a minute to the Bruges–Ostend Canal on which three large barges floated, each heavily laden with packing cases. He made two attacks on all three barges from astern and left them in flames before turning for home, making landfall at Ramsgate, and landing back at Southend at 13.20hrs. No enemy aircraft were encountered during the operations, but with cloud at 10/10ths at 1,000ft visibility was bad. Flight Lieutenant Mooney was reported missing from these operations.

17 JUNE

Local flying and air firing was carried out today by 121 Squadron; the weather was very good.

18 JUNE

At 04.35hrs, six aircraft of 121 Squadron, led by Squadron Leader Kennard, took off on a shipping reconnaissance patrol. The pilots flew at zero feet to Ostend, then down the coast to Calais, keeping about half a mile from the shore. Flak was very heavy from Calais, Ostend and Dunkirk. Two miles off Gravelines, the pilots sighted a big convoy of twelve tankers and two or three destroyers. The pilots approached as near as possible, but they were spotted by the enemy, which put up a tremendous flak barrage, so they aborted the patrol and turned back, landing at RAF Hawkinge at 05.30hrs, and returning home an hour later.

19 JUNE

Local flying and air firing were carried out by 121 Squadron today. In the evening a dinner was held in the mess.

In the Officers' Mess at 22.30hrs, Flight Lieutenant W. James Daley (106457) of 121 Squadron received an album made up and autographed by a large number of residents of Amarillo, Texas (his home town), from his squadron commander as a token of congratulations on the occasion of the award of the DFC.

20 JUNE

Pilot Officer Daley received his promotion today and he took Flight Lieutenant Mooney's place as commander of 'B' Flight of 121 Squadron, who went missing on the 16th as stated.

21 JUNE

121 Squadron spent the morning on convoy patrol. At 17.00hrs, the squadron took off on a 'ramrod', meeting the North Weald and Hornchurch Wings over Chelmsford, and making rendezvous with twelve Bostons over Martlesham. They were flying at 13,000ft as top cover. The bombers were on target when they dropped their bombs on to the docks at Dunkirk. Despite the flak being heavy in the area, no enemy aircraft were seen. The squadron landed home at 18.20hrs with nothing of importance to report.

22 JUNE

At 11.15hrs, eleven aircraft of 121 Squadron took off for RAF North Weald, where they took off again at 12.30hrs as part of the North Weald Wing on a 'roadstead'. They were to act as close escort to ten Bostons which were met over Martlesham at 12.45hrs, and then escorted them to their target; the docks at Dunkirk. On arrival over the target, the bombers split up; five to Dunkirk town and docks; and the others making in the direction of Ostend. Heavy flak was encountered from the shore batteries. No shipping or enemy aircraft were seen, and the squadron landed home at 13.52hrs.

Flight Lieutenant R.T. Apperley of 2830 Squadron, RAF Regiment, proceeded from this station to RAF North Weald, on attachment in accordance with instructions from Headquarters, 11 Group.

WAAF personnel began to arrive at this station in connection with the WAAF substitution scheme. Up to this date, it had not been Air Ministry policy to employ WAAF personnel at RAF Southend.

23 JUNE

Twelve aircraft of 121 Squadron took off at 05.00hrs on a 'rodeo'. The North Weald Wing was contacted over Southend and the Debden Wing over North Foreland at 500ft. After leaving the coast 121 Squadron climbed up to 15,000ft, and after skirting Dunkirk, they left France by Nieuport. No enemy aircraft or shipping was seen, but the flak was fairly heavy over the Dunkirk area. The squadron landed back at 06.25hrs.

Later in the morning, five aircraft went off on a flight to practise low attacks. While over the Blackwater River, Pilot Officer Julian Osborne crashed in the river, but fortunately was soon picked up by a fishing boat.

At 14.45hrs, twelve aircraft took off on a 'circus' operation. The North Weald and Debden Wings were contacted over Martlesham, and rendezvous was made there with twelve Bostons whose target were the docks at Dunkirk. 121 Squadron were rear support, and flew at 15,000ft after leaving the coast, arriving three minutes after bombing had taken place. The bombing was seen to have been successful with a heavy pall of black smoke over the area. The squadron then returned home, landing at 16.00hrs.

A manning exercise in connection with station defences was held from 18.00hrs to 20.00hrs inclusive, during which period, all defence positions were occupied by members of the RAF Regiment and station personnel. The results were satisfactory.

24 JUNE

Convoy patrols were carried out by 121 Squadron this morning off Clacton, but nothing of importance occurred.

25 JUNE

There was local flying only today.

26 JUNE

Local flying was carried out in the morning by 121 Squadron. In the afternoon six aircraft went on bomber interception practice, with two of the aircraft taking the part of the bombers, and the others as intercepting fighters.

At 17.15hrs, twelve aircraft took off as part of the North Weald Wing, with orders to patrol Beachy Head at 10,000ft. After that, the squadron proceeded to the mouth of the Somme, by this time flying at 27,000ft. From the Somme, the wing flew up to Le Touquet, just skirting the coast, and finally to Cap Gris Nez where they circled before returning, making landfall off Folkestone, and landing at home at 18.30hrs.

27 JUNE

All but one section of 121 Squadron was released at 13.00hrs. Flight Sergeant McCairns of 616 Squadron gave a lecture to intelligence officers and operational crews in the pilots' rest room in connection with his experiences on escaping from a prisoner-of-war camp in Germany.

28 JUNE

Local flying was carried out today.

29 JUNE

At 15.45hrs, twelve aircraft of 121 Squadron left on a diversion sweep as part of the North Weald Wing, which was contacted at Chatham at 16.00hrs. From there the wing flew to Pevensey, flying at zero feet for three minutes and then stepped up to 27,000ft by the time landfall was made at St Inglevert, three minutes after twelve Bostons (from 226 Squadron) had bombed the marshalling yards at Hazebrouck. After leaving St Inglevert, the wing flew 5 miles north of Cassell, and then towards home over Mardyck. Many Fw 190s were seen on the homeward journey and although individual engagements took place, no opportunity presented itself to the North Weald Wing to make an attack en masse. The heat was intense during these operations and three pilots had to return home before the squadron owing to overheated engines. The squadron landed at 17.18hrs. Several other wings operated on these operations, and for the first time, a US Army Air Force aircrew bombed a target in enemy-occupied Europe. Captain Charles Kegelman and his crew from the 15th Bombardment Squadron (Light), US Eighth Air Force, flew one of the Bostons that attacked the marshalling yards.

30 JUNE

121 Squadron carried out convoy patrols until 14.00hrs. Two convoys were involved, one 30 miles north of Harwich, the other just off Clacton.

Flying Officer (Acting Flight Lieutenant) S.R. Judd arrived at this station from 124 Squadron on posting for duty as station adjutant, replacing Flight Lieutenant A.R. Russell who proceeded to RAF Lympne to Command (a squadron leader post).

JULY

1 JULY

121 Squadron carried out an uneventful convoy patrol off Harwich in the morning.

Ten officers, twenty senior NCOs and sixty airmen of 130 Squadron arrived from RAF Perranporth, on instructions issued by Headquarters, Fighter Command (for intensive training).

2 JULY

The day was overcast and hazy. No flying was done in the morning, but in the early afternoon twelve aircraft of 121 Squadron took off to join with twelve aircraft from 130 Squadron for a practice flight together, led by Squadron Leader Kennard.

3 JULY

Nothing of importance today; the weather was not so good. A combined balbo was carried out with 121 and 130 Squadrons.

4 JULY

Nothing of importance in the morning; and at 13.00hrs the whole of 121 Squadron was released to celebrate American Independence Day.

5 JULY

No operational flights again today. Pilot Officer Cadman Padgett of 121 Squadron made a crash-landing at the aerodrome owing to the throttle jamming. The aircraft was badly damaged; the propeller blades snapped off, the port cannon broke off and damage to the undercarriage was considerable.

6 JULY

Sections of 121 Squadron went on convoy patrols in the morning and afternoon off Clacton.

7 JULY

Convoy patrols were carried out in the morning by 121 Squadron, but nothing to report. Eighteen aircraft and the crews of 130 Squadron returned to RAF Perranporth on cessation of its attachment to Southend.

8 JULY

Pilot Officer Gilbert Halsey and Sergeant Aubrey Stanhope of 121 Squadron were scrambled at 07.10hrs, and vectored on a course of 120°. They sighted a Ju 88 just north of Dunkirk and gave chase. It was not until the enemy aircraft was over Cap Gris Nez that both pilots were able to attack it. Halsey gave a four-second burst from line astern from 400 yards, but observed no results. Stanhope fired from the same distance and caused the enemy aircraft to weave. As he got nearer for another opportunity, the top rear gunner opened fire. Stanhope gave another burst and silenced the gunner. He closed in to 80 or 90 yards and opened fire again, and observed orange flashes coming from the port engine, and thick black smoke trailing from it. The aircraft went into cloud. Having expended their ammunition the pilots did not pursue the enemy further and returned home, landing home at 07.55hrs.

At 14.20hrs, twelve aircraft took off on an uneventful shipping reconnaissance flight.

The two remaining aircraft and crews of 130 Squadron had left for RAF Perranporth during the morning. A party of three senior NCOs and twenty-five other ranks of 130 Squadron followed by rail in the afternoon.

Pilot Officer C.W. Bray (68963) returned from a junior administrative course at RAF Stannington.

9 JULY
Local flying took place today.

10 JULY
Heavy rain all day, but there was one uneventful scramble by aircraft of 121 Squadron.

11 JULY
No flying today. Flight Lieutenant J.S.Wood was attached to the station to RAF Biggin Hill for duty as permanent duty pilot, on instructions received from Headquarters, 11 Group.

The first summer training camp for ATC personnel was opened up on the outskirts of the aerodrome and was placed under the command of Pilot Officer C.W. Bray. The approximate number of personnel expected to pass through the camp in each week was five officers and 100 cadets.

12 JULY
Twelve aircraft from 121 Squadron took off on a 'rodeo' as part of the North Weald Wing at 15.40hrs. Rendezvous was made with the wing over Southend five minutes later at 500ft. The wing then proceeded to make landfall at Boulogne at 24,000ft and continued to Le Touquet. Then they made a wide circuit out to the Channel and re-entered France by Cap Gris Nez, leaving the coast by Calais. No enemy aircraft were seen and no flak was experienced. The squadron landed at 16.45hrs.

At 18.40hrs, the twelve aircraft took off again as part of the North Weald Wing on a 'circus' operation. Rendezvous was made at Chatham at 18.55hrs at 500ft, and contact was made with twelve Boston bombers at Pevensey. The Hornchurch and Biggin Hill Wings also took part in this operation in which 121 Squadron was support cover and flew between 11,000 and 12,000ft. The target was the airfield at Abbeville, and the operation was carried out successfully. The squadron returned home at 20.00hrs, having encountered no any enemy activity.

13 JULY
In the morning twelve aircraft from 121 Squadron accompanied the North Weald Wing on a shipping reconnaissance flight to Flushing. Flak was very slight and no enemy aircraft were seen. At 11.30hrs, three Lysanders were flown to RAF Martlesham Heath to join 1488 (FG) Flight, then stationed there.

14 JULY
Sergeants Kelly and Blanding of 121 Squadron took off on a 'rhubarb' operation at 16.15hrs. The proposed target was north of Bruges, but with the weather being too good over the coast they experienced light flak straight away, and so decided to return home, landing at 17.26hrs.

At 17.30hrs, Pilot Officer Mahon and Sergeant Carpenter took off on a 'rhubarb' operation, making landfall at St Englevert, where, against light flak, the pilots shot up hangars and the aerodrome, which was in the process of having a great deal of construction work done to it. The pilots then proceeded south for 3 miles and came across a railroad in progress of construction, with a stationary train loaded with railroad implements. The gun post opened fire on the pilots but Pilot Officer Mahon fired back and silenced the gun. They then opened fire on the engine of the train and left it smoking and badly shot up. The pilots landed back at base at 18.20hrs.

Revd A.R. Bradshaw arrived on posting from 31 PD (Canada) to take over duties of chaplain of RAF Southend.

15 JULY

At 12.00hrs, twelve aircraft from 121 Squadron took off as high cover for the Hornchurch Wing which was doing a mass 'rhubarb'. Contact was made with the North Weald Wing at West Malling at 12.05hrs and then proceeded to Pevensey and crossed the Channel at zero feet for fourteen minutes, and then climbed to 10,000ft. Landfall was made at Le Touquet and the pilots turned right and came away again. On the way out about 2 miles west of Boulogne a green patch was spotted by some of the pilots in the sea, and on investigation, noticed that there was a pilot in the green patch of water. Coming down to water level it was seen that the pilot had no dinghy, but was waving cheerfully.

Squadron Leader Kennard ordered four aircraft to orbit the pilot, while he and the rest of the squadron climbed to 17,000ft to look for signs of any rescue boats. They saw four of them but heading in the wrong direction. By waggling their wing tips and circling around the boats, the squadron finally made them steer a course in the right direction towards the pilot in the sea. When the boats were within 300 to 400 yards of the pilot, the squadron was forced to turn for home for lack of petrol. On taking a last look round, Kennard could not see the pilot as he had drifted out of the green patch, but word was received later that he was rescued by the boats, which took a great risk in approaching so near the French coast. Three of the pilots landed at RAF Lympne, two at RAF Manston and the rest at RAF Southend at 13.45hrs.

At 17.55hrs, twelve aircraft took off again on a 'roadstead' operation in conjunction with the North Weald Wing, who were contacted over Southend. 121 Squadron immediately preceded 331 and 332 Squadrons, and made landfall a few miles off Ostend. Turning down the coast they went within a few miles of Flushing and Walcheren Island to look for enemy shipping. Two ships of the armed minesweeper class were sighted just off Watcherau Island, one a mile behind the other. The squadron attacked the first one which was about 500 tons, and was towing a target ship behind. The vessel had a funnel and a superstructure. All twelve pilots dived on it and gave it short bursts, and left it burning from stem to stern. Then the other squadrons attacked it and did further damage. No flak came from the vessel but a lot of heavy flak came from the shore. No enemy aircraft were sighted and the squadron returned home at 19.20hrs.

16 JULY

A few quiet days lay ahead for the pilots of 121 Squadron. Despite being at readiness, nothing of importance occurred.

18 JULY
Very bad weather today. There was one scramble but no enemy aircraft were seen owing to low cloud.

19 JULY
Twelve aircraft took off at 12.30hrs and flew to Debden to re-fuel and meet the North Weald Wing, and then flew across the Channel at 500ft, making landfall just a mile or two from Dunkirk. 121 Squadron was rear support for six Bostons, some six minutes ahead of them, who were bombing objectives at Lille. The wing was ordered to patrol the coast between Dunkirk and Nieuport, just keeping clear of the coast. It was while on the third patrol near Nieuport that Flight Lieutenant Edner saw two Fw 190s, and engaged one of them. He fired three separate bursts at it, finally leaving the enemy aircraft with smoke pouring from its engine. Hits were also seen to register on the fuselage. Pilot Officer Halsey and Pilot Officer Donald Young also had combats with two Fw 190s, but observed no strikes. Sergeant Sintetos was forced to land at Manston as his aircraft had been badly damaged by flak from ground defences. Flak was intense in the Nieuport area. Eleven pilots returned to Southend at 16.00hrs.

The first weekly summer camp training of four officers and seventy ATC cadets was completed today and they returned to their respective units, and appreciation was expressed to the station commander.

The second weekly summer training camp commenced today with the arrival of four ATC officers and eighty-three ATC cadets. The weather was not very promising and rain set in and continued until the early hours.

20 JULY
121 Squadron was scrambled twice this morning, but nothing of importance was reported.

21 JULY
Eleven aircraft of 121 Squadron took off this morning for RAF North Weald at 16.00hrs, and took off from there with the North Weald, Hornchurch, and Debden Wings on a 'rhubarb' operation, which took place at Ostend and Nieuport. Gun posts, factories, armoured lorries and trucks were the targets which came in for concentrated attention by 121 Squadron, and much damage was caused to those objects. Sergeant Kelly, Sergeant Sintetos and Pilot Officer Boyles had their aircraft hit by ground defences, with bullets penetrating the fuselages. Bullets only just missed Pilot Officer Boyles, passing through his cockpit. Pilot Officer Benjamin Taylor (on his first sweep) was shot down by ground fire, a bullet piercing his left leg just above the knee. Fortunately the bullet did not lodge, but passed through and exited the cockpit. The pilots landed home at 17.40hrs.

22 JULY
Four aircraft of 121 Squadron took off at 11.35hrs on a 'rhubarb' operation. The French coast was crossed 3 miles east of Dunkirk, and the Nieuport and Verieuse Canal was the target. On the canal were several barges, which opened fire on the Spitfires with machine guns. The pilots fired, causing explosions on four of the barges, which were left on fire and smoking heavily. Sergeant Blanding shot up a gun post on his way out. Flight Sergeant James Sanders received flak from the ground which pierced the

instrument panel in the cockpit, hitting his right hand and head, and also the port wing of his aircraft. However, he remained in control of the aircraft, and all aircraft landed home at 12.30hrs.

23 JULY
Four spitfires from 317 Squadron arrived from RAF Northolt for a day of air-to-sea firing practice.

24 JULY
Air-firing practice was carried out in the morning by 121 Squadron. At 11.30hrs, Pilot Officer Mahon and Sergeant Blanding went on a 'rhubarb' operation, leaving the coast at Littlehampton. Landfall was made just south of Ault, when they flew east and found the Le Touquet and Abbeville railroad. Experiencing light flak, the pilots shot up a factory and observed explosions on the second floor. Despite being hit by flak in the aileron and port wing, Sergeant Blanding destroyed a gun post, and a switch tower was attacked with success by Pilot Officer Mahon. The pilots then returned home, leaving the French coast by Berck Sur Mer, and landing at 12.40hrs.

Pilot Officer James Happel joined the squadron today.

25 JULY
The second weekly summer training camp of four ATC officers and eighty-three ATC cadets was completed today, when such personnel returned to their respective units.

The third weekly summer training camp opened today with the arrival of four ATC officers and seventy cadets.

An exercise called 'Asthay' was held to test the defences of the aerodrome. The exercise commenced at 23.59hrs in the evening and terminated at 05.30hrs the next morning, during which period the 'enemy' – the Southend Home Guard, supported by a company of the 8th Devons – attempted to capture the aerodrome.

Two hundred paratroops in battledress were dropped in the Canewdon area at around 22.00hrs, and were reported to be working their way towards the aerodrome. The Rochford Platoon Home Guard, 2810 and 2830 Squadrons, RAF Regiment, 121 Squadron (which had a party of forty standing at five minutes' readiness at Dispersal, kept under cover, but ready to act as a reserve anywhere inside the aerodrome perimeter), and all defence personnel including Royal Artillery, took up their defence positions.

Station personnel fell in at the side of the west hangar and were marched to their localities. Sentries were posted, and patrols were sent out. Complete silence was ordered from 23.30hrs as well as a total blackout. Blank ammunition was issued with strict orders that no weapon was to be discharged within ten paces of anyone (the ammunition was still lethal at that range). Thunder flashes and smoke were also issued.

The exercise was successful in that the enemy was unable to infiltrate the defences, mainly because of the difficulties encountered in crossing the terrain around the outskirts of the aerodrome, which lost them the element of surprise for a 'mass' invasion.

26 JULY
There was a scramble at 07.00hrs by aircraft of 121 Squadron, but the bandit was not contacted.

At 15.05hrs, twelve aircraft took off on a shipping patrol. The coast was left via Deal and landfall was made between Calais and Gravelines. An 'E-Boat' was sighted and was completely destroyed by the squadron who made a concerted attack on it. Heavy flak came from the coastal batteries. The squadron returned home at 15.55hrs.

At 16.15hrs, six aircraft set off again on a shipping reconnaissance approximately in the same place as the previous operation, and returned home at 17.00hrs with nothing to report.

27 JULY

Very bad weather in the morning, but some local flying took place in the afternoon when it brightened up a bit. However, at 16.30hrs, 121 Squadron took off to rendez-vous with the North Weald Wing on a 'rodeo', flying across the water to within a mile of Ostend at zero feet. From there they climbed and flew to Haamstede, and finally home via Calais. Flak was considerable at Calais and Dunkirk, but no enemy aircraft or shipping were seen. The squadron landed back at 17.55hrs.

28 JULY

In the afternoon twelve aircraft of 121 Squadron took off on a shipping reconnaissance flight with the North Weald Wing. Landfall was made south of Nieuport, and from there the pilots flew to Walcheren Island and back home over Gravelines. Flak was consider-able from the coastal batteries off Ostend, but no enemy aircraft or shipping was seen.

Warrant Officer W. Morgan (335768) (Admin.) was discharged from the RAF on appointment to a commission in the A&SD Branch as flying officer (on probation). Acting Flying Officer Terry was appointed Acting Flight Lieutenant on 1 July 1942.

30 JULY

In the afternoon, twelve aircraft of 121 Squadron took part in a 'circus' operation as part of the North Weald Wing acting as rear support for six Bostons that flew ahead to St Omer with the Debden and Hornchurch Wings. They made landfall at Berck Sur Mer when six Fw 190s were sighted. Three pilots attacked them: Flight Lieutenant Daley shot down one, and two others dived to get away. The other pilots, Pilot Officer Mahon and Sergeant Blanding, had no engagements.

31 JULY

At 14.10hrs, twelve aircraft of 121 Squadron took off on a 'circus' operation. Rendezvous was made with the North Weald and Tangmere Wings at Pevensey Bay, and they then flew at zero feet across the Channel but climbed to 15,000ft when they made landfall at Berck Sur Mer. Six Bostons had flown across a few minutes earlier to Abbeville. Enemy aircraft were sighted and attacked by the squadron with the result that Squadron Leader Kennard shot down one Fw 190 but was hit by enemy fire and was injured in the knee, hand and buttocks. His aircraft was seriously damaged; he was able, however, to crash-land his aircraft at RAF Lympne, from where he was taken to Maidstone Hospital. Pilot Officer Mahon shot down two Fw 190s, Sergeant Kelly destroyed one Me 109, and Flight Lieutenant Edner shot down two more Me 109s. Pilot Officer Boyles claimed a Me 109 as 'probable'. These victories took place over Berck Sur Mer and the north of the Somme. However, Pilot Officer Norman Young, who was flying Spitfire AA732, failed to return from the operation, having been shot down over Abbeville. The remaining aircraft landed at Hawkinge, Manson and Southend, the latter at 15.16hrs.

AUGUST

1 AUGUST

Local flying only was carried out today by 121 Squadron. At 10.00hrs, the third weekly summer training camp of four ATC officers and seventy cadets was completed, when such personnel returned to their respective units.

At 17.00hrs, the fourth weekly summer training camp opened with the arrival of six ATC officers and 102 cadets.

2 AUGUST

Six sections of two aircraft of 121 Squadron were scrambled during the day but had nothing to report. One section also carried out a convoy patrol.

Flight Lieutenant (Acting Squadron Leader) W. Dudley Williams, DFC was posted to 121 Squadron from 122 Squadron.

3 AUGUST

Two sections of 121 Squadron were scrambled in the morning, and convoy patrol was carried out by a third section, but returned with nothing to report.

Pilot Officer M.D. Assheton-Smith was attached to the RAF School of Intelligence at Harrow for the 29th RAF intelligence course 'A' by authority of Headquarters, 11 Group.

4 AUGUST

121 Squadron carried out local flying in the morning, and two shipping reconnaissances in the afternoon, but no action took place.

5 AUGUST

Blue Section of 121 Squadron (Flight Sergeant Sanders and Sergeant Phillip J. Fox) was scrambled from 06.20hrs to 09.20hrs but had nothing to report. During the morning formation and dogfight practice took place.

At 15.15hrs and again at 15.50hrs, Red Section (Sergeants Kelly and Blanding) was scrambled but again nothing to report. Pilot Officer John Brown was posted to 53 OTU.

6 AUGUST

Air Marshal T.L. Leigh-Mallory CB, DSC, Air Officer Commanding, 11 Group, visited the station today.

7 AUGUST

At 10.40hrs, Red Section (Flight Lieutenant Daley, DFC and Sergeant Kelly) of 121 Squadron acted as escort to a Supermarine Walrus on air-sea rescue duties. At 13.00hrs, Blue Section (Pilot Officer Gene Fetrow and Sergeant Stanhope) scrambled, but had nothing to report.

8 AUGUST

No operational flying was carried out today. The fourth weekly summer training Camp was completed today and such personnel returned to their respective units.

The fifth weekly summer training camp opened, with the arrival of three ATC officers and eighty-seven cadets.

The Officer's Mess at The Lawn, Hall Road, 3 miles from the aerodrome. *(Courtesy of 611 Squadron Association)*

Pilot Officer Colin H. MacFie of 611 Squadron. *(Courtesy of 611 Squadron Association)*

611 Squadron pilots at Southend. *Left to right*: Sergeants L.N. 'Tweakie' Askew, John Down, and A. Gillegan. *(Courtesy of 611 Squadron Association)*

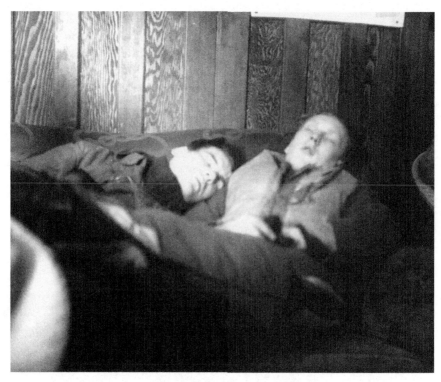

Sergeant Herbert Sadler and Pilot Officer Philip Pollard of 611 Squadron resting in the Dispersal Hut at Southend. They were killed on 5 February 1941 and 22 October 1941 respectively. *(Courtesy of 611 Squadron Association)*

Sergeant Bruce Thomas's damaged Spitfire P7609 at Southend. *(Courtesy of 611 Squadron Association)*

Sergeant Bruce Thomas standing by damaged Spitfire P7609. (He was killed on 18 May 1941.) *(Courtesy of 611 Squadron Association)*

Left to right: Squadron Leader Peter 'Tubby' Townsend, William 'Mac' Gilmour, DFM and Pilot Officer Nigel J. 'Mushroom' Smith of 611 Squadron at Southend. *(Courtesy of 611 Squadron Association)*

Flight Lieutenant Patrick Terrance O'Leary and Squadron Leader Leslie Sydney 'Sid' Ford of 403 Squadron. *(Courtesy of Joe Fukuto)*

Rochford Hall was requisitioned as the Sergeants' Mess. *(Author's Collection)*

Pilot Officer František Burda of 310 (Czech) Squadron. *(Courtesy of B & E Kudláček collection/www.fcafa.wordpress.com)*

Squadron Leader František Vancl, DFC of 312 Squadron. *(Courtesy of B & E Kudláček collection/www.fcafa.wordpress.com)*

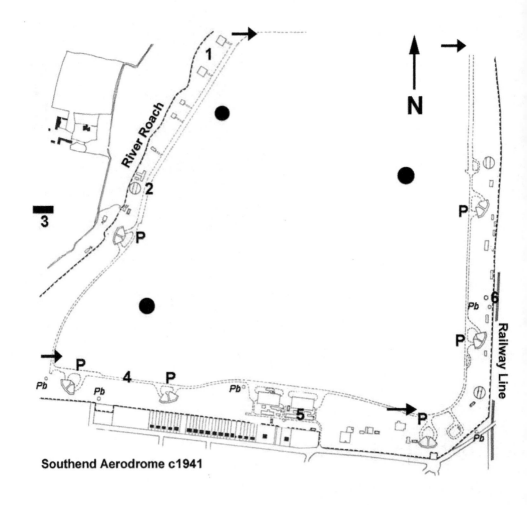

Southend Aerodrome c1941

Key to Map:
Black circle: Picket-Hamilton Fort
1. Bomb Stores
2. Flight Offices & Rest Room
3. LAA Position
4. Battle HQ & Station Control
5. Cook House & NAAFI
6. AA Gun Position
P. Aircraft Pens
Pb. Pillboxes
Black Arrows: Initiating Points (The Last Resort)
(Illustration by the Author)

Aerial photograph of the EKCO Works off Priory Crescent, Southend – note the camouflaged rooftops of the factory units. *(Courtesy of John Anderson)*

Squadron Leader Karel Mrazek, DFC of 313 Squadron. *(Courtesy of the Zdenek Hurt Collection)*

Pilot Officer František Hradil of 19 Squadron. *(Courtesy of the Zdenek Hurt Collection)*

264 Squadron Defiant and pilots at Rochford. *(Author's Collection)*

137 Squadron, 5 March 1943: *Left to right*: P/O Robert Leslie Smith, DFC, DFM; F/O Edward Lancelot Musgrave (RAAF); P/O Desmond Roberts (RNZAF); F/S John McGowan Barclay; W/O Arthur Gaston Brunet (RCAF); F/L John Michael Bryan; F/O Joseph Laurier DeHoux (RCAF); Sgt Aubrey Cartwright Smith; F/O John Edward McClure (RCAF); Sgt Norbury Dugdale; Sgt Thomas Arthur Sutherland; Sgt Ernest Alfred Bolster; F/O John Maude Hadow; S/L Humphrey St John Coghlan, DFC; F/S Hugh Leo O'Neill; and Sgt Robert Woodhouse. The dog was Lynn and belonged to Mike Bryan. *(Courtesy of Rob Bowater)*

A Westland Whirlwind of Blue Section of 137 Squadron. *(Courtesy of T.F. Smith)*

Armourers loading a Whirlwind of 137 Squadron at RAF Manston. *(Courtesy of T.F. Smith)*

Pilots of 611 Squadron. *Top row, left to right:* 'Doc' Sanderson; S/L Bitmead; F/Lt Watkins; Joker (the dog); F/Lt Buys; P/O Gardner; P/O Johnson. *On the wing, left to right:* Sgt 'Tubby' Townsend; F/O Sutton; P/O Duncan-Smith; P/O Pollard; P/O Appleton. *Under the wing, left to right:* F/Lt Mears; P/O 'Chips' Carpenter; Sgt Gilmour; Sgt Fair; Sgt Feely; Sgt 'Mushroom' Smith; Sgt 'Joe' Leigh. *Standing:* P/O Lamb and Sgt McHugh. *(Courtesy of 611 Squadron Association)*

Warrant Officer Arthur G. Brunet of 137 Squadron. *(Courtesy of T.F. Smith)*

Aubrey Cartwright Smith, DFM of
137 Squadron. *(Courtesy of T.F. Smith)*

George Buzz Beurling marking up his 'kills'.
(Courtesy of Robin McQueen)

Flight Lieutenant John M. Bryan of
137 Squadron. *(Courtesy of T.F. Smith)*

Johnny Lawton of 137 Squadron. *(Courtesy of T.F. Smith)*

Hugh Godefroy of 403 Squadron. *(Courtesy of Robin McQueen)*

403 Squadron at early readiness. *(Courtesy of Robin McQueen)*

Riggers and fitters. *(Courtesy of Robin McQueen)*

403 Squadron pilots. *(Courtesy of Robin McQueen)*

403 Squadron 'Wolf Jockeys'. *(Courtesy of Robin McQueen)*

Sergeant Alfred Allsopp with other pilots of 350 Squadron. *(Courtesy of R.J. Rooker)*

611 Squadron Spitfires. *(Author's Collection)*

James 'Johnnie' Johnson served with 19, 610 and 616 Squadrons and the Canadian Wing at Kenley. *(Courtesy of Robin McQueen)*

Squadron Leader Dean Hugh Dover, DFC and Bar, 403 Squadron. *(Courtesy of Robin McQueen)*

A Hurricane Mk IIB being fitted with its bomb load. *(Courtesy of The South East Echo)*

9 AUGUST

No operational flying again today. Air Chief Marshal Sir William Mitchell, KCB (commander of the New London Region ATC) visited Southend and inspected the ATC camp.

10 AUGUST

At 11.00hrs, six aircraft of 121 Squadron took part in a shipping reconnaissance, and a good deal of local formation flying and air firing took place during the day. At 16.20hrs four sections carried out convoy patrols.

Flight Lieutenant (Acting Squadron Leader) C.H. Gadney, Officer Commanding RAF Southend, was attached to Rollestone Anti-Gas School for a senior officers' gas course.

11 AUGUST

At 10.30hrs, various sections of 121 Squadron took part in practice interception. At 13.20hrs three sections carried out convoy patrols.

12 AUGUST

At 08.20hrs, four sections of 121 Squadron carried out convoy patrols.

13 AUGUST

Two shipping reconnaissances were carried out today by 121 Squadron, one in the morning and one in the afternoon. During the remainder of the day the pilots did air-to-air and air-to-sea firing.

14 AUGUST

At 10.10hrs, Red Section (Flight Lieutenant Daley and Pilot Officer Roy Evans) of 121 Squadron was scrambled but had nothing to report. Five sections carried out convoy patrols during the day. Sergeant Carpenter took ATC members for trips in a Tiger Moth.

Flight Lieutenant (Acting Squadron Leader) C.H. Gadney returned to the station on completion of the senior officers' gas course.

15 AUGUST

Thirteen aircraft of 121 Squadron took off at 14.15hrs. One aircraft was directed to orbit North Foreland at 12,000ft to act as relayer of messages between Operations and the squadron. The remainder of the squadron proceeded and made rendezvous just off Flushing as another squadron came out. Nothing of importance occurred, and they landed home at 15.25hrs. Majors Callahan and Stovall of the US Air Army Corps visited the squadron, arriving at 12.30hrs in connection with the transfer of American pilots of 121 Squadron to the US Air Army Corps.

The fifth weekly summer training camp was completed, and such personnel returned to their units.

The sixth weekly summer training camp opened with the arrival of three ATC officers and forty-five cadets.

16 AUGUST

At 13.15hrs, twelve aircraft of 121 Squadron took off on a shipping reconnaissance. They flew at zero feet and made landfall north of Ostend, flying along the coast and west of

Walcheren and to Schouwen. The pilots were fired upon by four barges in the bay at Haamstede. No attack was made on the barges and the squadron landed back at 14.50hrs.

Eighteen aircraft of 19 Squadron arrived at this station from RAF Perranporth for temporary duty.

17 AUGUST

At 12.40hrs, 19 Squadron took off on an offensive patrol and made rendezvous at a height of 2,000ft over Manston with three other squadrons. The squadrons crossed out at Pigwell Bay and began to climb until a height of 12,500ft was reached, which brought them over Gravelines. 19 Squadron's position was 1,000ft above the other squadrons up sun. From Gravelines the formation swept on to St Omer where three enemy aircraft were seen taking off. The squadrons made a sharp right-hand turn and came out again at Calais at a height of 12,000ft. The English coast was contacted at Dover and the squadrons crossed in at Southend. Flak was experienced over Calais, which was accurate for direction but not for height. Fifteen MTBs were sighted just off Calais. No combats were started, and the squadron landed back at Southend at 13.45hrs.

At 16.25hrs, twelve aircraft of 121 Squadron took off at 16.25hrs to rendezvous at the Naze with the rest of the wing and three Flying Fortresses at 10,000ft. Owing to the squadron not being informed that 'zero hour' had been put back fifteen minutes, they arrived at the rendezvous too early. They waited for the remainder of the North Weald Wing while the bombers went on to their objective. Eventually, the wing set course for Dunkirk, did a couple of circuits and then returned home. No enemy aircraft were seen.

18 AUGUST

No operational flying was carried out, but a small amount of practice flying was done.

Pilot Officer Paul M. Ellington and Pilot Officer Kenneth G. Smith joined 121 Squadron today from 58 OTU. Flight Lieutenant C.C. McCarthy-Jones was posted here to join 19 Squadron.

19 AUGUST

Operation Jubilee: an amphibious assault by Canadian, British, and US troops was mounted to seize temporarily the Channel port of Dieppe. Extensive air support was provided by RAF Fighter, Bomber and Coastal Commands, under the control of Air Marshal Leigh-Mallory, AOC, 11 Group, RAF Fighter Command.

At 08.40hrs, 121 Squadron took off and set course for Beachy Head together with 19 Squadron. From there they carried on to Dieppe and patrolled the area at 5,000ft. They were met with a good deal of opposition from a number of Fw 190s directly they reached the patrol line. Dogfights ensued and the squadron returned home in ones and twos. Three pilots failed to return from these operations: Pilot Officer Mahon, Pilot Officer Taylor (in Spitfire AD569) and Pilot Officer Fetrow. Later in the day, however, news was received that Pilot Officer Fetrow had baled out and was picked up by one of the convoy boats returning from the Dieppe Raid. He was unhurt. Four enemy aircraft were shot down and claimed as destroyed or damaged by the squadron. Flight Lieutenant Edner was the first to arrive back at Southend owing to damage to the tailplane of his aircraft caused by a cannon shell from combat with an enemy aircraft.

At 08.51hrs, twelve Spitfire MkVbs of 19 Squadron took off from this station behind 121 Squadron and crossed the English coast at Beachy Head at a height of 3,000ft and set course for Dieppe, reaching there at a height of 10,000ft as top cover. Eight Fw 190s were sighted above at 12,000ft and slightly to the west of Dieppe. The enemy aircraft at first made no attempt to engage, but as the squadron passed over Dieppe the Fw 190s came in to attack.

The squadron broke up into sections and several combats took place in which five of our pilots fired. Pilot Officer J. Henderson (Blue 3) fired at two Fw 190s which immediately dived steeply and Blue 3's engine cut out while trying to follow them. He then sighted two more enemy aircraft south-west of Dieppe at 10,000ft, both weaving, and climbed slightly above and up sun of them and made a diving attack. Although both enemy aircraft apparently saw him as they dived down steeply, Blue 3 followed and attacked, and as a result two streams of white smoke emitted from each side of the fuselage of the enemy aircraft which went into a vertical dive. The enemy aircraft was still in this position emitting white smoke when it was last seen at 6,000ft and was claimed as damaged. Pilot Officer Henderson was then attacked by two more Fw 190s and his aircraft received hits on the port mainplane and in the port machine-gun ammo tank. He had to take violent evasive action but landed home safely. Blue 3 reported that he observed a Spitfire explode in the air over Dieppe.

Squadron Leader P.B. Davies and Sergeant I.M. Mundy (Red Section) made an astern attack on a Fw 190 from about 500 yards' range and as a result the enemy aircraft immediately broke away from its leader and dived towards land. It was last seen at a height of 500ft in a fairly steep dive over land. It is thought by the pilots concerned in the engagement that the enemy aircraft was not likely to have made a safe landing, although no claim was made.

Flight Lieutenant C.F. Bradley (Blue 1) also attacked a Fw 190 with the result that the enemy aircraft flying at the time in a shallow dive immediately went into a steep vertical dive towards the sea when it was last seen at 2,000ft (no claim made). Blue 1 then sighted a Do 217 about to attack two ships off Bernard Le Grande at a height of 7,000ft and climbed to attack. He fired a two-second burst but was not in a position to observe any results.

Pilot Officer R. Royer (Free French) attacked two Fw 190s and fired a short burst at each without result. Pilot Officer Royer observed his No. 4 (Sergeant E.R. Davies) being attacked by two Fw 190s and black smoke was emitting from the Spitfire. This pilot was later picked up in the Channel, having baled out from his damaged aircraft. The squadron re-crossed the English coast at Beachy Head in twos and threes, and ten aircraft had landed by 10.30hrs. The squadron was flying too high for military observation but many fires were seen in Dieppe. Ships of all types were seen in and entering the harbour of Dieppe.

At 11.50hrs, aircraft of 19 Squadron and 121 Squadron took off again and crossed the English coast at Beachy Head, setting course for Dieppe. The weather had deteriorated since the morning. 121 Squadron flew at 2,000ft, just under the cloud base, and a good deal of flak was experienced from the land batteries. Flight Lieutenant Daley was hit by a shell which made a large hole in the starboard side of the tailplane. His engine cut out, and he was prepared to bale out when the engine restarted and he continued the patrol. The squadron landed home at 13.30hrs without further incident.

19 Squadron was at a height (above the cloud) of 4,000ft when the target area was reached, and as a turn was being made to port four or five unidentified aircraft were

sighted at 2,000ft and up sun. When the turn was made over Dieppe four Fw 190s
were sighted coming out of cloud at 3,500ft but on seeing the Allied formation they
turned away into the cloud. Two Do 217s were then sighted over the rear of the main
concentration of Allied shipping, bombs being dropped but well wide of their targets.
Blue 1 (Flight Lieutenant C.F. Bradley) fired at one of the Dorniers as it was entering
cloud from a range of 650–700 yards, but no results were observed.

The squadron re-crossed the English coast at Beachy Head and the twelve aircraft
landed home at 13.50hrs. Three Allied ships near Dieppe appeared to be burning, one
of which looked like a destroyer.

At 16.15hrs, the third sortie in the Operation Jubilee by the Spitfires of 19 and
121 Squadrons took off from Southend, again crossing the coast at Beachy Head, but
this time at 2,000ft under cloud. When 20 miles out to sea ten Fw 190s were sighted
above and ahead of the squadron at 3,000ft coming in for a head-on attack. Formation
was broken into sections and individual combats took place; Flight Lieutenant C.F.
Bradley (Blue 1) attacked the last of the ten enemy aircraft as they passed overhead
and as a result he saw a large piece fly off the enemy aircraft. It then turned on its back
and dived vertically towards the sea. Owing to a cannon stoppage Blue 1 was unable
to follow up his attack so he turned away to port and as he did so he saw a splash in
the sea. Blue 1 could not ascertain whether this was the enemy aircraft he had attacked
but the same was claimed as damaged with a request that it be upgraded to 'destroyed'.

Red 2 (Sergeant I.M. Mundy) attacked the centre aircraft out of three Fw 190s
and saw strikes of red flashes on the enemy aircraft's starboard wing near the aileron.
Owing to another Fw 190 behind him, Mundy was unable to obtain any satisfaction
in the way of a definite result of his attack. Pilot Officer J. Henderson also fired at two
Fw 190s but with no result, as did Pilot Officer R. Royer.

Sergeant J.W. Foster, flying as Blue 2, received hits on his starboard mainplane and
received a slight cut on his right leg from a cannon splinter. The squadron re-formed
with 121 Squadron after the combats and crossed in at Beachy Head, and landed at
home from 17.50hrs. The main concentration of shipping was seen to be well over
halfway back across the Channel. From the combats that had taken place during the day,
all pilots claimed that the enemy showed a disinclination to make a fight, and if they had
had a speedier aircraft there would have been an even greater number destroyed.

During the course of Operation Jubilee, Allied aircraft flew 2,614 sorties. German
ground forces and the Luftwaffe opposed the landings in strength and Allied ground,
air and naval casualties were heavy; during the course of 19 August the RAF lost 106
aircraft and three high-speed launches (HSLs).

Although the operation was unsuccessful, a number of vitally important lessons were
learned which were subsequently applied in the planning and conduct of landings in
the Mediterranean and the invasion of north-west Europe (Operation Overlord).

20 AUGUST

19 Squadron returned to RAF Perranporth on completion of duty. At 16.10hrs,
121 Squadron took off and made rendezvous with three other squadrons of the North
Weald Wing at Beachy Head at 10,000ft. The squadron was top cover and climbed
to between 28,000ft and 30,000ft, sweeping St Omer and Gravelines and in over
North Foreland. The Hornchurch and Kenley Wings took part in this operation.
121 Squadron returned to base at 17.35hrs having encountered no enemy aircraft.

21 AUGUST

At 11.15hrs, 121 Squadron took off to rendezvous at the Naze at 10,000ft with the rest of the North Weald Wing. The wing was intending to meet some Flying Fortresses about 80 miles out at sea on their returning from bombing Rotterdam. However, owing to a big mix up, the squadron was recalled to base shortly after making rendezvous, landing just after midday.

22 AUGUST

121 Squadron was released today except for some local flying. Sergeant Richard G. Patterson arrived here on posting from 116 Squadron.

The sixth weekly summer training camp was completed, and such personnel returned to units.

2830 Squadron, RAF Regiment, left by road to RAF North Weald, for two weeks' camp.

At 17.00hrs, the seventh weekly summer training camp of three officers and thirty-seven cadets opened.

23 AUGUST

No operational flying was carried out today.

24 AUGUST

Local flying today with the exception of a 'rhubarb' operation by Pilot Officer Happel and Sergeant Carpenter of 121 Squadron. They took off at 15.30hrs and landed at 16.45hrs, but had nothing to report.

25 AUGUST

No operational flying was carried out today. Sergeants Frank Fink and Frank Smolinsky arrived at this station to join 121 Squadron.

26 AUGUST

No operational flying owing to poor weather. Pilot Officer C. Sorrie (Engineering Officer) was posted here to join 121 Squadron from 1 PDC, West Kirby today. A detachment of 116 Squadron from RAF Heston, with two Lysander aircraft, also arrived at the station on attachment for calibration duties.

27 AUGUST

At 11.45hrs, 121 Squadron took off to rendezvous with three other squadrons of the North Weald Wing at the Naze. They flew at zero feet, making rendezvous on time at 12.02hrs. The wing flew at zero feet almost to the French coast, making landfall 2 miles north of Nieuport. The squadron climbed to 10,000ft, turning starboard and going parallel to the coast but 10 miles inland, until they reached Calais. From there they came out and towards Dover, landing at Southend at 13.10hrs. Two ships were seen entering Calais Harbour, and there was some flak at Dunkirk but there was nothing else of importance to report.

At 17.00hrs, the squadron, with the North Weald and Debden Wings, made rendezvous at Orfordness at approximately 5,000ft. From there they steered a course of 100° for 80 miles, and then orbited eight Flying Fortresses which had been bombing Rotterdam and were escorted back by the squadron, crossing the English Channel at

Orfordness and so back to base, landing at 18.30hrs. No enemy aircraft were seen. Pilot Officer Chester Grimm joined the squadron today from 59 OTU.

28 AUGUST
At 11.40hrs, 121 Squadron took off and made rendezvous with the North Weald Wing at 12.00hrs over Frinton at 12,000ft. From there they set course to reach the French coast at Mardyck, climbing to between 23,000ft and 25,000ft. Thence to south of Calais and out at Cap Gris Nez, and back over Dover. No enemy aircraft were encountered but there was some flak at Dunkirk.

29 AUGUST
At 09.50hrs, 121 Squadron took off and made rendezvous with the North Weald and Debden Wings at 15,000ft over Frinton. They proceeded to Mardyck, climbing to 25,000ft, and thence to Cassel, St Omer and out at Cap Gris Nez, where the top squadron of the wing were attacked by some Fw 190s. Returning, they crossed the English coast near Hythe.

There were two scrambles during the afternoon: Blue Section of 121 Squadron (Pilot Officers Sanders and Young) at 13.40hrs, and again at 14.40hrs, but no enemy aircraft were engaged as the 'Bogey' turned out to be friendly aircraft.

At 10.00hrs, the seventh weekly summer training camp was completed, and such personnel returned to their respective units.

30 AUGUST
At 09.05hrs, Blue Section of 121 Squadron (Pilot Officers Sanders and Young) were scrambled but returned having made no contact. Another scramble for the same section came at 09.40hrs, but again there was nothing to report.

31 AUGUST
The weather in the morning was 10/10ths cloud with some rain, clearing somewhat in the afternoon. Flight Lieutenant Daley and Pilot Officer John Slater were scrambled at 12.25hrs but had nothing to report.

SEPTEMBER

1 SEPTEMBER
At 06.40hrs, Red Section of 121 Squadron (Pilot Officers Padgett and Happel) were scrambled, and landed back at 07.15hrs with nothing to report.

At 11.25hrs, White Section (Sergeants Carpenter and Blanding) with Red Section (Pilot Officers Padgett and Happel) were scrambled, and although they saw what appeared to be a Ju 88 disappearing into the clouds at about 8,000ft flying west, they did not see it again. Convoy patrols were also carried out by sections of the squadron at 09.50hrs and 10.20hrs.

2 SEPTEMBER
A convoy patrol was carried out by two sections of 121 Squadron between 13.15hrs and 14.55hrs, but returned with nothing to report. A message was received that Flight Lieutenant Seldon Edner had been awarded the DFC.

3 SEPTEMBER

No flying owing to 10/10ths cloud for most of the day.

4 SEPTEMBER

A sweep by 121 Squadron, planned for 11.00hrs, was put back twice and then finally cancelled on account of the bad weather over the French coast.

At 10.30hrs, ten aircraft of 121 Squadron took off on a squadron balbo which was pronounced very successful.

5 SEPTEMBER

At 09.30hrs, twelve aircraft of 121 Squadron took off to make rendezvous with 333 Squadron at Beachy Head at 10.00hrs at 15,000ft. The squadrons then proceeded to the French coast, climbing to 25,000ft. Landfall was made at Cayeux, and they then swept towards Abbeville, re-crossing the coast at Cayeux and home over Dungeness. No flak or enemy aircraft were seen.

During the day, two sections were out on convoy patrol, and three sections were scrambled at different times, but proved fruitless with nothing to report.

However, when Blue Section (Pilot Officer Fetrow and Sergeant Fink) were scrambled at 14.40hrs, Pilot Officer Young, who was doing local flying near Biggin Hill at about 1,500ft, heard Operations giving instructions to Blue Section on the R/T and immediately started to climb and head in the direction of the enemy aircraft. He sighted a Ju 88 at about 20,000ft over base, being attacked by two other Spitfires. The enemy aircraft, leaving by north-east, was damaged and set on fire by these two Spitfires and started diving down. Pilot Officer Young followed it down and gave it two bursts of cannon fire, after which it crashed into the sea some miles east of the Naze. He circled over the spot and then returned home.

At 17.00hrs, the eighth weekly summer training camp of five officers and eighty-five cadets opened.

6 SEPTEMBER

At 11.00hrs, Air Chief Marshal Sir William Mitchell, KCB (commander of the New London Region ATC) visited the ATC camp.

At 16.15hrs, twelve aircraft of 121 Squadron took off to rendezvous over Colchester at 5,000ft with two other squadrons from the North Weald Wing for a diversion sweep. They proceeded to Orfordness to make rendezvous with the Debden Wing at 15,000ft, and then proceeded to Ostend, Nieuport, Dunkirk, and back via North Foreland to base but with nothing to report.

7 SEPTEMBER

At 09.10hrs, twelve aircraft from 121 Squadron took off to make rendezvous with the rest of the North Weald Wing and the Northolt Wing over Clacton. From there they proceeded to Ostend, climbing to 28,000ft, then on to Bruges, Ostend and towards Dunkirk before returning home via Dover. Some flak was experienced over Ostend. On the way back Sergeant Stanhope and Pilot Officer Fetrow saw eight Fw 190s and took shots at two of them, but observed no results.

At 14.10hrs, nine aircraft took part in a wing balbo with 331 and 332 Squadrons, but returned with nothing to report.

8 SEPTEMBER

No operational flying today.

9 SEPTEMBER

Continuous convoy patrols were carried out by five sections of 121 Squadron despite 10/10ths cloud at 1,000ft. At 15.50hrs, Black Section (Pilot Officers Young and Grimm) was scrambled but returned shortly afterwards with nothing to report.

10 SEPTEMBER

No operational flying today. Some practice interception was carried out by 121 Squadron, and in the morning Pilot Officer Frank Boyles and Sergeant R. Patterson were ordered up to destroy a loose barrage balloon, flying at about 6,000ft north of base.

11 SEPTEMBER

At 10.45hrs, two sections of 121 Squadron carried out a convoy patrol, but had nothing to report.

12 SEPTEMBER

No operational flying today. At 10.00hrs, the eighth weekly summer training camp was completed, and the ATC personnel returned to their units.

13 SEPTEMBER

At 09.05hrs, four sections of 121 Squadron carried out convoy patrol; the weather was 10/10ths cloud at 13,000ft.

At 15.20hrs, twelve aircraft took off on a shipping reconnaissance, crossing the English coast at Dungeness and setting course for Le Touquet. They did not cross the French coast, but flew along the coast to Dieppe, and then returned home, crossing the English coast again at Dungeness. The squadron flew at zero feet on both journeys, and had nothing to report.

14 SEPTEMBER

The weather was still 10/10ths cloud at 1,500ft for most of the day. Three sections of 121 Squadron were scrambled: Blue Section (Pilot Officer Smith and Sergeant Fox) at 12.50hrs, Red Section (Pilot Officers Slater and Grimm) at 16.45hrs, and Green Section (Pilot Officer Fetrow and Sergeant Stanhope) at 17.45hrs, but all had nothing to report upon their return.

15 SEPTEMBER

In the morning three sections of 121 Squadron carried out convoy patrol.

At 09.00hrs, Air Vice Marshal R.P. Mills visited this station regarding National Savings.

At 15.00hrs, ten aircraft of 121 Squadron met 331 Squadron over the base and proceeded towards the Belgian coast at zero feet. They made landfall at Blankenberge, and from there flew to Flushing, and back crossing the English coast at the Naze, with nothing to report.

At 17.55hrs, ten aircraft took off to lead a wing balbo with 331 Squadron from North Weald.

16 SEPTEMBER
Air-firing practice was carried out in the morning by 121 Squadron. At 16.00hrs, Air Commodore E. Digby Johnson AFC, AOA, Fighter Command, visited the station.

17 SEPTEMBER
Local practice flying only today. At 16.00hrs, Pilot Officer C.W. Bray was attached to RAF North Weald for duty as commandant of RAF Regiment Camp 'B'.

19 SEPTEMBER
No operational flying today. At 16.00hrs, 2810 Squadron, RAF Regiment, left by road for camp at RAF North Weald.

20 SEPTEMBER
One convoy patrol was carried out by aircraft of 121 Squadron at 12.05hrs. At 18.10hrs, Blue Section (Flight Lieutenant Edner and Pilot Officer Grimm) was scrambled, but had nothing to report.

21 SEPTEMBER
At 06.25hrs, Blue Section (Pilot Officers Halsey and Smith) of 121 Squadron was scrambled, but returned without incident.

At 13.35hrs, White Section (Pilot Officers Kelly and Slater) took off on a shipping reconnaissance to Haamstede and returned at 14.00hrs with nothing to report. The same section took off again at 14.52hrs, and flew via Flushing to Haamstede and shot up one flak ship which was left burning. Pilot Officer Slater's aircraft was hit in the glycol tank and was seen to crash into the sea.

22 SEPTEMBER
Apart from one scramble at 07.55hrs which reported nothing back, there was no operational flying. 121 Squadron started their move to RAF Debden.

At 11.30hrs, Flight Lieutenant E. Anthony arrived here on posting for duty as station medical officer. At 17.00hrs, ASO W.J. Bagley arrived here on posting for duty as code and cypher officer. At 18.00hrs, the advance party of one officer and forty other ranks of 350 (Belgian) Squadron arrived by rail from RAF Redhill.

23 SEPTEMBER
Personnel and aircraft of 121 Squadron left by rail and air on transfer to RAF Debden. The main party of twenty-two officers and 189 other ranks of 350 Squadron arrived by rail and air on transfer from RAF Redhill. The squadron was to be part of the Hornchurch Wing with 64, 122, and 453 Squadrons.

24 SEPTEMBER
Twelve sections (twenty-four aircraft) of 350 Squadron kept up a standing patrol between North and South Foreland at 1,000ft from 06.15hrs until 18.30hrs.

Major E. Debock and Commander R.A. Nyssens, staff officers, Belgian Air Force, arrived here for temporary duty with 350 Squadron.

25 SEPTEMBER
At 08.30hrs, one section of 350 Squadron was at readiness, and two sections were

at fifteen minutes. At 13.00hrs, the squadron was released off the camp except for one section.

26 SEPTEMBER
At 12.25hrs, six sections of 350 Squadron patrolled the west-bound Convoy 'Protem', north of Whitstable until 13.30hrs.

27 SEPTEMBER
Six sections of 350 Squadron kept up a standing patrol between North and South Foreland from 09.30hrs to 14.00hrs and from 15.15hrs until 19.05hrs; the Convoy 'Beacon' was patrolled going out of the Thames Estuary by four sections.

At 17.00hrs, six aircraft of 'B' Flight were scrambled to patrol over the base at 8,000ft, but were recalled at 17.20hrs as the enemy aircraft had turned back.

28 SEPTEMBER
Despite visibility being reduced to 600–1,000 yards and constant rain all day, one flight of 350 Squadron was at readiness from 08.30hrs until 13.00hrs, and one section was at readiness thereafter.

29 SEPTEMBER
'A' Flight of 350 Squadron was at dawn readiness and two sections patrolled Barrow Deep from 06.40hrs until 08.10hrs. Two further sections patrolled between North and South Foreland at 10,000ft between 08.20hrs and 09.45hrs.

The Convoy 'Protem', south of Southend and going north-east, was patrolled by three sections between 08.05hrs and 10.30hrs.

'B' Flight was at readiness at 13.00hrs. Blue Section were ordered to take off to patrol over the base at 17.05hrs until 17.50hrs, but had nothing to report.

30 SEPTEMBER
At 10.40hrs, Red Section of 350 Squadron was ordered to patrol base and returned at 11.30hrs with nothing to report. Enemy aircraft that had been plotted 40 miles south of base had turned back. At 12.45hrs, Red Section took off again on a patrol between North and South Foreland at 1,000ft, and returned at 14.20hrs.

A standing patrol between North and South Foreland was kept up from 16.00hrs until 19.15hrs by four sections and another patrol by one section was carried out over Barrow Deep at 10,000ft from 17.50hrs until 19.00hrs.

OCTOBER

The turning point of the war is generally regarded as being the winter of 1942–43. Then the German momentum came to an end and Britain and her Allies (now fighting Germany and Italy in Europe and Japan in the Far East) moved to the offensive: on the land in North Africa and Italy, at sea with the start of the successful campaigns against the U-boats, and in the air with the greatly increased strategic bombing offensive against the heart of Germany and the use of tactical air power on a large scale. That offensive continued to increase both against Germany and Japan throughout 1944 until the final victories of the Allies in 1945.

Meanwhile, in Germany, the fourth launch of the pilot-less rocket had been successful. When Hitler heard the news he gave the immediate go-ahead to mass-produce the rockets, and to build concrete launching bunkers in the Pas de Calais.

1 OCTOBER
Four sections of 350 Squadron patrolled North and South Foreland between 10.00hrs and 13.50hrs and two sections patrolled the same line from 16.50hrs until 18.40hrs.

2 OCTOBER
At 13.34hrs, twelve aircraft of 350 Squadron were airborne with 453 Squadron. They made rendezvous with the Debden and North Weald Wings at Orfordness at 14.00hrs with 350 Squadron as top cover at 15,000ft. The Belgian coast was crossed at Nieuport with the squadron at 27,000ft and the wings swept to Ypres, and out near Calais, orbiting once in mid-Channel, and returning at 15.05hrs.

Thirteen officers and eighty-six other ranks of 453 Squadron arrived by air and rail from RAF Hornchurch for temporary duty.

3 OCTOBER
No flying today – thick fog reduced visibility to 250 yards, and 350 Squadron was released off camp at 17.00hrs

4 OCTOBER
The foggy weather conditions continued today, but began to clear in the afternoon. Red Section of 350 Squadron took off at 15.40hrs to patrol a convoy, but returned as the weather outside the immediate vicinity of the aerodrome was unfit.

ATC cadets were given trips in the station Tiger Moth by pilots of 350 Squadron. The squadron was called to readiness at 17.18hrs for a possible 'roadstead'.

Flying Officer R.J. Woodroffe was attached here from RAF Kenley for duty as station adjutant.

5 OCTOBER
No flying today.

6 OCTOBER
At 08.35hrs, two sections of 350 Squadron patrolled over the Convoy 'Platform' which was south-east-bound from the Thames Estuary, and returning home at 10.40hrs.

From 10.20hrs until 12.50hrs, three sections of 350 Squadron patrolled over the Convoy 'Result', which was south-west-bound into the Thames Estuary.

From 15.30hrs until 18.25hrs, three sections patrolled the north-east-bound Convoy 'Platform', east of Felixstowe.

Pilot Officer R.Van De Poel (100999) was posted here from 124 Squadron on attachment to 'A' Flight of 350 Squadron.

7 OCTOBER
Early morning fog right down to the deck reduced visibility to 200 yards, but began to improve later, and Blue Section of 350 Squadron went on convoy patrol from 16.15hrs until 17.30hrs.

Acting Flight Lieutenant S.R. Judd was attached to the RAF School of Administration, Stannington, for 62 War Course (Senior Admin).

8 OCTOBER
Training flying was carried out today. Acting Pilot Officer G.A. Daniels arrived here on posting from No. 1 Officer's School, Cosford, for anti-gas/fire duties.

9 OCTOBER
Twelve aircraft of 350 Squadron were airborne at 07.51hrs as top squadron in the Hornchurch Wing. From Felixstowe, course was set for Dixmude and the wing swept to St Omer, south of Calais and Mardyck with the squadron at 29,000ft. Slight flak was experienced at Calais which was accurate but behind the squadron. On hearing that there were bandits at 8,000ft near Calais, the squadron orbited and Blue Section went down below cloud to investigate but saw nothing. The squadron was back home at 09.15hrs.

Five sections kept up a standing patrol from 14.25hrs and 18.50hrs.

Personnel of 453 Squadron returned to RAF Hornchurch on completion of duty.

10 OCTOBER
Black Section was scrambled and was airborne from 08.20hrs to 08.40hrs without seeing anything. Five sections, one of 'B' Flight and the rest of 'A' Flight, patrolled the Convoy 'Casing' in the estuary off Eastchurch, north-east-bound, from 09.15hrs to 12.40hrs.

11 OCTOBER
One section of 350 Squadron was at readiness at dawn, 'B' Flight was at immediate, and 'A' Flight was at fifteen-minute readiness at 08.30hrs.

At 13.37hrs, twelve aircraft took off on Rodeo 101, making rendezvous with 453 Squadron over Southend three minutes later. They flew to Felixstowe to join up with the North Weald Wing at 14.00hrs, and then proceed to Furness, sweeping just north of Cassel, and out at Gravelines, making a wide orbit in the Channel. On the way back to North Foreland, two Spitfires of 453 Squadron were seen to collide and go into the sea about 8 miles off the Foreland.

From 17.30hrs to 18.40hrs Red Section escorted the Convoy 'Beacon' which was south-bound, east of Southend.

Blue Section was scrambled at 17.30hrs but landed fifteen minutes later with nothing to report.

12 OCTOBER
The whole of 350 Squadron was at readiness at 06.15hrs and took off at 07.45hrs to act as an anti-flak squadron with 453 Squadron flying above. Rendezvous was made at Manston with four Westland Whirlwind bombers at 08.00hrs and the squadron received instructions to vector 090° to Ostend, where they flew to at sea level. Nothing but eleven fishing smacks were seen and the squadron, after orbiting, flew to Zeebrugge where they again orbited before returning. All aircraft were down by 09.15hrs.

The rest of the day was occupied by various patrols between North and South Foreland, Barrow Deep, and also the Convoy 'Waiter'.

At 18.35hrs, Blue Section took off on patrol between North and South Foreland but was recalled before reaching the patrol line. Blue 1 crashed on landing at Southend at 18.50hrs (the aircraft categorised 'A/C', the pilot was uninjured); Blue 2 landed safely at 19.00hrs.

13 OCTOBER
Five sections of 350 Squadron patrolled between North and South Foreland from 14.00hrs to 18.30hrs, all patrols being without incident.

14 OCTOBER
Red Section of 350 Squadron patrolled between North and South Foreland from 08.35hrs to 09.55hrs and from 17.30hrs to 18.30hrs without incident.

15 OCTOBER
From 09.25hrs, three sections of 350 Squadron patrolled the north-east-bound Convoy 'Platform', east of Southend, returning at 12.25hrs. At 12.10hrs, Red Section relieved a flight of Typhoons that were on patrol between Dungeness and Dover at low altitude, returning at 13.40hrs.

16 OCTOBER
From 12.15hrs, two sections of 350 Squadron patrolled the Convoy 'Result', east of Burnham, and into the estuary, returning at 13.55hrs. From 14.55hrs, Yellow Section patrolled 'Tennerden' at 10,000ft, returning at 16.10hrs.

Red Section was airborne at 16.15hrs to patrol between North Foreland and St Margaret's Bay but one aircraft returned with engine trouble after ten minutes. Green Section relieved Typhoons on patrol between North Foreland and St Margaret's Bay, and patrolled from 16.30hrs to 17.45hrs, themselves being relieved in turn by Red Section who landed at 18.25hrs.

17 OCTOBER
Six sections of 350 Squadron patrolled the Convoy 'Pilot', east of Southend, north-bound from 08.10hrs to 13.00hrs. Two sections patrolled between North and South Foreland from 11.00hrs to 13.00hrs.

At 14.20hrs, twelve aircraft of 350 Squadron, led by Flight Lieutenant A. Boussa (101465), DFC took off to make rendezvous over Hornchurch with 453 Squadron when the wing was detailed to act as close escort to eighteen Bostons in an attack on Le Havre. Rendezvous was made but the operation was cancelled and the squadron told to land as there was rain and fog over Hornchurch. 350 Squadron was in cloud at just 400ft.

Further news was received today of Flying Officer H.A. Picard (87693). It appears that he spent six days and six nights in his dinghy before being rescued by the Germans and had a slight wound to the knee. After some time in hospital in Paris, he was sent to Germany.

18 OCTOBER
No flying today. Flying Officer C.W. Bray ceased his attachment to RAF Regiment Camp, North Weald. At 10.00hrs, 50 per cent of personnel saw the film Next of Kin at the Odeon cinema in Southend.

19 OCTOBER
Training flying only was carried out today. At 10.00hrs, the remaining 50 per cent of personnel saw the film *Next of Kin* at the Odeon cinema.

20 OCTOBER
Green Section of 350 Squadron was airborne at 09.50hrs to patrol a convoy but was recalled due to bad weather after thirty minutes.

Red Section patrolled the north-bound Convoy 'Passage', east of Felixstowe, from 13.05hrs to 14.05hrs; Yellow Section patrolled from Ramsgate to Dover at low altitude from 15.35hrs to 16.25hrs; and Pink Section was up at 15.35hrs for a 'rhubarb' but was recalled because of the unsuitable weather.

21 OCTOBER
Red Section of 350 Squadron patrolled between North and South Foreland from 07.40hrs to 08.55hrs, and eight sections patrolled the Convoy 'Ribald', south of Southend, from 08.05hrs to 14.55hrs.

Blue Section patrolled between North and South Foreland from 17.05hrs to 18.10hrs. 'A' Flight patrolled Manston at 1,500ft from 17.30hrs to 17.55hrs.

22 OCTOBER
Seven sections of 350 Squadron patrolled the Convoys 'Totem' and 'Agent' from 08.35hrs to 13.05hrs.

23 OCTOBER
Yellow Section of 350 Squadron patrolled between North and South Foreland from 09.15hrs to 10.10hrs, landing afterwards at RAF Manston. Three sections patrolled between Deal and Dover at low altitude from 09.55hrs to 12.50hrs.

24 OCTOBER
Black Section of 350 Squadron patrolled the east-bound Convoy 'Carnage', north of Sheerness, from 07.55hrs to 08.25hrs. Blue and Red Sections patrolled the south-bound Convoy 'Status', east of Burnham, from 10.35hrs to 12.50hrs.

26 OCTOBER
At 12.45hrs, Operations were just ordering Red Section of 350 Squadron to scramble when a Dornier Do 217E, which was shot down by a gunner of the Anti-Aircraft Section (2830 Squadron) of the RAF Regiment, crashed into the Dispersal Hut. It completely wrecked the south part of the building, killing Warrant Officer T.E.M. Dyon, the squadron engineering officer, and injured two of the ground personnel. Three of the enemy crew were killed outright and one was admitted to hospital.

The squadron was moved into the West Dispersal previously occupied by a flight of 116 Squadron, and were soon reorganised.

At 15.45hrs, Blue Section patrolled the base below cloud and landed at 16.00hrs, and at 17.10hrs, Red Section patrolled the North and South Foreland until 18.25hrs.

27 OCTOBER
From 13.30hrs until 18.10hrs, five sections of 350 Squadron patrolled the Convoy 'Peewit', south-bound 10 miles off Southend.

28 OCTOBER

Red Section of 350 Squadron was scrambled at 16.05hrs to patrol the base below cloud in view of approaching enemy aircraft. Nothing was seen, and the aircraft landed at home at 16.30hrs.

29 OCTOBER

At 12.20hrs, the Air Officer Commanding, 11 Group, visited this station as did Mr Pierlot, the Belgian prime minister, the Belgian air attaché, Colonel Wouters, and other high-ranking Belgian officers. The whole station personnel paraded and after lunch in the mess the AOC presented the Distinguished Flying Cross to Squadron Leader D.A. Guillaume. The *Croix de Guerre* was awarded to Flying Officer H. Marchal (87678) (missing) and Sergeant (now Pilot Officer) J. Ester (127452) for the destruction of a Fw 190 on 30 July 1942.

The prime minister and party left after a march past by units on the station. The Minister of National Defence cited the squadron in the *Ordre du Jour de l'Armée*.

30 OCTOBER

No operational flying today. At 14.00hrs, the three members of the Do 217E crew who were killed when their aircraft was shot down on 26 October were buried at Sutton Road Cemetery.

31 OCTOBER

At 15.00hrs, Warrant Officer T.E.M. Dyon of 350 Squadron, who was killed on 26 October 1942, was buried at Brockwood Cemetery with an attendance of twenty officers, including Colonel Wouters. He was posthumously awarded the *Croix de Guerre*.

Red Section patrolled the Convoy 'Bacon' east-bound, east of Southend, for an hour from 12.30hrs.

NOVEMBER

1 NOVEMBER

Four sections of 350 Squadron patrolled North and South Foreland between 13.55hrs and 16.30hrs.

2 NOVEMBER

Local flying practice only was carried out today by 350 Squadron.

3 NOVEMBER

Blue Section of 350 Squadron patrolled the north-bound Convoy 'Platform' 10 miles east of Southend.

Acting Flight Lieutenant S.R. Judd ceased his attachment to the RAF School of Administration, Stannington, on completion of 62 War Course.

4 NOVEMBER

Adverse weather prevented flying until the 6th.

6 NOVEMBER

Twelve aircraft of 350 Squadron were airborne at 13.40hrs with 453 Squadron and made rendezvous with 122 and 64 Squadrons on a diversionary sweep (Ramrod 22). A second diversion was carried out according to plan except that the weather closed in over France and the ground could not be seen.

The wing had to be directed by the controller once landfall had been made. No enemy aircraft were seen and no flak was observed. All aircraft were down by 15.10hrs.

7 NOVEMBER

No flying today owing to adverse weather conditions.

8 NOVEMBER

Twelve aircraft of 350 Squadron were airborne at 10.30hrs on a main diversion sweep (Circus 235) and arrived at Felixstowe at 10.46hrs at 15,000ft but did not see the wing. Re-setting course they overtook the wing in the Channel and flew to Poperinghe, Armentières, Hazebrouck and St Omer, and came out over Gravelines. Very intensive and effective flak was encountered from Calais, dead in the centre of the formation. Flying Officer Georges Deltour (1299923), flying as Blue 3, was hit but managed to make a crash-landing at the edge of Manston Aerodrome, having no oil left. Nothing of special interest was seen on the sweep, and the rest of the squadron was all down by 11.45hrs.

Between 15.00hrs and 17.45hrs the Convoy 'Bacon' was patrolled by three sections, north of Sheerness.

9 NOVEMBER

No flying today.

10 NOVEMBER

Between 13.55hrs and 15.40hrs 350 Squadron patrolled London between Whitehall and the Mansion House on the occasion of the Lord Mayor's Luncheon.

11 NOVEMBER

No flying today owing to adverse weather conditions. 350 Squadron was released off camp at 13.00hrs.

12 NOVEMBER

With thick fog down to the deck today and visibility reduced to just 50 yards, there was no flying and 350 Squadron was released off camp at 13.00hrs.

Acting Pilot Officer G.A. Daniels of this station completed a fire-fighting course at Weeton.

RAF Southend beat RAF Hornchurch at soccer and hockey in the 11 Group Cup Matches.

13 NOVEMBER

The weather was still foggy with a slight improvement during the day, and a little formation flying practice took place. Again, 350 Squadron was released off camp at 13.00hrs.

The squadron celebrated the first anniversary of its formation today with a dance held at Station Headquarters. The party was a great success and was enjoyed by everybody.

Flight Lieutenant T.J. Tarry (RAF Regiment) arrived at this station on posting from 4077 AA Flight on its formation.

14 NOVEMBER

350 Squadron was released off camp for the whole day and attended a celebration luncheon in London given by the Belgian Government. Among the guests present were the Belgian prime minister, Air Minister Sir Archibald Sinclair, the Air Officer Commanding in Chief, the Air Officer Commanding, 11 Group, Colonel Wouters, and other high-ranking Belgian and British officers.

15 NOVEMBER

One section was at readiness, and two more sections of 350 Squadron were at fifteen minutes. The weather was still poor today.

16 NOVEMBER

Between 08.45hrs and 11.45hrs three sections of 350 Squadron patrolled the east-bound Convoy 'Casing', east of Southend. Between 11.25hrs and 13.30hrs two sections patrolled the east-bound Convoy 'Upward', east of Southend.

In addition to local flying and dusk landings by the squadron, Pink Section (Flying Officer André Plisnier (100654) and Flying Officer Francois Venesoen (107235)) carried out a 'rhubarb' over the Dieppe area with very successful results. Flying Officer Venesoen observed cement fortifications under construction near Veules les Roses and turning eastwards saw four detachments of German troops (about thirty in each) and shot up one detachment with good results. Near Sanqueville, a goods train was spotted going south, the engine of which he attacked and left it at a stand-still enveloped in clouds of steam. The section then flew northwards and over the aerodrome of St Aubin, spotted a Ju 52 flying south at about 400ft. Venesoen attacked the enemy aircraft head-on, observing hits, followed in by Plisnier who fired short bursts with slight deflection, and observed hits in the back of the fuselage. The aircraft crashed on the ground and burst into flames. They had to dodge medium flak from north of the aerodrome, and then turned westwards and headed towards the coast, where they met heavy tracer flak running parallel to the coast, but landed back at base without damage.

17 NOVEMBER

Local flying only today.

18 NOVEMBER

350 Squadron was at readiness from 15.00hrs but were not called upon. At 15.40hrs, three pilots for RAF Manston for advanced readiness for a fighter night.

19 NOVEMBER

A 'rhubarb' operation was undertaken by Pink Section (Flying Office Plisnier and Sergeant L. Harmel (1299917)) of 350 Squadron in the morning. They crossed the Belgian coast 8 miles east of Knocke in bad weather and steered south-south-east and followed the Bruges–Ghent railway until about 5 miles from Ghent. They were flying at about 400ft when they spotted a twin-engined aircraft at the same height and apparently coming in to land at the aerodrome south-west of Ghent. They identified it as a Me 110 and Flying Office Plisnier attacked it head-on, firing from 1,000 yards but with no visible results. Sergeant Harmel followed him in and attacked with deflection at a range of 150 yards closing to 20 yards and saw pieces flying off from around the port engine. Plisnier had turned and made a second attack, and this time the tailplane was blown off and the enemy aircraft turned over, swooped down and hit the ground, breaking into pieces. Pink Section then crossed out in cloud cover 2 miles east of Zeebrugge.

A second 'rhubarb' planned for the afternoon was cancelled owing to unsuitable weather.

20 NOVEMBER
With continuing bad weather, 350 Squadron was released off camp at 12.00hrs.

Flying Officer C.W. Bray of this station was posted to 1488 (FG) Flight at RAF Martlesham Heath, for administration duties.

21 NOVEMBER
Local flying and dusk landings were carried out today by 350 Squadron.

22 NOVEMBER
Six aircraft from 350 Squadron took part in a practice attack on Medway towns from 08.30hrs to 09.35hrs, beating up civilians, defence troops and vehicles, and the Civil Defence Services. Between 10.25hrs and 13.30hrs three sections patrolled the northbound Convoy 'Totem', north-east of Deal. Practice flying and dusk landings were also carried out.

23 NOVEMBER
Local flying only was carried out today by 350 Squadron.

Five members of the crew who were killed when a Wellington crashed near Pitsea on the night of 16/17 November 1942 were buried at Sutton Cemetery, Southend.

24 NOVEMBER
Eleven aircraft of 350 Squadron were called to readiness at 09.30hrs and at 10.00hrs took off on a 'roadstead' to provide anti-flak cover for four Hurri-bombers of 174 Squadron. They made rendezvous over Manston at 10.30hrs with the Hurri-bombers and eight Spitfires of 64 Squadron who were providing top cover for the operation.

They swept in at low level from Dunkirk to Knocke but no ships were seen. Very heavy flak was experienced along the coast, particularly in the neighbourhood of Ostend and Zeebrugge, and the squadron landed without damage or casualties at RAF Manston at 11.40hrs.

At 12.15hrs, the squadron took off again for Southend but were recalled and were down again fifteen minutes later.

At 15.20hrs, the squadron was airborne again on a 'rodeo' over the Abbeville area with seven Spitfires of 64 Squadron. Two aircraft of 350 Squadron were forced to return midway owing to engine trouble, and made their way home to RAF Southend. The rest of the formation crossed the Channel at Dungeness and climbed to 20,000ft over France. Nothing was seen, however, and the squadron returned without any results. The weather closed in and one aircraft lost the formation and landed at RAF Manston, and the other eight aircraft, which were unable to make base, landed at RAF West Malling at 16.20hrs, and spent the night there.

25 NOVEMBER

The aircraft of 350 Squadron left West Malling and landed back at RAF Southend at 12.15hrs. In the afternoon six aircraft took off for RAF Manston to maintain advanced readiness for fighter night but were recalled owing to the bad weather.

This station beat RAF North Weald at both soccer and rugby in the AOC 11 Group Cup matches.

26 NOVEMBER

Red Section of 350 Squadron took off at 09.00hrs to patrol the east-bound Convoy 'Passage' south of Southend, returning home at 10.10hrs.

27 NOVEMBER

No operational flying was carried out today; 350 Squadron was released off camp at 11.00hrs.

28 NOVEMBER

Local flying was carried out today. Flying Officers Plisnier and Venesoen of 350 Squadron joined a convoy at Southend on a four-day 'Goodwill' trip.

29 NOVEMBER

Between 09.40hrs and 12.45hrs three sections of 350 Squadron patrolled the Convoy 'Agent' east-bound off Southend.

30 NOVEMBER

From 09.35hrs to 10.50hrs, Green Section of 350 Squadron patrolled the east-bound Convoy 'Carnage' 5 miles east of Southend. At 10.35hrs, Red Section relieved Green Section and was ordered to land at Manston at 11.20hrs. At 11.15hrs, Blue Section took off on a patrol between North and South Forelands and nine more Spitfires of the squadron took off at the same time from Manston. The patrol was continued from RAF Manston by four more sections until 16.30hrs and all aircraft of the squadron were home by 16.45hrs.

DECEMBER

1 DECEMBER

From 09.20hrs to 12.45hrs, three sections of 350 Squadron patrolled the east-bound Convoy 'Platform' off Southend, and between 12.20hrs and 15.05hrs three sections patrolled the south-bound Convoy 'Result', east of Burnham. 'B' Flight carried out air-to-air firing during the morning.

At 16.35hrs, Red Section were scrambled and patrolled base for fifteen minutes as enemy aircraft were reported in the Crouch Estuary, but they landed later with nothing to report.

2 DECEMBER

'A' Flight of 350 Squadron was at readiness at dawn and at thirty minutes from 13.00hrs. They were called to readiness again at 16.00hrs and again at 16.30hrs but only for a few minutes in each case.

At 11.50hrs, Pink Section, and at 12.10hrs Purple Section, took off on 'rhubarb' patrols but they were forced to turn back at the French coast as the weather deteriorated. A fair amount of camera-gun practice was carried out during the day.

ASO W.J. Bagley (5407) (C&C) resigned his commission on medical grounds.

3 DECEMBER

350 Squadron was at readiness at dawn to take off for RAF Manston, but with fog closing in, a relaxed state was ordered at 13.00hrs and the squadron was released for training at 16.00hrs.

4 DECEMBER

At 08.25hrs, two sections of 350 Squadron took off for RAF Manston and 08.55hrs; they were joined by three more sections to carry out a convoy patrol. Cannon tests were also carried out during the day.

5 DECEMBER

350 Squadron was at readiness during the morning. Cannon tests were carried out in the afternoon.

Flight Lieutenant (Acting Squadron Leader) J.C. Stone (74509) arrived here on posting from RAF West Malling for duty as LDA.

6 DECEMBER

350 Squadron was at thirty-minute readiness all morning.

7 DECEMBER

In their last morning at RAF Southend, 350 Squadron carried out convoy patrols, and was released at 14.40hrs when the squadron began to move out to RAF Hornchurch during the afternoon. 453 Squadron had arrived at 11.30hrs from RAF Martlesham to replace 350 Squadron.

Major N.B. Collins (Royal Warwickshire Regiment, RARO) of this station was posted to RAF Llanbedr for duty as LDA.

8 DECEMBER

The weather was not too good, but 453 Squadron maintained convoy patrols outside the estuary in the morning.

At 20.00hrs, there was dancing for airmen and airwomen in the NAAFI restaurant at Medway Court.

9 DECEMBER

The first sweep of the month for 453 Squadron was carried out today, but no incident was reported.

10 DECEMBER

At 11.00hrs, six aircraft from 453 Squadron – Flight Lieutenant J.W. Yarra, DFM (402823) with Pilot Officers Ernest Esau (405472), Richard J. Darcey (408172), L.J. Hansell (403924), and M.H.I. De Cosier (405575), and Sergeant G. Stansfield (401543) – took off on a shipping reconnaissance and sighted an enemy convoy of merchant ships off Flushing which they attacked. During this sortie Flight Lieutenant Yarra and

Pilot Officer De Cosier were hit by flak and were lost. De Cosier's aircraft stalled while he was trying at a very low speed to gain height enough to jump, and dived into the sea. Although Yarra did bale out at 1,000ft, he hit and became caught in the tailplane. His parachute came out, but streamed behind the aircraft as it went down. He was seen to disengage before the aircraft hit the sea in flames and he was seen to fall into the water with his parachute streaming behind him unopened. His body was not recovered and he was accordingly reported as 'Missing Believed Killed'. Of the enemy ships, one of the Merchantmen was severely damaged and left burning fiercely, while a large number of men on the flak ships were killed, and many guns silenced.

At 20.00hrs, the ENSA Entertainers presented a Grand Variety Concert in the Concert Hall, Earl's Hall School.

11 DECEMBER
A bad day; there was no operational flying but a little practice flying was done before 453 Squadron was released for the rest of the day.

Corporal C. Wedley (920911) of 2830 Squadron was tried by district court martial for an offence under Section 40 of the Air Force Act.

12 DECEMBER
The weather improved, making a convoy patrol possible for 453 Squadron from 09.00hrs until 10.20hrs, followed by a sweep (as the third division of Circus 242). The squadron was not engaged by the enemy but the aircraft landed at RAF Manston owing to deterioration in the weather.

Section Officer Turton (1996) (C&C) arrived here on posting from RAF Tangmere.

13 DECEMBER
The pilots who were on yesterday's sweep returned from RAF Manston at intervals between 10.00hrs and 10.30hrs. Despite the rest of the 453 Squadron being at thirty-minute readiness all day, no further flying was possible owing to the weather conditions.

14 DECEMBER
The weather remained poor and beyond routine convoy patrols, which produced no incident, little flying was done. A replacement aircraft arrived to 453 Squadron, which was a good thing as most of those on strength were getting tossed out, and in view of the fact that the squadron was equipped with Spitfire Mk Vbs, no brand-new aircraft were procurable. Those in strength were elderly and consequently the amount of work that had to be done on them to keep them serviceable was abnormally high, with the result that a heavy strain was put upon a very much under-strength ground crew.

At 10.30hrs, Squadron Leader Simmonds presided over a Court of Inquiry which was held to inquire into loss of equipment.

At 20.00hrs, a dance for airmen and airwomen was held in the NAAFI restaurant, Medway Court.

15 DECEMBER
One flight of 453 Squadron was on aerodrome defence.

16 DECEMBER
453 Squadron was at thirty-minute readiness all day. Flight Lieutenant A.R. Russell

(72929) was posted to the station from RAF Biggin Hill, supernumerary for administration duties.

17 DECEMBER
Convoy patrols were carried out in the morning by 453 Squadron and one scramble
by Pilot Officer R.H.S. Ewins (405117) and Sergeant Stansfield. This was the first for
some time, but after flogging around the sky for fifty minutes, the section was told
that the enemy aircraft were actually 50 miles away, and so was recalled. During the
afternoon one section was scrambled at 1,500ft over the Canterbury area, but returned
with nothing to report.

18 DECEMBER
Low cloud and a threatening outlook restricted flying today. 453 Squadron was at
thirty-minute readiness, but released at lunchtime. Another replacement aircraft
arrived for the squadron in the afternoon, and a 'Victory' salvage drive was initiated on
the station.

19 DECEMBER
With clearer weather in the morning than the previous day, 453 Squadron was at
thirty-minute readiness, but the weather closed in again during the afternoon.
'B' Flight was on sixty-minute readiness for a fighter night.

20 DECEMBER
453 Squadron was ordered to be airborne within seven minutes and report to
RAF Hornchurch for briefing, but owing to poor weather they were re-directed to
RAF Manston, and later took part as second diversion of Circus 244. After ninety
minutes they returned with nothing to report.

In the afternoon one section was scrambled to orbit Manston at 25,000ft but was
recalled almost at once.

21 DECEMBER
A dirty day weather-wise; there was no operational flying and very little non-
operational flying.

22 DECEMBER
Another dirty day; just a little non-operational flying was carried out.

23 DECEMBER
453 Squadron took off to RAF Manston in the morning, but the sweep which had
been laid on was cancelled. Instead, a prolonged patrol was maintained over minesweepers in the Straits. This patrol was of considerably greater interest than many, as
not only was the work of the minesweepers well worth watching, but as the weather
was clear, enemy aircraft were clearly visible over the coast of France. None of them
approached, however.

A Christmas party was held in the Medway Court NAAFI for airmen and airwomen. The MC was Squadron Leader C.H. Gadney. A most entertaining evening of
dancing and games was thoroughly enjoyed by all.

24 DECEMBER
Probably fortunately, the weather ruled flying out almost entirely, but 453 Squadron managed to return from RAF Manston.

25 DECEMBER
No flying today. A most excellent Christmas dinner was provided, and thoroughly enjoyed and appreciated by all personnel, followed by a dance for airmen and air-women in the evening.

26 DECEMBER
No flying.

27 DECEMBER
About eleven hours of local flying was carried out by 453 Squadron with the improvement of the weather. They were released after lunch.

28 DECEMBER
Mixed weather; no flying today.

29 DECEMBER
453 Squadron flew to RAF Manston for convoy patrols and returned home. Flying Officer V.A. Lanos (81778) was attached to RAF Bridgnorth for a flying controllers' course, and Section Officer J.D. Savage (3995) was posted away to RAF Towyn.

30 DECEMBER
453 Squadron was at fifteen-minute readiness in the morning. A song and dance show for the station personnel took place in the Concert Hall, Earl's Hall School.

31 DECEMBER
453 Squadron carried out standing patrols north to South Foreland in the morning and returned home at lunch time.

At 10.28hrs, twenty-seven other ranks of 4077 AA Flight left by rail on transfer to RAF Great Sampford, and at 13.58hrs, thirty other ranks of 4027 AA Flight arrived on transfer from RAF Fairlop.

In the early afternoon 453 Squadron was called to 'Stand By' for a scramble but did not take off.

Flight Lieutenant A.R. Russell carried out an investigation into an outbreak of fire in the requisitioned property 'Ludworth' in Wells Avenue, Rochford, on 23 December.

Gas exercises were carried out on every Wednesday during the month.

Physical training was carried out daily by 2810 and 2830 Squadrons, RAF Regiment, 4077 AA Flight, and the WAAFs, with unarmed combat being taught on alternate days.

Sports events for the month:

The Station Soccer 1st XI played four matches, winning three and losing one.
The Station Soccer 2nd XI played four matches, winning two and losing two.
Inter-section Soccer: twenty-eight matches were played.
The Rugby Station XV played five matches, winning four and losing one.
The Hockey Station XI played five matches, winning two and losing three.
Netball (WAAFs) played two matches, winning one and losing one.
In the Inter-section Challenge Cup, RAF Southend won both rounds *v.* RAF Fairlop
and RAF Stapleford Tawney in all three matches, rugby, soccer and hockey.

4

1943

JANUARY

The winning of air superiority was crucial. It meant the end of the Luftwaffe as a decisive fighting force and ensured that the Allied invasion force could be safely landed in Normandy in June 1944 without significant interference from the air.

1 JANUARY
The New Year opened with a dull, cloudy day which was unfit for any flying. The process of recovery from recent festivities was therefore able to go forward without interruption.

Section Officer P. Barton (2532) was posted from this station to RAF Kenley (WAAF 'G'). A transfer of AA Flights was carried out today with 4077 moving to RAF Fairlop, and 4027 moving in.

2 JANUARY
The weather lifted today and 453 Squadron went on a sweep intended as a diversion for Circus 243 – a bombing attack on Abbeville Aerodrome. The rest of the wing was made up of 122 and 350 Squadrons. The squadron was airborne for ninety minutes, but the flight was uneventful, with no enemy aircraft or flak encountered.

3 JANUARY
Another fine day; convoy patrols and a great deal of practice flying were carried out by 453 Squadron, including cine-gun exercises, sector reconnaissances and formation flying for the benefit of the new pilots to the squadron.

2779 Squadron, RAF Regiment, arrived from RAF North Weald on an exchange with 2810 Squadron.

Pilot Officer Simpkins D.G.E. Branch, Air Ministry, visited the station.

4 JANUARY
The whole day was spent by 453 Squadron on convoy patrols flying out of RAF Manston. Over thirty-six hours were flown in thirty sorties. No enemy aircraft were seen, and no incidents were reported. The aircraft returned home in the evening.

At 09.35hrs, Lysander V9823 of 1488 (FG) Flight took off, and the pilot reported aileron and elevator controls jammed shortly after take-off. The aircraft crashed on landing in field adjacent to the aerodrome and burst into flames, becoming a total wreck. The pilot and crew were not injured. Finding the cause of the controls jamming proved impossible.

5 JANUARY
There was snow on the ground in the morning. Convoy patrols were carried out by 453 Squadron, but the weather quickly closed in and there was no flying in the afternoon.

At 15.15hrs, a Spitfire Mk IX (BS137) of 332 Squadron overshot the landing and collided with Spitfire Mk IX (BS445) which was 'parked' near the Watch Office. The latter aircraft also belonged to 332 Squadron. Both aircraft were extensively damaged, being categorised 'B' and 'E' respectively. The pilot was uninjured.

6 JANUARY
Snow, rain and sleet today; there was no flying.

Pilot Officer Baldwin, Equipment Branch, HQFC visited the station.

7 JANUARY
Snow, rain and sleet again today – no flying. At 20.00hrs, a variety concert by the 'Dominant Cs' was held at Earl's Hall School.

8 JANUARY
A very cold morning, but the weather was fine enough to allow some formation flying by 453 Squadron during the day. Cine-gun exercises were also carried out as well as further training for the less experienced pilots.

9 JANUARY
A short convoy patrol was carried out by 453 Squadron in the morning, which was followed by a sweep in which the squadron was airborne from 12.45hrs to 14.05hrs. The squadron returned to base without any noteworthy incident.

Flying Officer G.G.F. Smartt (114495) was posted here from 29 Squadron for medical duties.

10–12 JANUARY
Bad weather kept aircraft grounded all day.

11 JANUARY
Flight Lieutenant E. Anthony (87974) was posted to RAF Zeals for medical duties.

13 JANUARY
In the morning, the weather had cleared enough for a sweep by 453 Squadron as part of Circus 249 to St Omer. No engagement took place, but heavy and accurate flak was encountered from the Dunkirk area. The only damage, however, was to Flight Lieutenant Andrews' aircraft which had been holed in several places and remained unserviceable for a considerable time, much to his disgust.

3746 (Canadian) Echelon transferred to RAF Redhill, and was replaced by 3074 Echelon.

14 JANUARY
No flying today. Flying Officer A. Gilbert (117784) was posted here from RAF Hunsdon.

15 JANUARY

The day was devoted to convoy and minesweeping patrols by 453 Squadron, and practice flying including formation and aerobatics were also carried out.

Wing Commander McLeod visited the station from Headquarters, 11 Group. Flight Lieutenant (Acting Squadron Leader) F.W. Dowling (43604) was attached (pending posting) from RAF College to command the station.

16 JANUARY

453 Squadron carried out convoy and minesweeping patrols from RAF Manston in the morning. No enemy aircraft were observed and thus no incidents to report.

17 JANUARY

453 Squadron flew convoy patrols again from RAF Manston, and also an army co-operation exercise was carried out in the Etham and Folkestone area. The squadron was on readiness at night, but, although there was a raid with a number of enemy aircraft overhead and plenty of anti-aircraft fire, the weather unfortunately did not permit flying. It was fairly clear overhead, but there was a thick ground haze which reduced visibility to a very short distance. There had been many alerts during the past week, both during the day and the night, but it had not been possible to take advantage of them to open the squadron's record for enemy aircraft destroyed owing either to the weather or to the fact that the raiders had been too far away. On several occasions, reports had been received of enemy aircraft approaching, but they had been turned away before coming within reach.

18 JANUARY

The constant damp weather had a severe effect on the health of both ground and aircrews, the Australians in particular suffering from an epidemic of feverish colds which, while fairly short lived, were severe in their effects. Today, Sergeant F. Halcombe (416094) of 453 Squadron, normally an extremely careful pilot, had a taxiing accident when taking off from RAF Manston on a convoy patrol. Immediately afterwards he was taken to hospital and was released ten days later. It appeared from the medical evidence that at the time he was suffering from the onset of illness, which may explain the lapse in his concentration.

Flight Lieutenant (Acting Squadron Leader) C.H. Gadney, station commander, was posted to Headquarters, Fighter Command.

At 20.00hrs, an ENSA Concert was held at Earl's Hall School.

19 JANUARY

The weather was very bad, with rain and low cloud. This was just as well in view of the number of pilots who were in hospital and many of the ground crew were suffering from the prevailing epidemic. There were several alerts during the day, but no action.

20 JANUARY

It was still cloudy, but good enough to allow nearly twelve hours of practice flying. Both flights of 453 Squadron were at readiness all night, one here and one at RAF Manston. Although there were two alerts, neither flight was sent up.

Flight Lieutenant N.F. Cook (44041) was attached (pending posting) from RAF Middle Wallop for accountant duties. Flight Lieutenant O'Connor, catering officer, HQFC visited the station today.

21 JANUARY

Prolonged convoy patrols were carried out by 453 Squadron. This was a remarkable achievement considering that many of the pilots were sick, but in all, fifty-two and a half hours of flying was done.

22 JANUARY

What could be mustered from 453 Squadron was at readiness in the morning, but was released in the afternoon.

23 JANUARY

The epidemic reached its height with thirteen pilots of 453 Squadron in hospital. The weather was very thick with fog, however, and no flying could be done.

At 13.00hrs, the Fighter Command Rifle Demonstration Flight arrived at this station. All available personnel attended the very interesting and instructive demonstration.

24 JANUARY

Dense fog; 453 Squadron released in the afternoon.

25 JANUARY

Convoy patrols and practice flying was carried out by 453 Squadron. Flight Lieutenant J.E. Garrish (83626) was attached to Headquarters, Fighter Command (pending posting) for accountant duties.

A satisfactory salvage drive was made in all sections on the station.

26 JANUARY

453 Squadron carried out convoy patrol in the morning from RAF Manston without incident and a patrol over Canterbury at 10,000ft for thirty minutes in the late afternoon yielded no results, returning in poor visibility to a half-laid flare path.

27 JANUARY

Dirty weather meant very little flying was done. A station dance was held in the Concert Hall, Earl's Hall School.

28 JANUARY

Another day of adverse weather meant very little flying was done. Pilot Officer L.A. Harvey (84591) was posted here from RAF Hornchurch for physical fitness duties.

At 15.00hrs, a talk and discussion on the Beveridge Report was given by a lecturer of the Regional Committee, London, in the Concert Hall, Earl's Hall School.

29 JANUARY

Dirty weather meant only one convoy patrol could be carried out by 453 Squadron in the morning.

30 JANUARY

Again only one convoy patrol was carried out by 453 Squadron in the morning. Squadron Leader J.C. Stone, commander, RAF Regiment was attached to RAF North Weald.

31 JANUARY

Gales today – no flying. Squadron Leader John Ratten (405111) sent the thanks of 453 Squadron to Sir Courtauld Thompson, with whom many of the pilots stayed at his house in Burnham.

At 10.00hrs, the film *Coastal Command* was shown to RAF, WAAF and ATC personnel in the Odeon Cinema, Southend, followed by a presentation by the station commander to Cadet Flight Sergeant N.A. Bull, 1312 Squadron ATC, for his help during the crash of a Dornier Do 217 at Southend on 26 October 1942, followed by a march past at which the salute was taken by the station commander.

Gas exercises were carried out weekly during the month.

Physical training was carried out daily by 4027 (AA Flight), 2779 and 2810 Squadrons, RAF Regiment, and 453 Squadron.

Sports events for the month:

The Station Soccer 1st XI played four matches.
The Station Soccer 2nd XI played five matches.
Inter-section Soccer: twenty-eight matches were played.
The Rugby Station XV played three matches.
The Hockey Station XI played one match.
Netball (WAAFs) played one match.

FEBRUARY

1 FEBRUARY

The weather was not very good but one convoy patrol was carried out by 453 Squadron together with a certain amount of practice and air-to-air firing.

2 FEBRUARY

High wind made all flying out of the question.

3 FEBRUARY

At 10.07hrs, 453 Squadron took off on Circus 258. Their role was escorting Venturas to Cambrai, but it became abortive owing to weather with 10/10ths cloud at 7,000ft as far as could be seen over France and Belgium. The squadron was home again at 11.37hrs.

At 15.08hrs, the squadron took off again to take part on Circus 259. Their role was escorting twelve Venturas to Abbeville. The weather was 6/10ths cloud at 4,000ft over the Channel area. Flak was experienced which was accurate for height but slightly behind them. The Venturas dropped their bombs and bursts were observed on the target. The squadron was back home at 16.47hrs.

Flight Lieutenant S. Pike (84173) was posted here from RAF North Weald for PDP duties.

At 20.00hrs, the RAF Gang Show No. 6 entertained large audiences at the Concert Hall, Earl's Hall School.

4 FEBRUARY

453 Squadron was at readiness all day, but a fair amount of fog didn't lift as expected and subsequently a sweep that was laid on for the afternoon was cancelled.

Section Officer V.M. Turton (1996) was attached to RAF North Weald for cypher duties.

5 FEBRUARY

453 Squadron was on 'roadstead' readiness at dawn, but there was no incident. A sweep was again laid on for the afternoon but cancelled owing to fog which was still hanging about. The squadron was released at 11.00hrs.

6 FEBRUARY

Heavy rain in the morning restricted flying, and one convoy patrol was carried out by 453 Squadron in the afternoon.

Pilot Officer Thornley played football in the afternoon for the Royal Australian Air Force versus the New Zealand Combined Services. The RAAF lost 8–5 after a stiff fight. A radio commentary by Pilot Officer Smith was transmitted to Australia.

7 FEBRUARY

The weather was still very difficult for flying with high wind and occasional heavy rain. 453 Squadron made a short convoy patrol in afternoon.

8 FEBRUARY

The weather was much the same as the previous day, and again, 453 Squadron made a short convoy patrol in afternoon.

9 FEBRUARY

A Dornier Do 217 passed over the aerodrome at 08.40hrs. 453 Squadron had a section on aerodrome defence but although the enemy aircraft had dropped bombs in the neighbourhood of Romford, the section received no information of its presence until they saw it crossing the perimeter track. It was then, of course, too late for anything to be done.

It should, perhaps, be mentioned that Flight Sergeant Wood of 'B' Flight had an earlier view of the enemy aircraft. He was machine-gunned as he was cycling from the Sergeants' Mess. He did not get hit, but he complained that he could not steer his bicycle because of the strikes he saw on both sides of the front wheel!

Pilot Officer V. Lanos (31772) ceased his attachment to RAF Bridgnorth for a flying controllers' course.

At 16.00hrs, Flight Lieutenant Donald Andrews (404795) and Pilot Officer Esau, of 453 Squadron, went on a special shipping reconnaissance. They swept the coast and harbours of Ostend, Flushing, West Kappelle, Zeebrugge and Blankenburg, and brought back considerable shipping information. Intense flak was experienced at Flushing and West Kappelle. They were flying at zero feet except over the port areas when they climbed up to the cloud base. The weather was 10/10ths cloud with a base varying from 500ft to 700ft with several rain showers. Visibility was 3 miles approximately below cloud but very hazy. They landed at RAF Manston at 17.20hrs.

1 (Typhoon) Squadron was forced, by inclement weather, to land here just after 16.00hrs. The last aircraft to come in had difficulty in getting its wheels down. After flying round for some twenty minutes, the wheels did actually lock in the 'down' position, but the pilot was not aware of this as the indicator lights had failed. To make

matters worse, the flaps also failed to operate. The aircraft, coming in from east to west, did not touch down until almost at the western perimeter and then ran through barbed wire and rubble, and turned over, ripping the tail unit off. The pilot, who was extricated from the cockpit with some difficulty, was uninjured. His aircraft was categorised 'E'.

At 20.00hrs, the first performance of the newly formed station concert party, *Southend Scroungers*, was well received by a large audience at the Concert Hall.

10 FEBRUARY
Flying postponed because of bad weather.

13 FEBRUARY
A slight improvement in the weather gave 453 Squadron the opportunity for some practice formation flying.

13/14 FEBRUARY
Ten Ju 88s were spotted close to Southend, searching for shipping. The enemy aircraft joined up with fifteen more and moved northwards, but not before the Bofors guns at Burnham-on-Crouch brought one down.

14 FEBRUARY
453 Squadron was on 'roadstead' readiness at dawn and on convoy patrols during the day.

15 FEBRUARY
Eleven aircraft from 453 Squadron made rendezvous with bombers acting as close escort to Dunkirk on Circus 265. No enemy aircraft or flak was seen owing to 10/10ths cloud at 9,000ft to 10,000ft over the target area. The bombing was abandoned and the wing withdrew.

Pilot Officer G.A. Daniels (130769) was attached to RAF Redhill for gas duties.

At 10.00hrs, ENSA presented a show in the Concert Hall, Earl's Hall School.

16 FEBRUARY
At 12.25, 453 Squadron took off on a sweep (Rodeo 169). They crossed the coast at 23,000ft, with the weather 10/10ths cloud at 5,000ft over Channel and French coastal areas. They swept the Dunkirk, St Omer, Berck, Boulogne and Cap Gris Nez areas, and although no enemy shipping was seen, six enemy aircraft were spotted by 350 Squadron in the Berck area 5,000ft below when they were going out from Boulogne. The squadron was home by 13.39hrs.

17 FEBRUARY
At 09.50hrs, 453 Squadron took off on Circus 269. They made rendezvous with the wing over Clacton at 1,000ft, but when east of North Foreland, they ran into cloud which increased to 10/10ths at 6,000ft, and another layer of 9/10ths at 12,000ft from mid-Channel to as far inland as could be seen. The wing remained between these layers until they were three minutes from the target when the decision was made to turn back as there was no improvement in the weather. They made landfall at Clacton at 10.12hrs, and landed home at 10.53hrs.

At 19.30hrs, an airmen and airwomen's dance was held at Earl's Hall School.

18 FEBRUARY

At 15.00hrs, Flight Lieutenant Griffith, adjutant at the RAF Wing in Russia, gave a talk in the hall, on the work of the RAF in Russia.

At 16.00hrs, a 'circus' involving 453 Squadron was laid on, but owing to heavy weather was cancelled. The squadron was also going to do night readiness and practice flying at RAF Manston, but this, too, was cancelled owing to the weather.

19 FEBRUARY

A heavy ground mist lay for much of the morning. One flight of 453 Squadron was on fifteen-minute readiness at 13.15hrs, but as the weather did not improve was released at 15.18hrs.

20 FEBRUARY

One section of 453 Squadron was on readiness in the morning, although the weather was very misty. A show laid on for 13.00hrs was postponed until 14.00hrs and again at 16.00hrs. At 17.00hrs it was cancelled altogether and the squadron was released.

21 FEBRUARY

Heavy fog all day; no flying. Section Officer V.M. Turton (1996) ceased his attachment to RAF North Weald.

22 FEBRUARY

Dense fog made flying too hazardous until it broke on the 26th.

24 FEBRUARY

Flying Officer V.A. Lanos was posted to Headquarters, 13 Group.

25 FEBRUARY

Section Officer V.M. Turton (1996) was attached to RAF Manston for cypher duties. 2830 Squadron, RAF Regiment, returned from RAF North Weald on completion of their training, and 2779 Squadron, RAF Regiment, transferred back to RAF North Weald.

26 FEBRUARY

A big day's flying for 453 Squadron with a three-part 'circus':

The squadron took off on Circus 274, making rendezvous with 350 Squadron over the base and then proceeding to Clacton to make contact with bombers. Course was then set for Dunkirk at zero feet for six minutes, climbing to 10,000ft over the target area. Broken cloud was experienced 15 miles off the French coast, increasing to 10/10ths inland at 3,500ft. They crossed out at 10.00hrs, but no bombing took place owing to unfavourable weather conditions. 453 Squadron parted from the bombers over the estuary, and landed back at base at 10.50hrs.

At 14.01hrs, the second part of Circus 274 started with contact with 350 Squadron over the base and setting course for Clacton at zero feet to make rendezvous with bombers. They flew at zero feet for three minutes, climbing to between 10,000 and 11,000ft over the target, which was reached at 14.37hrs. The bombers released their 'eggs' on a left-hand turn then made straight for home, dropping down to sea level.

Several bombs were seen to burst in the target area. Flak experienced was accurate and heavy. They crossed in about 2 miles south of Bradwell Bay at 14.58hrs, and 453 Squadron left to return home.

At 16.35hrs, the third part of Circus 274 started with another contact with 350 Squadron and again setting course for Clacton at zero feet to make rendez-vous with bombers at 16.45hrs. They then headed for Dunkirk at zero feet for four minutes, climbing to 12,000ft over the target, and into accurate medium-heavy flak from the target area. With bombs dropped from 10,000ft, they crossed out at 17.11hrs making for Clacton, and losing height all the way, crossed in at zero feet at 17.32hrs where the squadron parted with the bombers in the estuary and landed home eleven minutes later.

27 FEBRUARY

In the late morning, a 'circus' was carried out by 453 Squadron with bombs again being dropped by the escorted bombers in the target area. The squadron was not engaged except by fairly heavy and accurate flak. On returning from these missions, the squadron remained on 'roadstead' readiness until 19.00hrs.

At 13.50hrs, 453 Squadron took off on Circus 575. Rendezvous was made with 350 Squadron over the base and they flew at zero feet to Clacton where they contacted the bombers and set course for Dunkirk. On the drop, many bombs were seen to burst on target. The squadron landed back at base at 14.59hrs, but remained on 'roadstead' readiness until 19.00hrs.

28 FEBRUARY

There was a heavy ground mist in the morning which prevented flying.

Gas exercises were carried out weekly during the month.

Physical training was carried out daily by 2810 and 2830 Squadrons, RAF Regiment, 4027 AA Flight, 116 and 453 Squadrons, and 1488 (FG) Gunnery Flight.

Sports events for the month:

The Station Soccer 1st XI played four matches, winning three and drawing one.
The Station Soccer 2nd XI played three matches, winning three.
Inter-section Soccer: twenty-eight matches were played.
The Rugby Station XV played five matches, winning two and losing two.
The Hockey Station XI played four matches, winning three and losing one.
Badminton was being played by all ranks.
Cross-country running had commenced and a team was being formed.
A boxing team was being formed and was in training.
Table tennis, billiards and darts facilities had been made available for all ranks, and matches arranged with service units.

MARCH

1 MARCH

At 08.50hrs, seventeen aircraft of 453 Squadron flew to Battle Station Westcott, landing there forty minutes later for exercises to prepare for Operation Spartan. Their road convoy of ten vehicles and two tankers followed, arriving at 18.00hrs.

Pilot Officer A.C. Freeman (134843) was posted here from 2783 Squadron, Heston, to join 4027 (AA) Flight.

5 MARCH

An Oxford (DF357) of 1657 CU Stradishall overshot on landing and ran into a trench in the north-west corner of the airfield, wrecking the port undercarriage. The fuselage was also damaged and the aircraft was classified category 'B'. The pilot and three passengers were uninjured.

13 MARCH

Flight Lieutenant A.R. Russell (72929) was attached to RAF Hawkinge for administrative duties. 453 Squadron returned to the station on completion of exercises for Operation Spartan.

14 MARCH

Operation Spartan: 453 Squadron took part in operations from RAF Southend during the afternoon; 'A' Sweep was a 'rodeo', sweeping Hardelot, Desvres and Cap Gris Nez at 19,000ft, orbiting mid-Channel and returning via Dover. No incidents were worthy of reporting. 'B' Sweep was a 'ramrod' escorting Whirlibombers to bomb the marshalling yards at Abbeville, which succeeded without incident.

15 MARCH

Three aircraft of 453 Squadron did thirty minutes' night flying.

At 20.00hrs, an ENSA show *Tommy Get Your Fun* was given in the Concert Hall at Earl's Hall School.

16 MARCH

453 Squadron carried out standing patrols in the Barrow Deep area during the afternoon.

17 MARCH

453 Squadron was on convoy and standing patrols from midday until dusk. Pilot Officer I.T. Hayes (122541) was posted to RAF Castletown for electrical engineering duties.

The AOC, 11 Group, visited this station to carry out a general inspection. At 20.00hrs, a St Patrick's Night station dance was held in the Concert Hall at Earl's Hall School.

18 MARCH

453 Squadron carried out patrols in the Barrow Deep area in the late afternoon and evening.

19 MARCH

453 Squadron carried out patrols in the Barrow Deep area in morning.

20 MARCH

Operations called for one section of 453 Squadron to be scrambled at 09.30hrs. The aircraft orbited the base until landing at 09.47hrs with no incident to report. Patrols in the Barrow Deep area were carried out from mid-afternoon until dusk. Following these, the squadron was at sixty-minute readiness for fighter nights.

21 MARCH

No flying today owing to bad weather. Flight Lieutenant A.R. Russell ceased his attachment to RAF Hawkinge.

22 MARCH

Eight aircraft of 453 Squadron took part in some practice army air support flying, which took about two hours. Standing patrols were carried out during the afternoon.

Flight Lieutenant G.H. Blair (118673) was attached from 4027 (AA) Flight on transfer to 4077 (AA) Flight, pending posting to Command, replacing Flight Lieutenant T.J. Tarry (84486), who was attached to 4027 (AA) Flight on transfer from 4077 (AA) Flight, pending posting to Command.

23 MARCH

Some local flying by 453 Squadron included cine-gun, aerobatics and dive tests; standing patrols were carried out during the afternoon.

Flight Lieutenant T.A. Wiese (79019) was attached to RAF Gravesend for intelligence duties.

24 MARCH

453 Squadron carried out an abortive sweep to Abbeville, where they turned back 5 miles from the French coast owing to bad weather conditions.

25 MARCH

453 Squadron carried out standing patrols during the morning, and after noon, they took off to escort Whirlibombers to bomb the marshalling yards at Abbeville.

26 MARCH

Two aircraft of 453 Squadron carried out their last 'rhubarb' operation in the Knocke to Dixmude area from RAF Southend. In a successful attack, they seriously damaged one locomotive, caused damage to a second, and damaged one barge.

27 MARCH

453 Squadron transferred to RAF Hornchurch this morning via rail and road. At 08.10hrs, a special train arrived at Southend from Ayr carrying the first party from 222 (Natal) Squadron. They took over the Spitfire Mk Vbs from 453 Squadron and maintained one section on readiness for airfield defence from 15.00hrs. 4027 (AA) Flight left for CTC Castle Toward for No. 7 Combined Operation Courses.

28 MARCH

Convoy patrols by two flights of 222 Squadron were carried out between 10.20hrs and 15.35hrs, and a few sector reconnaissances were also flown. The remainder of the squadron arrived by air at 13.10hrs. The aircraft were being modified and the squadron letters painted on, etc. A little local flying was carried out.

29 MARCH

Convoy patrols were carried out by 222 Squadron from 06.55hrs until 13.30hrs. Two sections led by the commanding officer made a reconnaissance over the Channel between Dover and Calais, flying by way of the estuary, and down the coast, but saw nothing.

Sergeant Norman Swift in Spitfire BR370 of 453 Squadron crashed at Southchurch owing to a fuel shortage while flying a reconnaissance. He sustained some injuries including a fractured femur, head injuries and concussion, and was taken to Southend General Hospital. The aircraft was written off.

At 20.00hrs, ENSA gave the show *Saloon Bar* in the Concert Hall at Earl's Hall School.

30 MARCH

A fine but hazy day; 'A' Flight of 222 Squadron (three sections of two aircraft) was scrambled at 08.25hrs, and were airborne within two minutes. They maintained a patrol between Southend and Folkestone, and landed home without incident at 09.35hrs. Convoy patrols were carried out by 'B' Flight from 08.45hrs until 14.30hrs and by 'A' Flight again from 11.10hrs until 13.45hrs.

31 MARCH

After a rainy night the morning was dull. 'B' Flight of 222 Squadron was at dawn readiness. Convoy patrols were commenced by 'A' Flight at 10.10hrs. At approximately 12.00hrs, Yellow Section (Flying Officer Clements (Yellow 1) and Flying Officer Cryderman (Yellow 2)) were orbiting the Convoy 'Carnage' about 15 miles south-east of Felixstowe when Yellow 1 saw a radial engine and odd bits of engine fall out of the sky, followed seconds later by what appeared to be bombs which exploded in the sea. Shortly afterwards four parachutes were seen descending about a mile east of the convoy. Yellow 2 promptly gave out a Mayday on their position, and then three more parachutes were seen coming down. Yellow 2 remained orbiting the area while Yellow 1 returned to the convoy. Blue 1 (Flight Lieutenant Tripe) was sent out to bring Yellow 2 home when it was discovered that his R/T was u/s. No signs of any rescue of the downed aircrew were seen up to the time they left the scene an hour later. Yellow Section landed at Southend at 13.10hrs and 13.20hrs respectively. (There was no follow-up report to the incident with the stricken bomber.)

Gas exercises were carried out weekly during the month.

Physical training was carried out daily by 2810 Squadron, RAF Regiment, 4027 AA Flight, 116 and 453 Squadrons, and 1488 (FG) Flight.

Sports events for the month:

The Station Soccer 1st XI played two matches, and winning both.

The Station Soccer 2nd XI played three matches, winning two and drawing one.

Inter-section Soccer: thirteen matches were played.

The Rugby Station XV played five matches, winning three and losing two.

The Hockey Station XI played five matches, winning three and losing two.

Badminton is being played by all ranks.

The cross-country running team had been being formed and was in training for the 11 Group competition.

The WAAFs played and lost the only netball match played this month.

Table tennis, billiards and darts facilities were being used by all ranks, with matches having been arranged with service units.

APRIL

1 APRIL

The twenty-fifth anniversary of the Royal Air Force. 222 Squadron, with 3074 Echelon, left for RAF Martlesham. At 08.30hrs, a colour hoisting parade and march past of all units and sections was held at this station. During the parade an address was given by the station commander on the work of the RAF.

At 12.00hrs, a special dinner was prepared and the officers and senior NCOs waited upon the airmen and airwomen. At 20.00hrs, in continuation of the twenty-fifth anniversary celebrations, a station dance took place in the Concert Hall, Earl's Hall School.

2 APRIL

Flight Lieutenant A.R. Russell (72929) A&SD was posted to RAF Manston for administrative duties.

3 APRIL

A Defiant (AA435) of 515 Squadron, Heston, overshot upon landing. The aircraft ran into barbed-wire entanglements in north-west corner of the airfield and tipped up on its nose. The propeller and undercarriage fairings were damaged and the aircraft was classified as category 'A/C'. The engine failed shook load test and had to be changed. The pilot was uninjured.

Pilot Officer F.A. Higgins (123784) A&SD was attached to the station from RAF Biggin Hill for administrative duties. Flying Officer I. McInnes (109502) was posted here from 29 Squadron, RAF West Malling, for duty as assistant duty pilot.

10 APRIL

638 and 1576 Squadrons ATC arrived for a seven-day Easter camp.

11 APRIL

Section Officer P.E. Barton (2532), WAAF (G) was attached to Headquarters, 11 Group, for a code and cypher course.

13 APRIL

At 20.00hrs, an ENSA Show *Over to You* was presented at Earl's Hall School Concert Hall. Pilot Officer F.A. Higgins (123784) A&SD ceased his attachment from RAF Biggin Hill.

17 APRIL
638 and 1576 Squadrons ATC departed Southend having completed their Easter camp. 656, 106, 1390, 1474 and 1580 Squadrons ATC arrived to begin their Easter camp.

18 APRIL
Section Officer E.M. Webb (3220), WAAF (G) was attached to Headquarters, 11 Group, for seven days on a code and cypher course.

19 APRIL
Warrant Officer R. Stafford (501951) (Station Armament) was posted to RAF Pocklington.

20 APRIL
At 08.45hrs, a successful station defence exercise was held in which the local military units participated with the RAF Regiment and station personnel. The exercise terminated at 13.00hrs.

At 18.00hrs, the Rt Revd the Lord Bishop of Chelmsford dedicated the Church of St Christopher on the main camp. Revd J.F. Cox, assistant chaplain-in-chief, and the Venerable Ellis N. Gowing, Archdeacon of Southend, assisted. The chief constable, representing the Southend Constabulary, was also present. This body presented the church with four stained-glass windows. The chancel screen was given by the Officers' Mess. The redecoration and woodwork was the work of four airmen of 2810 Squadron: Corporal Farmer, LAC Bell, LAC Robson, and LAC Murphy. These four airmen also donated a sanctuary lamp.

21 APRIL
Pilot Officer C.A. Maple (130764) A&SD was posted here from RAF Biggin Hill as a relief for Pilot Officer G.A. Daniels (130769) who was posted to Headquarters, 83 Group.

24 APRIL
As part of four days of local and practice flying, 124 Squadron from RAF North Weald carried out air-firing practice at Southend and Clacton Ranges.

656, 106, 1390, 1474 and 1580 Squadrons ATC completed Easter camp.

2035 Squadron ATC arrived at the station.

25 APRIL
Section Officer E.M. Webb (3220) WAAF (G) was posted to Headquarters, 11 Group. Section Officer C.M. Turnbull (3015) WAAF (G) was posted in as replacement, but would take up duties following attachment to Headquarters, 11 Group, for a seven-day code and cypher course. Warrant Officer S. Piner (200748) was posted to the station from RAF North Weald for duty as station armament warrant officer.

A Spitfire Mk VI (BR189) of 124 Squadron approached to land at Southend and in doing so collided with a blister hangar in East Dispersal. The port and starboard undercarriage oleo struts were knocked off, but the aircraft remained airborne and, after making another circuit of the airfield, crash-landed. The propeller and both main planes were extremely damaged and the aircraft categorised 'B'. The pilot, Sergeant Johnson, was uninjured.

26 APRIL
Squadron Leader Donald E. Kingaby, DSO, DFM (the only RAF pilot to be awarded the DFM three times) arrived from RAF Hornchurch on posting to command the station, to replace Squadron Leader F.W. Dowling (43604) A&SD who was awaiting a posting overseas. At 20.00hrs, ENSA presented *Youth on Parade* at Earl's Hall School.

28 APRIL
Flight Lieutenant S. Pike (84175) was posted to RAF Farnborough for PDP duties.

29 APRIL
Flight Lieutenant T. Barrington (81752) A&SD arrived here from RAF Biggin Hill on posting for administration duties.

30 APRIL
2035 Squadron ATC completed Easter camp today.

Gas exercises were held weekly during the month.

Physical training was carried out daily by 2810 and 2830 Squadrons, RAF Regiment, 116 Squadron, 1488 (FG) Flight and WAAFs.

Sports events for the month:

The Station Soccer 1st XI played four matches, winning two, drawing one and losing one.
Inter-section Soccer: Eight matches were played.
The Station Hockey XI won the only match played this month.
Badminton was being played regularly by all ranks.
Cricket practice had started, and the first station match was played on Saturday 1 May.
Table tennis, billiards and darts facilities were being used by all ranks, and matches had been arranged with service units.

MAY

1 MAY
4027 (AA) Flight moved to RAF Kingscliffe, and 4189 (AA) Flight arrived here from RAF Aldermaston as relief. Squadron Leader Kingaby opened the Wings for Victory week at Rayleigh, Essex. RAF personnel attended the parade.

2 MAY
Section Officer O.M. Turnbull (3015) WAAF (G) ceased attachment to Headquarters, 11 Group, on completion of a code and cypher course, and took up her posting at this station.

8 MAY
Flight Lieutenant (Acting Squadron Leader) F.W. Dowling (43604) was posted to West Kirby.

9 MAY

Flying Officer J.C.E. Roberts (87118) A&SD was posted to the station from RAF Ballyhalbert, supernumerary for administration duties.

10 MAY

At 20.00hrs, ENSA presented *All in the Picture* in the Concert Hall, Earl's Hall School.

13 MAY

2830 Squadron, RAF Regiment, moved to Brandy Bay, Dorset. At 20.00hrs, the RAF Gang Show performed in the Concert Hall, Earl's Hall School.

14 MAY

The station's Wings for Victory week started today with a target of £1,000.

15 MAY

Squadron Leader Kingaby opened the Rochford Wings for Victory week. RAF personnel attended the parade.

16 MAY

RAF personnel from this station attended a Drumhead Service at the Hockley Wings for Victory week parade.

Flying Officer J.C.E. Roberts (87118) A&SD was attached to 5003 Works Squadron for administration duties.

A Spitfire Mk Vb (BL821) of 331 Squadron, RAF North Weald, made a heavy landing at Southend causing failure of the starboard oleo leg-locking unit. The aircraft was classified category 'A' and repairs were carried out by personnel of 331 Squadron.

17 MAY

4189 (AA) Flight was absorbed into 2810 (AA) Flight on this day.

18 MAY

This station played soccer against the 22nd Anti-Tank Regiment at Southend Stadium in aid of this station's Wings for Victory week.

At 19.30hrs, a fundraising station dance for the Southend Wings for Victory week was held at Earl's Hall School.

At 18.00hrs, the body of a German airman was washed up on the foreshore at Shoebury. The only effect found on him was an identity disc (No. 57359/326).

21 MAY

At 20.00hrs, a further station dance in aid of Wings for Victory week was held at Earl's Hall School. The target of £1,000 was beaten, the total figure raised being £1,247 19s 2d.

23 MAY

The station chaplain, Squadron Leader (Revd) A.R. Bradshaw, conducted a Drumhead Service at Rochford for their Wings for Victory week. RAF personnel attended the parade.

25 MAY
At 11.00hrs, the German airman, washed up on the foreshore at Shoebury on the 19th, was buried at Sutton Cemetery (Grave No. 13502).

28 MAY
A Spitfire Mk Vb (EN905) of 124 Squadron, North Weald, made a heavy landing at the aerodrome after a failure of the oleo locking unit. The port hydraulic jack, port mainplane and flap were also damaged and the aircraft was categorised 'A/C'.

29 MAY
Pilot Officer D.J. Graham (137768), RAF Regiment, was posted here from RAF Kingscliffe.

30 MAY
A Spitfire Mk Vb (EN788) of 315 Squadron, Northolt, made a heavy landing here, causing starboard oleo leg pintle bolts to shear off. The starboard mainplane and flap were also damaged and required replacement.

Gas exercises were held weekly during this month.

Physical training was carried out daily by 2810 Squadron, RAF Regiment, 287 Squadron (an anti-aircraft co-operation squadron, which had arrived from RAF Croydon), and the WAAFs.

Sports events for the month:

The Station Cricket 1st XI played four matches, winning two, drawing one and losing one.
Inter-section Cricket: three matches were played.
The WAAF cricket team was being formed.
Cricket practice was carried out three times a week at the nets at Station Headquarters.
Tennis was provided free on hired courts, and a station team was being formed.
Badminton was being played regularly by all ranks.
Table tennis, billiards and darts facilities were used by all ranks.

JUNE

2 JUNE
Sergeant R.S. Sunnocks (911681), the photographer at the station, was mentioned in despatches. (*London Gazette*, 2 June 1943.)

6 JUNE
Pilot Officer C.A. Maple (130764) A&SD was attached to 11 Group School, Beddington, for a station personnel course.

7 JUNE
Section Officer P.E. Barton (2532) WAAF (G) was posted to RAF Manston for WAAF

(G) duties (a flight officer post). At 20.00hrs, ENSA presented the play *Dangerous Corner* at the Concert Hall, Earl's Hall School.

8 JUNE
Flying Officer J.C.E. Roberts (87118) A&SD was posted to 11 Group, supernumerary for administration duties.

9 JUNE
The Nore Lightship was removed today and replaced by the present Nore Fort. Orders were issued that Southend Pier be blown up in the event of the enemy coming close to landing, and the army rigged demolition charges between the two pier heads.

11 JUNE
Section Officer A.F. Holloway (3257) WAAF (G) was posted here from RAF Heston.

12 JUNE
137 Squadron and 3054 Echelon arrived from RAF Manston this morning and spent the day settling down. The squadron, flying Westland Whirlwinds, was in the process of being re-equipped with Hurricane Mk IVs.

13 JUNE
A little flying was carried out by 137 Squadron during the day and in the evening. Flight Lieutenant John M. Bryan (102570), Flying Officer John E. McClure (J/15505) with Warrant Officers Arthur G. Brunet (J/17907) and Joe H. Ashton (J/17890) of 137 Squadron flew to RAF Manston and operated from there during the night as follows: Flight Lieutenant Bryan (up at 01.07hrs, down at 02.30hrs) took off to bomb POLX Aerodrome (halfway between Abbeville and Gervais). He did not succeed, however, in locating the target so dropped two 250lb bombs on railway tracks near Abbeville. He was engaged by searchlights and flak but returned unscathed to Manston. The three other pilots turned back before crossing the French coast owing to unfavourable weather conditions.

14 JUNE
Pilot Officer C.B. Brook (130814) A&SD was attached to the station from RAF Northolt, for anti-gas/fire duties.

Six Whirlwinds of 137 Squadron flew to RAF Manston in the evening and operated from there as follows: Warrant Officer Ashton (up at 00.50hrs, down at 02.15hrs) set out to bomb POLX Aerodrome, which he eventually found owing to obstruction and other lights being switched on. He dived from 8,000ft to 700ft, firing a six-second burst of cannon fire and releasing two 250lb bombs, which were seen to explode on the south side of the runway. A number of strikes were seen in the vicinity of an enemy aircraft entering the runway that had its navigational lights switched on. No flak or searchlights were experienced.

Flying Officer McClure (up at 02.25hrs, down at 03.15hrs) dropped two 250lb bombs on a barge near Dixmude from 100ft, claiming it as destroyed. After searching unsuccessfully for trains and then shipping, he returned home.

Flight Lieutenant Bryan (up at 02.25hrs, down at 03.45hrs) found a train in the Roulers area, and dropped two 250lb bombs in a dive from 3,000ft to 100ft which appeared, however, to overshoot. He then made three attacks with cannon, seeing strikes on the engine causing intense steam and a brilliant three-second flash. Quite a lot of flak was experienced during this sortie.

Flying Officer Joseph L. DeHoux (J/15145) (up at 02.25hrs, down at 03.30hrs) patrolled the area from Poperinghe–Ghent–Ypres, and finally found two barges near Roulers on which he dropped two 250lb bombs from tree-top height, observing a big red explosion with debris flying in all directions. Another two barges were claimed as destroyed by him.

Warrant Officer Brunet (up at 00.55hrs, down at 02.05hrs) took off to bomb the Amiens-Glisy Aerodrome, but was unable to locate the target. He attacked a stationary goods train at Felixecourt with a two-second burst of cannon and dropping a 250lb bomb, observing strikes on the engine, whilst experiencing light flak from both ends of the train. On the way home, he inadvertently passed over Abbeville Aerodrome at 200ft and was greeted with intense and accurate light flak and searchlights, his aircraft receiving a hit on the fuselage. He dropped his other bomb very close to the runway.

Flight Sergeant John Barclay (655794) (up at 00.55hrs, down at 01.55hrs) set course for Abbeville, but returned to base owing to the weather being unsuitable; a large amount of cloud over the French coast.

15 JUNE

A few Hurricane Mk IVs were delivered to 137 Squadron today, despite the intention to keep the Whirlwinds until the end of the moon period before handing them over to 263 Squadron. The following Whirlwinds operated from RAF Manston during the night: Squadron Leader John B. Wray (37834) (up at 00.00hrs, down at 01.00hrs), on the way out to attack POLX Aerodrome, crossed the French coast at Cayeux and immediately afterwards a Fw 190 crossed in front of him. He fired a short burst from close range and saw a flash on the enemy aircraft's tail but could not observe any further results owing to the dazzling effect on his guns. He then dropped two 250lb bombs on POLX Aerodrome which was unlit, and pulled away without interference from any flak.

Flying Officer McClure (up at 00.05hrs, down at 01.30hrs) dropped two 250lb bombs on the centre of the Amiens-Glisy Aerodrome.

Flight Lieutenant Bryan and Flying Officer DeHoux (up at 01.20hrs, down at 02.40hrs) dropped four 250lb bombs on Coxyde-Furnes Aerodrome without observing results but intense light flak was experienced. The pilots then separated and Flying Officer DeHoux cannoned a tug and two barges on the Ghent-Bruges Canal, observing many strikes. After making a shipping reconnaissance to Gravelines, he returned to base. Flight Lieutenant Bryan attacked two barges in the same canal, seeing strikes and flying debris. He then made three attacks on a goods train, obtaining several strikes all over the engine and fire truck. Flak and searchlights were experienced by both pilots on crossing the enemy coast both ways.

Warrant Officer Brunet (up at 02.25hrs, down at 03.20hrs) could not find Coxyde-Furnes Aerodrome and bombed two barges on the Ypres Canal, scoring a direct hit on one and seeing the other keeled over on its side. There was plenty of flak and searchlights from coastal areas.

16 JUNE

A Hurricane Mk I (V7744) of 287 Squadron, while taxiing, collided with a Spitfire Mk Vb (W3829) which was parked on the edge of the airfield. The port mainplane of the Hurricane was badly damaged and the aircraft was classified category 'A', the mainplane being replaced by personnel of 287 Squadron. Spitfire W3829 of RAF Northolt was also classified category 'A', the oil tank, cowling and one coolant pipe being damaged. Repairs were carried out by personnel of 3054 Servicing Echelon.

Operations for the night due to be carried out by 137 Squadron from RAF Manston were cancelled owing to adverse weather conditions and the six Whirlwinds returned home early the following morning.

17 JUNE

Local flying began with 137 Squadron using the Hurricane Mk IVs during the day, and during the night offensive operations were carried out as follows: Squadron Leader Wray (up at 23.59hrs, down at 00.55hrs) dropped two 250lb bombs on POLX Aerodrome in a dive from 8,000 to 6,000ft, with bursts seen close to the runway.

Warrant Officer Ashton (up at 00.40hrs, down at 02.05hrs) saw the flare path of POLX Aerodrome lit up and so dropped two 250lb bombs in the middle of the runway from 600ft and fired a four-second burst of cannon at the hangars, obtaining strikes.

Flight Lieutenant Bryan (up at 00.50hrs, down at 02.09hrs) dropped two 250lb bombs on the runway of POLX Aerodrome in a dive from 7,000 to 3,000ft.

Warrant Officer Brunet (up at 00.11hrs, down at 01.05hrs), on the way out to POLX Aerodrome, sighted two 'E-Boats' 2 miles off Quend Plage. He attacked the second boat, dropping two 250lb bombs in a beam attack. They struck the water 15 to 20ft short, causing the boat to lift and turn 90° to face the shore and then stop. He then cannoned the same target, seeing strikes.

Flight Sergeant Barclay (up at 00.22hrs, down at 00.45hrs), after orbiting the base, landed again as his electrical equipment was u/s.

Flying Officer John Luing (121527) (up at 00.25hrs, down at 01.44hrs) bombed the southern runway of POLX Aerodrome in a shallow dive from 4,500 to 2,000ft.

Flying Officer McClure (up at 01.07hrs, down at 02.29hrs) saw lights on at the same aerodrome, and dropped his two 250lb bombs, seeing them burst in the centre of the runway.

Flying Officer DeHoux (up at 01.13hrs, down at 02.14hrs) bombed the same aerodrome with hits either on or very near to the runway.

Flight Sergeant Barclay (up at 02.00hrs, down at 03.12hrs) could not locate the aerodrome but saw a stationary train of twenty covered trucks in a siding at Rue. He released two 250lb bombs from 200ft while cannoning the target, observing explosions and multiple strikes among the wagons. Three light flak positions in the vicinity opened fire on him and his aircraft was hit, though not causing serious damage.

18 JUNE

The weather was suitable for 'rhubarb' operations and eight Whirlwinds of 137 Squadron took off during the afternoon but were all forced to return before reaching the French coast owing to insufficient cloud cover.

19 JUNE

Night operations again took place from RAF Manston with 137 Squadron. Flying Officer DeHoux (up at 01.10hrs, down at 02.50hrs) saw several leading-in lights on the Amiens-Glisy Aerodrome and, diving from 6,000ft to deck level, released two

250lb bombs on the perimeter track. He then dived from 3,000 to 1,000ft on a stationary train seen in a marshalling yard south-east of Amiens, firing his cannons and obtaining strikes on the engine.

Flight Sergeant Barclay (up at 01.10hrs, down at 02.40hrs) bombed the runway at POLX but was experiencing trouble with searchlights before getting there.

Warrant Officer Ashton (up at 01.05hrs, down at 02.40hrs) also bombed the runway of the same aerodrome, going in just before Sergeant Barclay.

Flying Officer Luing (up at 01.20hrs, down at 02.45hrs) orbited the Amiens-Glisy Aerodrome for about ten minutes but there was no activity there and so dropped two 250lb bombs from 500ft on to the aerodrome, seeing them burst amongst hangars and buildings on the western side. His aircraft was illuminated by searchlights but no flak was experienced.

Flight Lieutenant Bryan (up at 02.20hrs, down at 03.50hrs) dropped his bombs on Abbeville Aerodrome, seeing them hit the runway. Searchlights and flak was received, and after an unsuccessful search for trains, he returned home.

Warrant Officer Brunet (up at 02.25hrs, down at 03.40hrs) bombed Abbeville Aerodrome but was unable to observe the results.

20 JUNE

The Wings for Victory week, Southend-on-Sea: several officers spoke at various Southend cinemas during the week. Flying Officer Harvey presented prizes at the Boxing tournament at the Bandstand on the Cliffs.

Practice flying with Hurricanes was continued during the day by 137 Squadron, and six Whirlwinds were later flown to RAF Manston ready for night operations.

Section Officer Turnbull (2013) WAAF (G) was posted to RAF West Malling, and was replaced by Acting Section Officer P.J. Sullivan (6514) WAAF (G) who arrived here from RAF Hunsdon.

21 JUNE

The six Whirlwinds sent to RAF Manston yesterday returned at first light, unsuitable weather conditions having made operations impossible.

137 Squadron carried out local and formation flying with the Hurricanes during the day.

In the evening the Whirlwinds went to RAF Manston for night operations as follows: Squadron Leader Wray (up at 01.15hrs, down at 02.00hrs) led the attack and dropped two 500lb eleven-second delayed-action bombs on POLX Aerodrome without observing results.

Flight Lieutenant Bryan (up at 01.35hrs, down at 03.05hrs) released two 500lb bombs from 500ft on POLX Aerodrome; the bursts were seen on or near runway. Searchlights and flak was experienced during the attack.

Flying Officer Luing (up at 01.55hrs, down at 03.10hrs) followed in next with similar results as did Warrant Officer Ashton (up at 01.40hrs, down at 03.10hrs).

Flight Sergeant Barclay (up at 02.08hrs, down at 04.00hrs) could not locate POLX Aerodrome but dropped his two 500lb bombs from 100ft on a stationary goods train just north of Rue. He claimed it as a direct hit as a huge grey cloud of steam and dirt flew up. On his return home, the starboard exactor jammed in the 'fully open' position and the engine lost power. While trying to land, the other engine failed owing to lack of petrol and Sergeant Barclay could not get his undercarriage down, and made a forced landing in a field near RAF Manston Aerodrome. He was unhurt, but the aircraft had to be written off.

At 20.00hrs, ENSA presented *Floating Around* at the Concert Hall, Earl's Hall School.

22 JUNE

During 22 and 30 June, the moonlight period having finished, the Whirlwind aircraft of 137 Squadron were handed over to 263 Squadron, and 137 Squadron became non-operational. A number of pilots were sent on a training course on the Hurricane Mk IV at RAF Milfield, and some pilots were posted to other squadrons. At Southend, the rest of the pilots continued practice flying with little of importance occurring over the next few days.

24 JUNE

At 20.00hrs, a station dance in aid of the Southend-on-Sea Wings for Victory week was held at Earl's Hall School.

28 JUNE

Pilot Officer G.B. Brooke (130814) A&SD ceased his attachment from RAF Northolt. At 20.00hrs, the WAAF's fourth anniversary dance was held at Earl's Hall School.

29 JUNE

A Lysander III (R9001) of 1488 (FG) Flight made a forced landing due to engine failure on Ray Sand, map reference M.4919. The aircraft crashed on landing and the pilot, Sergeant Shaw (RCAF) was injured and the target towing operator, AC1 Murphy, received slight injuries; both were taken to Chelmsford General Hospital. The pilot reported that the aircraft had been airborne for twenty minutes when the engine 'cut dead' without any warning. Prior to the cut the engine had been running smoothly, oil pressure and temperature being normal. Investigation at the site of the crash did not reveal cause of failure and the Group engineer officer gave instructions for the engine, if salvaged, to be returned for examination. The aircraft was classified category 'E'.

30 JUNE

Sergeant E.A. Bolster was posted to 247 Squadron; Flight Sergeant R. Woodhouse to RAF Milfield as an instructor; Sergeant W.J. Evans to Station Headquarters, Southend; and Flying Officer R.S. Flynn, the medical officer, was posted overseas, his place being taken by Flying Officer J.E. Morgan. Flying Officer P.H.B. Unwin arrived here from 59 OTU on posting to 137 Squadron.

Gas exercises were carried out weekly during the month.

Physical training was carried out daily by 2810 Squadron, RAF Regiment, 1 and 2 Hispano and Bofors Flights, 137 and 287 Squadrons, and the WAAFs.

Sports events for the month:

The Station Cricket 1st XI played four matches, winning two and losing two.
Inter-section Cricket: Four matches were played.

Cricket practice was carried out three times a week at the nets at Station Headquarters.
Tennis was provided free on hired courts.
Badminton was being played regularly by all ranks.
Table tennis, billiards, snooker and darts facilities were being used by all ranks, and
tournaments had been arranged to take place in the NAAFI.

JULY

1–7 JULY
Very little to report during this period. Only eight pilots of 137 Squadron were available, the rest being still at RAF Milfield. Local flying was carried out and on 4 July,
firing of 40mm guns took place at Leysdown Range. Hurricanes were also flown at
different times to RAF Friston for the harmonisation of guns and on the 5th the CO
flew to RAF Sawbridgeworth with other pilots to look at on the ground, and try to
recognise from the air, a collection of dummy tanks.

Squadron Leader Wray, Flying Officer DeHoux, Warrant Officer Ashton and Flight
Sergeant Thomas A. Sutherland (655932) left for RAF Milfield for the course; Flight
Lieutenant Alexander Torrance (64932), Flying Officers Bernhard Soulsby (126629) and
John T. Davidson (114577) and Flight Sergeants Aubrey C. Smith (156929) and Albert
Witham (1336599) returning therefrom to RAF Southend. It was learnt with pleasure
that Flight Lieutenant McClure was awarded the DFC for his work with 137 Squadron.

During the month the following pilots arrived here to join 137 Squadron: Flying
Officer Richard Curtis (63456), Pilot Officers R.W. Clarke (J/26500), H.G. Dickson
(J/26498), and R.A. Johnstone (J/22310) (all Canadians), Flight Sergeant Ronald
Wright (411878) (Australian), Flight Sergeant Charles Points (655554), and Sergeants
Lewis Boucher (658891), Jack Hayes (547410) and James Shemeld (1120717).

8–15 JULY
There was no operational flying during this period, but a large amount of practice
flying was carried out by 137 Squadron, including low flying, camera gun, formation
and low cross-country.

9 JULY
The only raid of the day was a low-level attack close to the aerodrome. High-explosive
bombs exploded in the vicinity of the EKCO works, including Thornford Gardens
and Sherbourne Gardens (both adjacent to the rear of the works), where properties
were damaged with fatalities, notably 29 Thornford Gardens, which was destroyed.
The EKCO Platoon, among their normal duties, assisted the ARP, police and Civil
Defence in rescue operations.

12 JULY
Pilot Officer W.J. Carr (62427) A&SD was posted to the station from RAF Saffron
Walden, supernumerary for administration duties.

13 JULY
Pilot Officer D.G. Graham (137768) RAF Regiment was posted here from RAF
Kingscliffe (2877 Squadron).

15 JULY
Flight Lieutenant T.J.M. Barrington (81752) A&SD was posted to Headquarters, 84 Group.

16 JULY
Flying Officer L.A. Harvey (84591), physical fitness officer, in an exchange posting, was sent to Andover for duty at Greenham Common while Pilot Officer C.H. Alexander (141967) was posted here in the exchange.

137 Squadron carried out low-flying attack practice during the day and aircraft from 'B' Flight flew to Bradwell Bay Aerodrome in the evening, and night-flying practice was carried out from there.

17 JULY
40mm cannon- and rocket-firing practice were carried out at Leysdown Range by 137 Squadron, occupying the pilots for most of the day. Night-flying practice took place from Bradwell Bay, again by 'B' Flight.

18–22 JULY
Practice flying, mainly consisting of low flying, was continued during this period by 137 Squadron. Four aircraft of 'A' Flight took off for RAF Manston for night-flying practice which had to be cancelled, however, owing to unfavourable weather conditions.

19 JULY
At 20.00hrs, ENSA presented a concert Go for It at the Concert Hall, Earl's Hall School.

20 JULY
At 14.00hrs, the Fighter Command Demonstration Flight (2713 Squadron, RAF Regiment) carried out a very instructive demonstration on the station. Personnel from all sections attended.

21 JULY
At 19.30hrs, a station dance was held at the Concert Hall, Earl's Hall School.

23 JULY
Flight Lieutenant Bryan, Pilot Officer Brunet, and Flying Officers Gordon S. Chalmers (131146) and Davidson of 137 Squadron flew to RAF Manston to carry out a 'rhubarb' operation. This was the first of this type of operation undertaken by Hurricane Mk IV aircraft using the 40mm cannons and proved highly successful. The four aircraft took off from RAF Manston at 13.10hrs. The Belgian coast was crossed in cloud at 15,000ft 2 miles west of Nieuport and a goods train was attacked near Cotemark by all pilots and the engine disintegrated. Two other goods trains were found at Statiestrate. Bryan and Chalmers attacked one, seeing strikes and leaving it covered in dirty black smoke. Brunet and Davidson dealt with the other, resulting in its engine's disintegration with the boiler knocked off the bogies. Intense light flak was experienced here. Near Lightervelde, Brunet and Chalmers shot up a large army lorry, and at Thielt a small train was attacked by all pilots and was left emitting black smoke. Two barges were cannoned next and badly damaged and the four aircraft crossed out at Nieuport in cloud

and returned to this station via RAF Manston, landing at 15.00hrs. The weather was 10/10ths cloud, base at 800ft with good visibility.

24 JULY

Today, six aircraft again flew to RAF Manston for 'rhubarbs'. Flight Lieutenant Bryan leading Pilot Officer Brunet, Flight Sergeants Witham and Clarence Neal (413236) of 137 Squadron, took off from RAF Manston at 13.10hrs and landed there by 14.30hrs to carry out an attack on transport targets in the Bruges-Ghent area. The Belgian coast was crossed 2 miles north of Nieuport in cloud at 2,000ft and all pilots attacked a goods train on the Thourot–Ostende line leaving it thoroughly broken up. Another train was found on the outskirts of Deynze and, again, all pilots were responsible for leaving it emitting smoke and steam up to 400ft. As the last pilot was finishing his attack, Brunet sighted three Fw 190s about 3 miles away at deck level. He warned the others over R/T and they all turned into the enemy aircraft with the intention of getting into cloud. Brunet got in a four-second burst of machine-gun fire and six 40mm shells from 1,000 yards, closing to 200 yards on one of the enemy aircraft from nearly head-on. Although no strikes were observed, the Fw 190 pulled suddenly away with a lot of bluish-grey smoke pouring from it.

Flight Sergeant Witham was attacked whilst climbing and, realising he could not reach cloud cover without being shot down, attempted a stall turn at 1,200ft, but went into a spin only finally being able to pull out at 300ft. Climbing for cloud (the base of which was 1,500ft) he was again attacked just before entering it, a cannon strike removing about 14in from one of his propellers. Flight Lieutenant Bryan, seeing all aircraft now safe, ordered them to base and, setting course for Dunkirk in and out of cloud, he went on alone to attack a goods train near Kruiske, observing strikes on the engine, with pieces flying off. As he broke away, he felt a bang in his port wing and saw a hole evidently caused by a Bofors shell. His ASI pipe was also severed. He also received light flak when crossing out at Furnes.

Flying Officers Davidson and Soulsby were airborne from RAF Manston at 14.10hrs and headed for railway and barge targets in the Bruges-Boulers area, but with the weather having cleared up, were forced to abandon the operation and landed back at RAF Manston at 14.20hrs.

In the meantime, practice low flying was continued at RAF Southend, but an accident put a halt to it when Sergeant J.A. Hayes (547410) hit the sea with his propellers and crash-landed on the ground, writing off the Hurricane but fortunately receiving no injury to himself.

25 JULY

Practice flying was carried out by 137 Squadron, including local flying for the new pilots, and low flying, formation and camera gun.

26–28 JULY

137 Squadron continued practice flying over the next few days, mainly comprising cross-country, camera gun, low flying and formation.

29 JULY

A big programme of firing RPs and 40mm cannon was carried out by 137 Squadron at Leysdown Range during the day with very good results.

30 JULY
A fair amount of practice flying was carried out by 137 Squadron, mainly consisting of low flying.

Squadron Leader J.C. Stone (74569), RAF Regiment, was posted to RAF Castle Camps for duty as LDA.

31 JULY
Low and formation flying and camera-gun practice was carried out by 137 Squadron during the day. A most unfortunate accident occurred during dogfight practice in the morning, resulting in the loss of Flight Sergeant Barclay and one Hurricane. He was out as No. 1 to Pilot Officer R.A. Johnstone and diving from 2,000ft on order to shake him off, but could not pull out of the dive and hit the ground, his aircraft bursting into flames near Maldon, Essex. Barclay must have been killed instantly.

Flying Officer G. Wallis, engineering officer, was replaced in an exchange posting by Pilot Officer D.P.L. Moore.

ATC Camps 3 July 1943–10 July 1943
Flying Officer Burton of 1389 Squadron and sixteen other ranks of 376 Squadron attended summer training camp.

17 July 1943–24 July 1943
One officer and fifty other ranks of 1389 Squadron and one officer and twenty other ranks of 1163 Squadron attended summer training camp.

24 July 1943–31 July 1943
One officer and fifty-one other ranks of 12(F) Squadron and one officer and twenty-three other ranks of 337 Squadron attended summer training camp.

Gas exercises were held weekly during the month.

Physical training was carried out daily by 2810 Squadron, RAF Regiment, 137 and 287 Squadrons, 3054 Echelon and the WAAFs.

Sports events for the month:

The Station Cricket 1st XI played five matches.
Inter-section Cricket: two matches were played.
Tennis is provided free on hired courts.
Inter-section Tennis: the station team played two matches (mixed).
Athletics: daily training for personnel participating in local sports meetings.
Badminton was being played regularly by all ranks.
Table tennis, billiards, snooker and darts facilities were being used by all ranks in the NAAFI.

AUGUST

1 AUGUST

Flight Lieutenant E.J. Poole (85240) GD was posted here from RAF Eastchurch for PDP duties.

Flight Lieutenant Bryan of 137 Squadron was awarded a Bar to his DFC for his consistent good work and leadership with the squadron. His score to the present was one Do 217 destroyed and one Fw 190 probably destroyed (both shared), thirty-five locomotives destroyed or damaged, two minesweepers, one 'E-Boat' and five barges damaged, besides bombing of enemy aerodromes, etc. Flying Officer DeHoux also received the DFC for his excellent work with 137 Squadron.

Quite a lot of practice flying took place during the day, mainly comprising formation cloud flying, cross-country, camera-gun attacks and low-flying formation.

2 AUGUST

Practice flying was continued by 137 Squadron throughout the week and it was learnt that the squadron would be returning to RAF Manston on 8 August.

Flight Lieutenant (Acting Squadron Leader) A.A. Dodd (89907), RAF Regiment, was posted here from RAF Castle Camps for duty as LDA.

At 20.00hrs, ENSA presented *Merry Go Round* at the Concert Hall, Earl's Hall School.

6 AUGUST

Squadron Officer D. Smith (36) WAAF carried out a Group staff visit of the WAAF section. Flight Lieutenant L. Arnold (100654) (Engineering) made a staff visit of the Electrical Section.

8 AUGUST

137 Squadron and 3054 Servicing Echelon moved to RAF Manston.

9 AUGUST

Pilot Officer S.B. Simpson (51402) (Technical Engineering) was attached to the station from RAF Hornchurch for duty as station engineering officer.

11 AUGUST

2810 (AA) Squadron, RAF Regiment, 1, 2, and 3 Hispano Flights, proceeded to RAF Filey for a two-week course of anti-aircraft basic training.

13 AUGUST

In another day of staff movement, Flying Officer R. Foulsham (101616) (Catering) left this station to attend a catering officers' conference at Headquarters, 11 Group.

Flying Officer G.H. Warren (112819) (Equipment) was posted here from RAF Hornchurch for duty as station equipment officer, and Flying Officer (Acting Flight Lieutenant) D.W. Compton (103313) (Equipment) was posted to RAF Gatwick for equipment duties.

14 AUGUST

2766 Squadron, RAF Regiment, arrived from RAF Merston.

16 AUGUST
At 20.00hrs, ENSA presented *Bobbie Hind and his Band* at the Concert Hall, Earl's Hall School.

17 AUGUST
1488 (FG) Flight (eight officers, seventeen senior NCOs, and seventy-seven other ranks) were transferred here from RAF Martlesham Heath. Pilot Officer A.L. Nelson (130760) A&SD was posted to the station from RAF Martlesham Heath for gas/fire duties.

19 AUGUST
Flight Lieutenant T.J.M. Barrington (81752) A&SD was posted here from Headquarters, 84 Group, for administration duties.

22 AUGUST
Flight Lieutenant I.A.V. Maling (100624), GD was attached to the station from 6 AACU, Castle Bromwich.

25 AUGUST
At 19.30hrs, a station dance was held in the Concert Hall, Earl's Hall School, for all ranks.

1 and 2 Hispano Flights of 2810 (AA) Squadron, RAF Regiment, proceeded from RAF Filey to Felixstowe for a seven-day firing course.

27 AUGUST
Pilot Officer C.A. Maple (138764) A&SD was posted to RAF North Weald for gas/fire duties.

30 AUGUST
At 20.00hrs, ENSA presented *Mumming Birds* at the Concert Hall, Earl's Hall School.

31 AUGUST
Flight Officer D.R. Pitts (1900) WAAF carried out a Group visit of the WAAF Section.

A Republic Aviation P-17 Thunderbolt (16367) piloted by Lieutenant G.A. Compton flew in to RAF Southend for refuelling, but overshot on landing, and the pilot applied the brakes too hard causing the aircraft to nose-over. The propeller was damaged and the engine required shock load testing, but the pilot was unhurt.

At 15.14hrs, a station exercise 'Beetumup' was held in conjunction with troops from the Southend and Shoebury Garrison. The object was to test the station defences and to carry out orders as laid out in the revised Battle Scheme dated August 1943.

At a 'Post Mortem' conference about 'Beetumup', the weak points were brought to light, but umpires generally agreed that the station defences were sound at the four points chosen for the attacks and that these attacks were repelled by day but with slight infiltration by night.

Gas exercises were held weekly during the month.

Physical training was carried out daily by 2766 Squadron, RAF Regiment, 1488 (FG) Flight, 287 Squadron, Station Headquarters and the WAAFs.

Sports events for the month:

The Station Cricket 1st XI played two matches and won both.
Inter-section Cricket: three matches were played.
Tennis was provided free on hired courts.
Badminton was being played regularly by all ranks.
Table tennis, billiards, snooker and darts facilities were being used by all ranks in the NAAFI, games room, Officers' Mess and Sergeants' Mess.
Rugby, soccer and hockey trial matches were being held for the winter season.

SEPTEMBER

1–6 SEPTEMBER
Normal station activities were carried out; nothing of particular interest to record.

7 SEPTEMBER
The Southend Wing: at 09.00hrs, 611 Squadron, led by Squadron Leader William Douglas (90896), arrived with twenty-four pilots and eighteen Spitfire Mk Vs from RAF Coltishall, and spent the day settling in.

610 Squadron, led by Squadron Leader Laury, DFC also arrived in the morning from RAF Bolt Head with twenty-eight pilots and seventeen Spitfire Mk Vs. To accommodate the squadrons, 1488 (FG) Flight relinquished their Dispersal.

During the day Group Captain Morgan, DSO, DFC, Wing Commander Flying at RAF Coltishall and Squadron Leader Newbury, DFC and Bar arrived to fly with the 'Southend Wing'.

During the afternoon there was preliminary warning that the wing might be required for an operation during the evening, but this was finally cancelled. Meanwhile, the station intelligence office was transformed into the wing Briefing Room.

8 SEPTEMBER
Shortly after breakfast a briefing was held and at 09.30hrs the Southend Wing took off for Part II of Ramrod S.41, as close escort to seventy-two Martin B-26 Marauders. The wing consisted of twelve aircraft of 611 Squadron and twelve aircraft of 610 Squadron, along with an independent four (nicknamed the 'Terrible Four') comprising Group Captain Morgan, Wing Commander Lucas, DFC, Squadron Leader Kingaby and Squadron Leader Newbury.

Everything went according to plan and the bombing appeared very good, with hits being observed on dispersal buildings and the perimeter. Light flak was experienced on the way to and from the target. Four Fw 190s tried to decoy the escort from the bombers, but dived away when threatened. Wing Commander Lucas' aircraft was attacked by one of six enemy aircraft, receiving hits on the starboard wing causing the ammunition to explode. When 10 miles south of Dunkirk he was attacked by a Me 109 with under-slung cannons, but managed reach RAF Manston, where his aircraft was categorised 'B'.

A Marauder was seen to go down into the sea west of the Goodwin Sands on the return journey and the crew were seen to be picked up an ASR launch. The wing landed back at RAF Southend at 11.05hrs with the exception of Wing Commander Lucas, who arrived after lunch from RAF Manston in a Magister.

During the afternoon, another briefing was held, and at 17.05hrs the wing, composed as this morning, took off on Ramrod S.42. Their role was close escort to twelve out of a formation of eighteen Mitchell bombers to the gun positions in the Cap Gris Nez area. Moderate heavy flak bursting below was experienced near Hardelot on the way in, and again near Boulogne on the way home. Near-direct hits were seen on the gun posts but there were some near misses. No enemy aircraft were seen or plotted and the wing landed back at RAF Southend at 18.15hrs.

At 19.00hrs, all pilots had to attend the Briefing Room, and at dusk they returned to Dispersal. It had been whispered that tomorrow should be the 'big day'. The squadron's release came through but at the same time orders were received that all aircraft had to have distinctive markings in the form of three black-and-white stripes painted on the main planes parallel to the fuselage. All crews immediately got to work with string, chalk, brushes and distemper, and by midnight the job was completed.

9 SEPTEMBER

Operation Starkey: all personnel were called at 03.45hrs, and after an early breakfast at 04.15hrs, the machines of the Southend Wing were warmed up and ready on the line by 05.00hrs. Unfortunately a dawn mist descended and did not clear sufficiently until 08.00hrs, causing the wing to miss the first show.

At 08.20hrs, however, the wing, consisting of the 'Terrible Four', twelve aircraft of 611 Squadron and twelve aircraft of 610 Squadron, took off to patrol between Calais and Le Touquet 15 miles inland at 12,000ft. This area was patrolled between 08.45hrs and 09.30hrs and a number of accurate bombing attacks were observed on the docks, harbours and beaches. Twenty to thirty enemy aircraft were seen flying inland at 15,000ft over the Calais area but no contact could be made with them. The wing returned home at 10.05hrs.

At 14.20hrs, the wing, comprised as before, took off on a 'ramrod' to act as close escort to bombers to Merville Aerodrome. Rendezvous was made on time and course set. Ten enemy fighters were seen on the way flying at 20,000ft 2 or 3 miles ahead, but they made no attempt to intercept the bombers. Heavy flak came up near the target where the bombing appeared slightly off; many bursts were seen north of the aerodrome. On the return journey a vertical heavy flak barrage was put up near Dunkirk and seven enemy aircraft followed the formation at 20,000ft but did not attempt to attack. The wing returned home at 15.45hrs. Again, nobody had an opportunity to fire.

At 17.05hrs, the wing again took off for a 'ramrod' hoping the third time would prove lucky. Rendezvous was made with the other fighter wings but the bombers did not turn up, causing the wing to be recalled and it landed home at 17.50hrs. More disappointment to everybody and then at 18.30hrs, an order was received instructing that the exercise was completed and the squadrons were to return to RAF Coltishall the next day. Work was immediately started washing off the black-and-white distemper and to return all the ammunition to the store.

Flight Lieutenant Barrington (administrative officer) was posted to RAF Heston.

10 SEPTEMBER

A very foggy morning. The aircraft of 610 Squadron should have taken off at 10.00hrs, with the road party departing immediately afterwards, and the rail party leaving after lunch. However, owing to the bad weather, only the 'private cars' party got away, leaving this station at 14.00hrs. At 17.00hrs, the aircraft took off, but could not get through a very thick bank of fog and cloud that extended over the whole of the eastern counties, and landed back at the station to everybody's delight. Without exception, the visitors enjoyed their stay and spoke admiringly of the way in which the station organisation had dealt with the sudden influx of visitors.

11 SEPTEMBER

Fog and low cloud prevented flying today.

12 SEPTEMBER

During the past forty-eight hours, the following messages were been received from Air Vice Marshal Saunders, OB, CBE, MC, DFC, MM, AOC, 11 Group:

Please convey to all pilots, ground crews and control staff my appreciation of the whole hearted and enthusiastic way in which they have responded to every demand made upon them during the last few weeks. Splendid results in air fighting have been obtained during the relatively few occasions when weather conditions did not interfere with our planned operations. I share with you the keen disappointment you will feel so much enthusiasm and effort was not permitted by bad weather alone to reap the harvests of victories which otherwise I know would have resulted.

From Commanding General Eighth Air Support Command:

I desire to express our appreciation of the support given by your groups to units of this Command which engaged in Operation Starkey. The high degree of co-operation and co-ordination and the excellent escort given to our units contributed immeasurably to the success of the missions. It would be appreciated if you would convey our appreciation to those squadrons which supported our units.

From Starkey Air Force Commander:

On completion of this operation I would be grateful if you would accept and convey to all your squadrons, pilots and ground crews my sincere appreciation for the whole hearted and splendid work carried out by them with so much enthusiasm and success in this operation and in spite of bad weather conditions particularly today. I share with them the disappointment they will feel that so much bad weather robbed them of the added experience and victories they would otherwise have obtained. It is now considered opportune to state briefly what exercise Starkey in fact was. It was an exercise designed to bring the Hun fighters to battle. It is known that the number of enemy fighters has increased considerably and the intention was to reduce their number in general air combat. Although the exercise proved most useful information for future combined operations, the real purpose was not achieved. The enemy were wily fish and would not rise to the bait. Instead of countless dogfights our pilots had to be content with 'stooge' patrols.

13 SEPTEMBER

A bright morning heralded the end of a very pleasant week for 611 Squadron at Southend. At 10.00hrs, the squadron took off and landed at RAF Coltishall forty minutes later. The rail party and the transports left immediately after packing and clearing up, arriving in there time for supper.

Pilot Officer Simpson, the station engineering officer, was posted to RAF Ford.
At 20.00hrs, an ENSA concert was given on this station.

16 SEPTEMBER

234 Squadron arrived with Mustangs from RAF West Malling for fourteen days of air-firing practice. In the evening the RAF Gang Show gave an entertaining performance.

17 SEPTEMBER

Air-to-air firing practice was carried out most of the day by 234 Squadron. In the evening a Sergeants' Mess dance was held in Earl's Hall School.

18 SEPTEMBER

The weather was unsuitable for air firing, and only a few pilots of 234 Squadron were able to do any practice firing. In the evening a dance was held in the Officers' Mess.

19 SEPTEMBER

With an improvement in the weather, 234 Squadron were able to carry out air-to-air firing practice every day until the end of the month.

26 SEPTEMBER

This station participated in the 'Battle of Britain' celebrations in Southend, and an RAF detachment marched with members of the Royal Navy, Army, Civil Defence, etc. to a church service held in the town. This was followed by a march past, the salute being taken by Squadron Leader Kingaby, Officer Commanding, Southend.

27 SEPTEMBER

In the evening an ENSA concert was given in the Concert Hall, Earl's Hall School.

30 SEPTEMBER

At 20.00hrs, RAF Station, Hornchurch Concert Party gave a show.

Gas exercises were held weekly during this month.

Physical training was carried out daily by the Bofors Flight, 2 and 3 Hispano Flights, 2766 Squadron, RAF Regiment, 1488 (FG) Flight, 287 Squadrons, and the WAAFs.

Sports events for the month:

The Station Cricket 1st XI played two matches, winning one and losing one.
The Station Soccer XI Team was chosen after a trial game: Possibles *v.* Probables.
The Station Rugby XV Team was chosen after three practice games.

The RAF XI and WAAF hockey XI teams were chosen after practice games.

Tennis was provided free on hired courts.

Badminton was being played regularly by all ranks in the gymnasium at Station Headquarters.

Table tennis, billiards, snooker and darts facilities were being used by all ranks in the respective games rooms.

OCTOBER

1 OCTOBER
234 Squadron carried out air-to-air firing all day today.

2 OCTOBER
234 Squadron carried out air-to-air firing from 10.00hrs until 16.00hrs. The following ATC squadrons were attached to the station for the purpose of competing for the station commander's annual trophy: 337 (Hammersmith); 640 (Southend); 930 (Westcliff); 1115 (Southend); 1312 (Southend); 1474 (Billericay); and 1341 (Thames Estuary).

The athletic part of the competition took place on the sports ground of the Southend High School and was won by 337 Squadron of Hammersmith.

The WAAF, which had been accommodated in Earl's Hall School, was transferred to the priory today.

3 OCTOBER
A bright and sunny day; 234 Squadron carried out air-to-air firing from early morning until last light.

The ATC squadrons completed the annual competition by demonstrating their efficiency in signalling, aircraft recognition, physical training, general knowledge and drill, all of which took place at the Earl's Hall School. The proceedings terminated with a squadron parade and march past to the band of the Southend ATC Wing. The salute was taken by Air Vice Marshal Sir William G.S. Mitchell, KCB, CBE, DSO, MC, AFC and the trophy presented by Squadron Leader Kingaby to the winning Squadron, 1312 Squadron (Southend).

4 OCTOBER
Air firing and air tests were carried out all day by 234 Squadron. Squadron Leader Richard Barnett (26222) informed the squadron today that they would soon be going overseas, but he being a dominion (New Zealand) pilot would not be allowed to go with them. He had been with the squadron only a short time, but had proved himself a fine leader and was highly respected by every member.

5 OCTOBER
There was no flying today as heavy mists continued throughout the day. Squadron Leader Barnett was preparing to leave the next day to take up his posting for duties as commanding officer of 501 Squadron. A farewell party was held in the mess and was a great success.

The move of the Station Headquarters from Earl's Hall School to Manners Corner Flats commenced today.

6 OCTOBER

Flight Lieutenant Ernest 'Dave' Glaser, DFC, Flight Commander of 'B' Flight, 234 Squadron, was appointed Acting CO pending the posting of a new squadron commander. Air firing took place in the morning, but bad weather closed down flying for the afternoon. Another loss to the squadron was Sergeant Harris, who was posted away to join 124 Squadron.

The move of the Station Headquarters was completed today, and a station dance was held in the evening.

7 OCTOBER

Air-to-air firing was carried out all day, completing the course at RAF Southend for 234 Squadron.

The Sergeants' Mess moved from Rochford Golf Club House to Manners Corner Flats. The administration staff and the majority of the senior NCOs other than aircrew were now housed within easy distance of the airfield.

8 OCTOBER

234 Squadron received instructions to move to RAF Hutton Cranswick the next day, together with 3038 Servicing Echelon. The squadron was to be re-formed there.

9 OCTOBER

All the ground crew and equipment of 234 Squadron left by rail today. The weather was too bad to fly the aircraft there.

10 OCTOBER

Bad weather continued until 13 October; all aircraft were grounded.

12 OCTOBER

The main party of 350 Squadron arrived from RAF Hawkinge, but the weather was still too bad for their aircraft to fly in.

13 OCTOBER

Seventeen aircraft of 350 Squadron flew in during the afternoon despite the continuing bad weather.

14 OCTOBER

All aircraft were grounded owing to the persistent bad weather.

15 OCTOBER

The weather improved a great deal today, and 350 Squadron began air-to-air firing practice with nineteen sorties being flown throughout the day. At 11.30hrs, 234 Squadron moved to RAF Hutton Cranswick.

16 OCTOBER

Air firing was continued today by 350 Squadron with exceptional weather conditions, twenty-nine sorties being flown today, and another twenty-five the next day.

18 OCTOBER

17 Armament Practice Camp (APC). RAF Southend became 17 Armament Practice Camp today by re-designating 1488 (Fighter Gunnery) Flight. Their aircraft were four Lysanders: Mk I (R2638), Mk II (N1227), Mk III (T1741), and Mk IIIA (V9795); two Masters: Mk II (AZ707) and Mk III (W8848); a Martinet Mk I (NH972); and a Spitfire Mk IX (MK184). 17 APC was commanded by Pilot Officer Robert Hugh Barber (42385), previously of 46 Squadron, and then current commander of AP Camps at RAF Warmwell and RAF Martlesham Heath, to train pilots, including American P-51 pilots, on the new gyro-gunsight.

350 Squadron continued air firing today with forty-nine sorties being flown. An aircraft recognition lecture was given in the evening.

19 OCTOBER

Air firing today by 350 Squadron with eleven sorties being flown. A lecture on range, line and deflection was given by Squadron Leader Boussa, DFC. An aircraft recognition lecture was given in the evening.

20 OCTOBER

350 Squadron carried out a number of successful sorties over the next few days: forty-nine today, twenty-nine on the 21st, forty-nine on the 23rd and twenty-six on the 24th.

25 OCTOBER

The weather was very bad today, and there was no flying. Orders were received for 350 Squadron to return to RAF Hawkinge.

ENSA gave a concert *The Show Boat* in the Rochford Senior School, kindly lent for the purpose by the Essex County Council.

26 OCTOBER

349 Squadron arrived from RAF Friston for air-firing practice. Major General Liardet, Director General of Ground Defences, arrived to inspect 2766 RAF Regiment Squadron.

The main party of the ground staff of 350 Squadron returned to RAF Hawkinge, having completed the air-firing practice course. The departure of the aircraft was delayed owing to bad weather.

27 OCTOBER

The weather remained very bad; no flying was possible until 31 October. Section Officer M. Longshaw was posted to this station as assistant adjutant. The body of a German airman was picked up the beach at Foulness. It had been in the water for some time but was thought to be that of a sergeant.

29 OCTOBER

The body of the German airman, picked up on the 27th, was buried at Sutton Road Cemetery, Southend.

31 OCTOBER

With an improvement in the weather, the remainder of 350 Squadron, including aircraft, returned to RAF Hawkinge.

Gas exercises were held weekly during the month.

Physical training was carried out daily by the Bofors and Hispano Flights, 2766 Squadron, RAF Regiment, 1488 (FG) Flight, 287 Squadrons, and the WAAFs.

Sports events for the month:

The Station Soccer XI played six matches, winning five and losing one.
Inter-section Soccer League: six matches were played.
The Station Rugby XV played three matches, winning one, losing one, and drawing one.
The Station (RAF) Hockey XI played three matches, winning one, losing one, and drawing one.
The Station (WAAF) Hockey XI played two matches, winning one, and losing one.
Tennis was provided free on hired courts.
Table tennis, billiards, snooker and darts facilities were being used by all ranks in the respective games rooms.

NOVEMBER

1 NOVEMBER
A very quiet start to the month; nothing of interest was recorded. Group Captain Moore, from Headquarters, 11 Group, visited the station.

9 NOVEMBER
349 Squadron returned to RAF Friston on completion of air-firing practice.

10 NOVEMBER
2834 and 2703 (AA) Squadrons, 83 Group, Tactical Air Force (TAF), arrived and were accommodated in winter quarters.

15 NOVEMBER
The Allied Expeditionary Air Force (AEAF) was formed to control the RAF and USAAF units during the forthcoming Invasion of Europe, under the command of Air Chief Marshal Sir Trafford Leigh-Mallory.

RAF Fighter Command was renamed Air Defence Great Britain; Air Marshal R.M. Hill was appointed AOC-in-C.

16 NOVEMBER
66 Squadron arrived for armament training until the end of the month. No operational flying was carried out, and the squadron went all out on air firing training. During this period both the squadron adjutant (Flying Officer R.H. Mann) and the squadron intelligence officer (Flying Officer S.P. Lucas) were unfortunately posted from the squadron to 135 Airfield Headquarters. Both had been with the squadron for a considerable time, and everyone was sorry to hear that they were to be no longer with them. Rumours had also been heard that the squadron was to be transferred to the Tactical Air Force, but nothing was stated officially. It was a period of chaos and

reconstruction in the affairs of the squadron. A piece of good news welcomed by the whole squadron was that Flight Lieutenant G. Kilcombe, the 'B' Flight commander, had been awarded the DFC.

17 NOVEMBER
Flight Lieutenant Mercer (medical officer) arrived here from RAF Detling.

18 NOVEMBER
Two postings away from the station today: Flight Lieutenant Smart to RAF Hawkinge, and Squadron Leader Holloway to RAF Manston.

19–21 NOVEMBER
Normal station routine; nothing of interest was recorded.

22 NOVEMBER
ENSA presented the play *Othello* in the Concert Hall of the EKCO Radio Factory in Priory Crescent, Prittlewell.

23 NOVEMBER
Squadron Leader Rawnsley, agricultural officer, visited the station.

24 NOVEMBER
2831 Squadron, RAF Regiment, arrived from RAF Shoreham for training.

25–29 NOVEMBER
Normal station routines were carried out until the end of the month. On the 26th, a Spitfire (MH422) of 129 Squadron crashed at the aerodrome.

30 NOVEMBER
66 Squadron returned to RAF Hornchurch on completion of air-firing practice. 3026 Servicing Commandoes arrived to service 317 (Polish) Squadron, which was due to arrive on 2 December for air gunnery practice.

Gas exercises were held weekly during the month.

Physical training was carried out daily by the Bofors and Hispano Flights, 2766 Squadron, RAF Regiment, and 17 APC.

Sports events for the month:
The Station Soccer XI played seven matches, winning three and losing four.
Inter-section Soccer: eight matches were played.
The Station Rugby XV played five matches, winning one, and losing four.
The Station (RAF) Hockey XI played six matches, winning two, losing three, and drawing one.
Table tennis, billiards, snooker and darts facilities were being used by all ranks in the respective games rooms.

DECEMBER

2 DECEMBER
At 13.25hrs, sixteen aircraft of 317 (Polish) Squadron, led by Squadron Leader Franciszek Kornicki (P-0695), arrived from RAF Northolt for air-to-air firing practice. All the pilots were present at the lecture on the firing programme and range instructions.

3 DECEMBER
The adverse weather meant that no flying could be carried out. Instructional films on air-to-air and air-to-ground firing were shown to the pilots of 317 Squadron. In the course of the day, all pilots attended lectures on photo camera, 20mm cannon and machine gun.

4 DECEMBER
With the improvement of the weather air-to-air firing was carried out by 317 Squadron during the whole of the day. Altogether 35,246 rounds of ammunition were spent.

5 DECEMBER
This morning films of the previous day were shown and flying on air-to-air firing continued by 317 Squadron.

6 DECEMBER
Air-to-air firing was continued throughout the day by 317 Squadron. ENSA presented *Dorchester Follies* in the Concert Hall of the EKCO Radio Factory.

7 DECEMBER
In the morning, a lecture was given on the harmonisation of guns and machine guns, and later in the day flying on photo attacks were carried out by 317 Squadron as well as some pigeon shooting.

8 DECEMBER
The weather was unsuitable for flying and lectures on 40mm Vickers 'S' gun, ammunition for Browning machine gun and 20mm cannon took place. This station was visited by the Group senior medical officer.

9 DECEMBER
The bad weather spell continued. The pilots of 317 Squadron attended a lecture on gun cleaning, and later in the day pigeon shooting took place. The physical fitness officer of the South-Eastern Command visited the station.

10 DECEMBER
The weather improved enough today to allow air-to-air firing practice to be resumed by 317 Squadron. Pilot Officer Butler was posted to RAF Hornchurch, and Pilot Officer Grassby was posted here from RAF Hornchurch, as MT officer.

11 DECEMBER
Today air-to-air firing both with guns and machine guns was carried out by

317 Squadron. Flight Sergeant Zych was involved in a flying accident. He had taken off with his section on firing practice, but on returning his engine failed and he had to force-land. Although he was unhurt, his aircraft sustained serious damage.

The body of a German airman was washed ashore at Foulness Island at 16.45hrs. According to effects found it would appear to be that of 510/57358 Ober Gefreiter Herbert Mechsner (b. 23 April 1923). Medical opinion gave cause of death as due to drowning. The body had not been in the sea for more than forty-eight hours. There was an alert on Southend on Friday 10 December when bombs were dropped. Several people expressed the opinion that a machine was seen to dive into the sea at approximately 19.45hrs. It was observed that the watch found on the body of the German airman had stopped at about this time.

A station defence exercise 'Noel' was held between approximately 20.00hrs and 02.00hrs.

12 DECEMBER
There was no flying today owing to the bad weather. Films of the previous day's flying were shown. In the afternoon revolver shooting took place.

13 DECEMBER
Air-to-air firing was continued today by 317 Squadron.

14 DECEMBER
Flying consisted of two aircraft of 317 Squadron doing photo attacks. The other pilots were engaged in watching films of the previous day's firing.

15 DECEMBER
Air-to-air firing was continued today. The burial of the German washed ashore at Foulness on the 11th, took place at Sutton Road Cemetery, Southend.

16 DECEMBER
The air firing course ended for 317 Squadron today, but they were unable to return to Northolt owing to bad weather.

17 DECEMBER
Continuous bad weather meant that 317 Squadron was still at the station.

18 DECEMBER
With a slight improvement in the weather, sixteen aircraft of 317 Squadron, led by Squadron Leader Kornicki, took off for RAF Northolt in the afternoon. Despite the very difficult flying conditions all the aircraft landed safely after the forty-minute flight.

20 DECEMBER
Nothing of importance to record. ENSA presented *Music Hall 1943* in the Concert Hall of the EKCO Radio Factory.

21 DECEMBER
222 Squadron arrived from RAF Hornchurch for air-firing practice.

23 DECEMBER

Air-to-air firing began today for the pilots of 222 Squadron. The assistant command salvage officer visited this station. The station sick quarters moved from 'Retford' to 'Greenways', which offered larger accommodation.

24 DECEMBER

Air-to-air firing continued today by 222 Squadron, the last before they enjoyed a break over the Christmas period.

25 DECEMBER

Christmas Day. An excellent dinner was served in each of the three messes and was thoroughly enjoyed by all. A grand party and dance was held in the evening at Medway Court. The Station Voluntary Band was in attendance.

26 DECEMBER

Air-to-air firing continued today by 222 Squadron. A dance was held in the Sergeants' Mess.

27 DECEMBER

222 Squadron returned to RAF Hornchurch on completion of air-firing practice.

28 DECEMBER

A fancy dress dance was given in the evening by the WAAFs.

30 DECEMBER

Command Defence Officer Brigadier C.R. Britten, MC visited the station and inspected RAF Regiment personnel.

31 DECEMBER

At 14.23hrs, a Flying Fortress (23089) of 338 Bomb Squadron 'V' USAAF, Snetterton Heath, was forced by lack of fuel to land at the aerodrome. The aircraft was returning from operations and the No. 1 oil radiator had been hit by flak, thus putting No. 1 engine out of action. The aircraft was categorised 'A/C' and required a new engine and oil radiator. The pilot, Lieutenant Ingram, and a crew of nine were uninjured.

Gas exercises were held during the month.

Physical training was carried out daily by the Bofors and Hispano Flights, 2766 Squadron, RAF Regiment, 287 Squadron and 17 APC.

Sports events for the month:
The Station Soccer XI played two matches, winning one and drawing one.
Inter-section Soccer: eight matches were played.
The Station Rugby XV team played three matches, winning one, and losing two.
The Station (RAF) Hockey XI played three matches, winning one, and losing two.
Table tennis, billiards, snooker and darts facilities were being used by all ranks in the respective games rooms.

5
1944

JANUARY

During 1944, four V1 flying bombs fell in the borough; one near Blenheim Chase, Leigh, killing nine people; and three at Bournes Green, Thorpe Bay, without the loss of life. The flying bombs, or doodlebugs as they were often referred to, could be instantly recognised by the droning sounds they made as they flew across the sky. When the propulsion ceased, and no flames extended from the rear, it would only be a matter of minutes before they would drop down and crash, exploding on impact. However, as terrifying and devastating as the effects of these flying bombs were, they were not as frightening as the rockets that had been developed and would soon follow. They appeared from nowhere with no warning at all.

3 JANUARY
413 R&SU arrived at the station to complete the formation of their unit.

5 JANUARY
124 (Baroda) Squadron arrived with their Spitfire Mk VIIs at this station from RAF West Malling for armament practice. Since 1941, the squadron had operated several variants of the Spitfire on bomber escort and high-altitude reconnaissance duties.

6 JANUARY
The '12th Night Dance' for all station personnel was held in the dining hall at Medway Court.

10 JANUARY
A rifle- and pistol-shooting competition commenced today between Station Headquarters, 17 APC, 287 Squadron and the RAF Regiment.

11 JANUARY
This day marked the beginning of the air operations designed to support the Allied invasion of France (Operation Overlord).

14 JANUARY
The rifle- and pistol-shooting competition had run satisfactorily, and there had been some keen competition.

15–17 JANUARY
Normal routine duties.

18 JANUARY
124 Squadron returned to RAF West Malling today.

20 JANUARY
501 Squadron with 3037 Echelon arrived from RAF Hawkinge for armament practice.

21 JANUARY
Flight Lieutenant N.W. Wickham, FCO of this station assumed the duties of air-sea rescue officer.

21/22 JANUARY
The Luftwaffe launched Operation Steinbock, a bomber offensive against targets in the UK – primarily London – in retaliation for RAF Bomber Command attacks on Berlin. Although attacks on the capital continued until the night of 20/21 April 1944, the results of this 'Baby Blitz' were poor and Luftwaffe losses at the hands of Fighter Command's night-fighters were heavy.

From late April, German attacks switched to the ports of southern England, in which shipping for the forthcoming Allied invasion of north-west Europe was already massing. However, once again the offensive yielded little tangible results for the Luftwaffe, at a high cost in men and machines.

25 JANUARY
A district court martial was held at the station today to try AC1 Meager (1865527) and Corporal Attwell (1200531).

26 JANUARY
A signal was received today about posting away of the station adjutant, Flight Lieutenant S.R. Judd, to 51 OTU, Hawarden, and the posting in of Flight Lieutenant N.E. Houghton from Combined Headquarters, Dover.

27 JANUARY
The Group public relations officer visited the station.

28 JANUARY
Squadron Leader Shewry from the Air Ministry ADO visited the station. The Flying Fortress that landed here on 31 December 1943 took off today, having been fitted with a replacement engine.

29 JANUARY
Section Officer Sullivan WAAF (G) was posted away. Flight Lieutenant N.E. Houghton reported to the station for duty as station adjutant.

In the late evening the aerodrome was attacked by enemy aircraft. Some 300 incendiaries were dropped but fortunately there were no serious casualties, and the damage caused was almost negligible.

31 JANUARY
Normal routine duties.

Gas exercises were held during the month.

Physical training was carried out daily by the Bofors and Hispano Flights, 2766 Squadron, RAF Regiment, 287 Squadron and 17 APC.

Sports events for the month:
The Station Soccer XI played four matches, winning three and drawing one.
Inter-section Soccer: eight matches were played.
The Station Rugby XV played three matches, winning one, and losing two.
The Station (RAF) Hockey XI played three matches, winning one, and losing one.
2834 Squadron, RAF Regiment received swimming instruction at Romford Baths.
Table tennis, billiards, snooker and darts facilities were being used by all ranks in the respective games rooms.

FEBRUARY

The US Strategic Air Forces in Europe began a sustained daylight offensive in February 1944 aimed at destroying the Luftwaffe on the ground by attacking the German aircraft industry, and in the air by combat. With escort all the way to the target, fewer bombers were lost while at the same time the Luftwaffe suffered increasingly heavy losses to the escort fighters.

1–2 FEBRUARY
Normal routine duties.

3 FEBRUARY
2703 Squadron, RAF Regiment, moved to RAF Catterick.

4 FEBRUARY
501 Squadron left for RAF Hawkinge today. In the late evening the aerodrome was attacked by enemy aircraft. Fortunately very few incendiaries fell and many which did failed to ignite, and as with last week, no high-explosive bombs were dropped on the aerodrome.

6 FEBRUARY
41 Squadron arrived from RAF Tangmere for armament practice.

7–9 FEBRUARY
Normal routine duties.

10 FEBRUARY
A lecture was given in the afternoon by an American officer on 'America and the American Life'.

11 FEBRUARY
A Flying Fortress (231694) of 511 Squadron USAAF Polebrook, piloted by Lieutenant Frank W. Turbyne, returning from operations over Frankfurt with casualties aboard,

came in to RAF Southend. On landing, the aircraft overshot and crashed into the defence post on the embankment of Warner's Bridge at the south-east corner of the airfield, and caught fire. The crew of eleven were assisted from the aircraft and admitted to hospital. The aircraft was burnt extensively and categorised 'E', and subsequently moved from the road and back on to the airfield.

12 FEBRUARY

2834 Squadron, RAF Regiment, moved out today. In the late evening there was an enemy attack in the vicinity but fortunately nothing was dropped on the aerodrome.

15–18 FEBRUARY

Normal routine duties. In the evening a dance was given by WAAF personnel on the station, and was well attended.

20 FEBRUARY

41 Squadron returned to RAF Tangmere today on completion of air firing. A Tiger Moth (DE374) of the squadron flipped over on to its back whilst taking off. The apparent cause of the accident was due to the aircraft becoming airborne too soon. Four main planes, fin, rudder, fuel tank, starboard front interplane strut and propeller were damaged. The aircraft was categorised 'A/C'. The crew was uninjured.

Eight officers from various squadrons reported to the station for a week's course with seventeen APC on the new gyro gunsight.

A Consolidated B-24 Liberator (2100340) of 578 Squadron USAAF Wendling, returning from a mission to Berlin, force-landed with 'wheels up' owing to lack of fuel, in a field near Paglesham, Essex (map reference M. 3713). One member of the crew of ten had been injured by enemy action. The nose of the aircraft and the underside of the fuselage was extensively damaged. A second B-24 (#340), also from 578 Squadron, had suffered severe damage from enemy aircraft fire, losing two engines. The pilot nursed the crippled plane across the Channel, losing height all the way to a crash-landing at Southend Aerodrome.

21 FEBRUARY

Pilot Officers Finlay and Garruthers were posted here for flying control duties.

22 FEBRUARY

312 (Czech) Squadron, led by Squadron Leader František Vancl, DFC (operating as part of the 2nd Tactical Air Force as a fighter-bomber unit with Spitfire Mk IXs), arrived at this station today for air-firing practice.

23 FEBRUARY

No flying was carried out today owing to adverse weather. Pilot Officer Fletcher reported to the station on posting as MT officer.

24 FEBRUARY

The bad weather continued; no flying today. A visit was received by Flight Lieutenant Joy, Command physical fitness officer.

25 FEBRUARY

With slightly better weather, 312 Squadron carried out practice ground strafing.

26 FEBRUARY

With 10/10ths cloud at 2,000ft and visibility reduced to 2 miles, three sections only of 312 Squadron carried out practice ground strafing.

27 FEBRUARY

312 Squadron carried out practice ground strafing.

28 FEBRUARY

312 Squadron carried out practice bombing today. The first gyro gunsight course was completed today, and a fresh batch of pilots reported to this station.

29 FEBRUARY

312 Squadron carried out bombing practice and air-to-air firing.

Gas exercises were held during the month.

Physical training was carried out daily by the Bofors and Hispano Flights, 2766 Squadron, RAF Regiment, 287 Squadron and 17 APC.

Sports events for the month:

The Station Soccer XI played five matches, winning all.
The Station Rugby XV played three matches, winning two, and losing one.
Inter-section Rugby: eight matches were played.
The Station (RAF) Hockey XI played four matches, losing all four.
Table tennis, billiards, snooker and darts facilities were being used by all ranks in the respective games rooms.

MARCH

1 MARCH

312 Squadron carried out practice ground strafing, and one section on cannon test.

Posting Notice was received this morning attaching the commanding officer, Squadron Leader Kingaby, to RAF Kenley for flying duties. The advance party of 2729 RAF Regiment, TAF, arrived.

An Oxford Mk II (HN143) of 287 Squadron landed at the aerodrome with damage to the aircraft consisting of a broken top starboard front Perspex panel, a dent in the top of the nose of the fuselage and slight damage to the underside of the port mainplane. The damage might have been caused by a sudden and violent change in atmospheric pressure as there were no abrasions in the vicinity of the damaged areas. The aircraft was categorised 'A'. The pilot was uninjured, but his passenger suffered slight facial injuries.

Squadron Leader B.P.A. Vallance reported here (supernumerary) to take over duty as commanding officer.

2 MARCH

312 Squadron carried out practice dive-bombing, and two sections also practised ground strafing.

3 MARCH

312 Squadron moved out today to RAF Mendlesham, Suffolk. The squadron went on to operate over France, softening up targets in preparation for the invasion and then supporting the D-Day landings.

17 APC held a dance in the evening to which all sections of the station were invited.

4 MARCH

Squadron Leader Kingaby and Squadron Leader Vallance, the new station commander, completed the handing over today.

In the evening, a dance was held in the Officers' Mess to which lady guests were invited, and it also served as a farewell party for Squadron Leader Kingaby, who was returning to operational flying.

6 MARCH

331 (Norwegian) Squadron arrived from RAF North Weald for flying practice with 17 APC. Flying Officer E.C. Skinner was posted here for code and cypher duties.

7-12 MARCH

With adverse weather conditions, the bombing training for 331 Squadron was carried out on only three days during their seven-day attachment; one day only suitable for air-to-ground firing.

13 MARCH

331 Squadron and its Echelon returned to RAF North Weald.

14 MARCH

313 Squadron and its Echelon arrived for flying practice with 17 APC.

15 MARCH

Sergeant Bedrich Kratkoruky (110669) of 313 Squadron from RAF Mendlesham intercepted a Heinkel He 111 over Canvey Island in the early hours. He chased it towards Southend and attacked it. The enemy aircraft lost height with both engines smoking, and crashed into the sea off Shoeburyness.

Sergeant Pilot Jindrich Konvicka (788221) of 313 Squadron overshot on landing at this station in Spitfire Mk IX (MK609) and crashed at the boundary at the north-west side of the airfield. The undercarriage was torn off, the port wing was torn off, and the starboard wing and the propeller were damaged. The aircraft was categorised 'E'. The pilot escaped injury.

Information received this morning was that an Air Field Construction Flight was to be accommodated on the station.

Acting Section Officer D.B. Midforth was attached to the station (supernumerary) for assistant adjutant duties.

16–17 MARCH
Normal routine duties.

18 MARCH
A district court martial was held today for AC1 Stoves, 413 R&SU.

A Spitfire Mk IX (MJ639) of 17 APC nosed into the ground while waiting for take-off due to the slipstream of another section taking off. The propeller was damaged and the engine shock load test; the aircraft was categorised 'A'. The pilot was uninjured.

19–21 MARCH
Normal routine duties.

22 MARCH
At approximately 01.20hrs, a Ju 88 was shot down and crashed at Wakering. The aircraft burned extensively; four bodies were recovered from the wreckage.

23 MARCH
4790 AC Works Flight arrived.

24-25 MARCH
Normal routine duties.

26 MARCH
A Spitfire Mk IX (MH720) of 332 Squadron, RAF North Weald, taxied into a starter trolley. The propeller was damaged, port wheel fairing damaged, and engine shock load test. The aircraft was categorised 'A'. The pilot was uninjured.

27 MARCH
Four German airmen from the aircraft shot down on the 22nd were buried at Sutton Cemetery.

313 Squadron moved out today having completed their course. Flight Lieutenant J.N. Marchbank was posted here for flying control duties.

28 MARCH
Eighteen aircraft of 310 (Czech) Squadron, along with its Servicing Echelon, arrived at this station during the afternoon from 134 Airfield. Sergeant Bedrich Froehlich (788257) followed along behind, with Sergeant Karel Posta (787624) as passenger in their Tiger Moth, landing an hour later.

The commanding officer visited Headquarters, 11 Group, to attend an administrative conference.

29 MARCH
Damp and cloudy weather meant there was no flying practice for 310 Squadron. A Spitfire Mk IX (MJ893) of 17 APC Southend landed with the 'wheels up'. The port and starboard main planes were damaged; the fuselage wrinkled around the cockpit and the propeller was damaged. The aircraft was categorised 'B'. The pilot was uninjured.

30 MARCH

A great improvement in the weather today and 310 Squadron carried out twelve bombing practice sorties and three flights also engaged in local flying.

31 MARCH

Air-to-ground firing sorties were practised for most of the day by 310 Squadron. However, on returning to Southend, Flying Officer Karel Zouhar (130858) in Spitfire Mk IX (MJ291) found that although his undercarriage was working, the locking pins failed to work. After informing 'Ops' he decided to land. The starboard wing tip, flap, IFF aerial and port undercarriage jack were damaged.

A second crash at this station today occurred when a Hurricane Mk IV (KZ398) of 287 Squadron landed with the port wheel retracted, causing damage to the port wing tip, flap and pressure head. Both aircraft were categorised 'A' and neither of the pilots sustained any injury.

Gas exercises were held during the month.

Physical training was carried out daily by the Bofors and Hispano Flights, 2766 Squadron, RAF Regiment, 287 Squadron and 17 APC.

Sports events for the month:

The Station Soccer XI played four matches, winning all four.
Inter-section Soccer: four matches were played.
The Station Rugby XV played two matches, winning one, and losing one.
Inter-section Rugby: eight matches were played.
The RAF Station Hockey XI played three matches, losing all three.
Swimming instruction was given twice weekly for the RAF Regiment.
Tennis had just commenced being playing on a hired PSI court.
Table tennis, billiards, snooker and darts facilities were played at Medway games room, Sergeants' Mess and Officers' Mess.

APRIL

1 APRIL

A dull morning with rain at intervals. No flying was done by 310 Squadron except by one pilot on a weather test at 10.30hrs, and a flight in the squadron's Auster to RAF Biggin Hill and back to obtain spares for MJ291.

An exercise code-named 'Paragen' was held during the night when all station personnel manned their defence localities and the aerodrome was attacked by units of 33 RHU.

2 APRIL

No flying was done today; another dull day with rain and visibility was very low.

3 APRIL
Sixteen aircraft of 310 Squadron left for Appledram (near Chichester). Two of the aircraft (MJ722 and MJ291) remained here as they were still undergoing repairs.

4 APRIL
222 Squadron arrived from RAF Hornchurch for bombing practice with 17 APC. A visit was made by Flying Officer Shields from RAF Biggin Hill, who lectured the WAAF on welfare.

5-6 APRIL
Normal routine duties.

7 APRIL
A visit was made by Pilot Officer Hayle, Headquarters, ADGB, on electrical engineering duties.

8 APRIL
Normal routine duties. In the evening a dance was held at the Officers' Mess, to which many local residents were invited.

10 APRIL
Normal routine duties.

11 APRIL
222 Squadron left the station, and instructions were received by signal that three Polish squadrons of 135 Airfield would be stationed here the next day for three days each, for firing practice with 17 APC.

12 APRIL
302 (Polish) Squadron arrived for firing practice until 14 April. Twelve of their aircraft took off on a 'ramrod' as close escort for bombers to an airfield south-east of Bruges. Heavy moderate flak was experienced, and all aircraft returned safely. The remainder of the squadron carried out local flying.

13 APRIL
Twelve aircraft of 302 Squadron took off on a 'ramrod' on target and withdrawal support.

A district court martial held today for the trial of AC2 M. Brook (1097346), of 17 APC.

A Hurricane Mk IV (LE398) of 287 Squadron landed here with the undercarriage retracted. The propeller, flaps, radiator, oil cooler, and air intake were damaged, and the aircraft was categorised 'B'. The pilot was uninjured.

14 APRIL
317 (Polish) Squadron arrived for firing practice until 17 April.

15-16 APRIL
Normal routine duties.

17 APRIL

A Spitfire Mk IX (MA840) of 317 Squadron overshot on landing because the flaps failed to operate. On investigation the membrane of the flaps selector was found to have broken. Damage was caused to the fuselage, main planes, undercarriage and propeller, and the aircraft was categorised 'B'.

Information was received from Headquarters, 11 Group, that 2766 Squadron would be moving out from Southend on the 22nd.

18 APRIL

308 (Polish) Squadron arrived for firing practice until 20 April.

19 APRIL

The advance party of 2766 Squadron, RAF Regiment, departed for RAF Harwell. A Spitfire Mk IX (MJ450) of 17 APC crashed upon landing, the engine having cut out. Severe damage was caused to the fuselage and main planes, and the aircraft was categorised 'E'. The pilot was uninjured.

20 APRIL

In the evening a farewell dance was held for 2766 Squadron.

21 APRIL

Normal routine duties.

22 APRIL

The main party of 2766 Squadron left to join the advance party at RAF Harwell.

22 APRIL

66 Squadron arrived at 132 Airfield for bombing and ground strafing practice. The weather was fine and many practice sorties were carried out from their first day here.

23 APRIL

Normal routine duties.

24 APRIL

A district court martial was held today for the trial of Corporal Parkes (1027814), Station Headquarters, who was acquitted of all charges.

A Spitfire Mk IX (EN565) of 66 Squadron landed badly after carrying out a dive-bombing exercise. The main planes were badly strained and fuselage frames were also believed to have been strained. The aircraft was categorised 'B'.

25 APRIL

W.e.f. 01.00hrs, RAF North Weald took over the responsibility for all cypher messages for this station, and the Cypher Office at 17 APC Southend was closed. Flying Officer McCaul, Headquarters, 11 Group, cypher officer, visited the station to superintend the closing of the section.

66 Squadron flew back to 132 Airfield during the morning.

26 APRIL
Flying Officer E.C. Skinner (code and cypher officer) proceeded on his posting to RAF Hawkinge.

27 APRIL
A visit received from Mr Campfield of No. 10 Works Area, when the question of de-requisitioning certain properties belonging to the station was discussed.

28–30 APRIL
Normal routine duties.

Gas exercises were held during the month.

Physical training was carried out daily by 287 & 291 Squadrons, 17 APC and the WAAFs.

Sports events for the month:

The Station Soccer XI played two matches, winning both.
Inter-section Soccer: four matches were played.
The Station Hockey XI played and lost the only match of the month.
Swimming: organised classes were given for the RAF Regiment.
Tennis was played regularly on a hired PSI court.
Cricket practice had commenced at the nets at Station Headquarters.
Table tennis, billiards, snooker and darts were played by all ranks in the respective games rooms.

MAY

1–2 MAY
Normal routine duties.

3 MAY
The station was still without a visiting squadron for practice with 17 APC after 66 Squadron left on 25 April, but the number of officers attending the weekly gyro gunsight course had been doubled in this week.

4–5 MAY
Normal routine duties.

6 MAY
A Hurricane Mk IV (KZ6028) of 287 Squadron, piloted by Sergeant Thomas, taxied into a barbed-wire fence during a high wind. Only the propeller was damaged and the aircraft was categorised 'A'. The pilot was uninjured.

7 MAY
Normal routine duties.

8 MAY

The station commander attended a conference of station commanders at Sector Headquarters, RAF North Weald.

A Spitfire Mk IX (LF807) of 17 APC Southend and piloted by Pilot Officer Chevers (RCAF), who was attached to them on a course, collided with a Drogue. Damage was done to port mainplane, port tailplane, elevators and rudder, and the aircraft was categorised 'A'. The pilot was uninjured.

9 MAY

Lieutenant Mears, naval administrative officer of Headquarters, ADGB, visited the station in connection with the naval attachment, which was to be here for some time to come.

10 MAY

At 20.30hrs, a telephone call was received from the RTO to the effect that ten officers, ten senior NCOs and 186 other ranks of 991 Squadron had been at this station since 16.30hrs, but had been unable to make contact with the receiving unit.

The movement was apparently so secret that the squadron themselves did not know to whom they were reporting and the receiving unit also was not informed. Arrangements were immediately made to bring the squadron and its equipment into the station and all were provided with a hot meal and placed into their billets by 23.00hrs.

Martinet 585 of 17 APC Southend, piloted by Warrant Officer Gibson, taxied into a starter trolley, causing damage to the engine.

11 MAY

A stricken Flying Fortress (107147) PU-C *Sweet Melody* of 36 (US) Squadron was returning from Saarbruecken, Germany; flak had knocked out the navigator's oxygen, one outboard engine and had blown off one of the bomb bay doors during its second bomb run. The pilots, Lieutenant Anthony Cecchini and Lieutenant Edward J. Veigel, had flown back at very low altitude across the Channel to the English coast, where they located Southend Aerodrome. Making a landing with only two engines running, the aircraft just missed a concrete ammunition building, crashed through a fence, and in doing so lost the landing gear, and bellied into a ditch. All the crewmen survived the difficult landing, and were hospitalised at Southend General Hospital. Despite the damage the aircraft was salvageable.

12 MAY

At 11.15hrs, 19 Squadron arrived for week of bombing and gunnery practice, giving the pilots and their ground crews (122 Airfield Echelon) a brief but welcome respite from operational duties. They spent the day settling in to their new quarters. An informal squadron 'get together' was held in the evening at 'the local', where everybody seemed in good form (especially towards the end of the evening).

13 MAY

19 Squadron carried out individual dive-bombing practice throughout the day. The weather was good but hazy. A station party was held in the mess in the evening and, judging by appearances, 'hay hitting' time was thoroughly enjoyed by the squadron officers. Both the army and the navy were well represented among the guests.

14 MAY

Air-to-ground firing practice was carried out by 19 Squadron. Flight Lieutenant Bird, DFC and Bar joined '19 Pursuit'.

15 MAY

A morning of practice dive-bombing was carried out by 19 Squadron in sections of fours, with air-to-air firing in the afternoon. Pilot Officers Wendt and Staples joined the squadron today.

A Spitfire (MK312) of 17 APC Southend and piloted by Flight Lieutenant D.C. Deuntzer who was attached here on a course, taxied into a dispersal bay causing damage to the propeller spinner, the port oleo leg fairing, and the air intake cowling. The pilot was uninjured.

16 MAY

A little air-to-air firing and low-level bombing practice was carried out in the morning, but bad weather prevented any flying in the afternoon. A film on air-to-air firing, and the pilots' cine films of their practice were shown afterwards.

A visit was received from the chief armament officer, Headquarters, ADGB.

17 MAY

Ground strafing was carried out individually and in sections of four aircraft by 19 Squadron during the morning, but the exercise was abandoned due to damage done to aircraft by flying stones, etc. Air-firing practice was carried out in the afternoon.

18 MAY

Practice dive and low-level bombing was carried out in sections of four aircraft by 19 Squadron. The aircraft damaged yesterday were flown to RAF Puntington for repairs.

A visit was received from Flight Lieutenant Joy, physical fitness officer, Headquarters, ADGB.

19 MAY

More practice dive-bombing was carried by 19 Squadron. A fairly thick haze gave added interest to the bombing. In the evening most officers attended a quiet party held in a rather distant 'local'.

20 MAY

With heartfelt regret, 19 Squadron packed its bags in the morning and said goodbye to Southend. None of the men seemed very keen to resume the old camp life. 122 Squadron, led by Squadron Leader E. Joyce, DFM, arrived from RAF Puntington for a week's course of dive-bombing and gunnery practice with 17 APC.

21 MAY

Bombing practice was carried out for most of the day by 122 Squadron. A contingent of RAF personnel from the station took part in the Rochford 'Salute the Soldier' parade.

Martinet 588 of 17 APC Southend and piloted by Flight Lieutenant Khan whilst taxiing collided with a Spitfire Mk IX (MK286) piloted by Pilot Officer Cooper, who was attached here on a course. The fuselage and tail unit of the Spitfire was extensively damaged, and damage was also caused to the mainplane. The aircraft was categorised 'E'. The Martinet suffered damage to the centre section and starboard oleo leg and the port mainplane, and was categorised 'A/C'. Neither of the pilots were injured.

22 MAY

Air-to-ground, low-level, and dive-bombing practice was carried out by 122 Squadron. The squadron was joined by Flight Lieutenant Exel, and Lieutenant Nyerrod was posted away as captain of 65 Squadron to fill a flight commander post.

A visit was received from Squadron Leader MacIver, Headquarters, 11 Group, to survey the requisitioned property, and it was agreed that approximately fifty properties could be de-requisitioned. Squadron Leader MacIver was accompanied by Flight Lieutenant Simpson, Headquarters, ADGB, who was primarily interested in discussing the proposed alterations to the Watch Office.

23 MAY

The same practices as the day before were carried out by 122 Squadron. A Lightning E6Y (267435) of 402 Squadron and piloted by Lieutenant Coenen was forced to land here after receiving damage due to enemy action. The port and starboard engine propellers, and fuselage were all damaged and the booms strained. The undercarriage and rudders had been cannon shelled. The aircraft was categorised 'E'. The pilot was uninjured.

24 MAY

A hazy start to the day meant that 122 Squadron could only begin to practice air-to-air firing in the afternoon. Flying Officer Hargreaves, a new pilot, joined the squadron from Group Support Unit.

25 MAY

A clearer day than yesterday and 122 Squadron carried out bombing practice in the morning, and air-to-air firing in the afternoon.

26 MAY

A cloudy morning meant there was no flying done in the morning, but ten dive-bombing sorties were carried out in the afternoon by 122 Squadron when the cloud had dispersed sufficiently.

27 MAY

Another cloudy start to the day, and again, no flying could be done until the afternoon, when 122 Squadron carried out air-firing practice.

A two-day course for NCOs and ATC cadets commenced today, consisting of twenty boys, and a further twenty reported for a week's course on the station. Squadron Leader Holliday, Headquarters, ADGB, and Squadron Leader Commons, Air Ministry photographic representatives visited this station today.

28 MAY

Following a very interesting informal lecture given on the gyro-sight, 122 Squadron packed up and returned to RAF Puntington. The monthly full-scale gas exercise was held on this station today.

30 MAY
The Revd A.R. Bradshaw, station chaplain, proceeded on posting to RAF Wyton.

31 MAY
Normal routine duties.

Gas exercises were held during the month.

Physical training was carried out daily by 287 and 291 Squadrons, 17 APC and Station Headquarters personnel.

Sports events for the month:

The (RAF) Station XI Hockey Team played and lost the only match this month.
Parties of twenty a time were given swimming instruction from 10.00hrs–10.30hrs, Monday–Friday at the Westcliff Open-air Bath.
Tennis was played regularly on a hired PSI court, and the station team was being formed.
Squash facilities were provided in Southend.
The Station Cricket XI played five matches, winning four and losing one.
Inter-section Cricket: three matches were played.
Tug-o-War: the station team had been formed, and participated in two local sports tournaments versus local service units. They won the first, and were runners-up in the second.
Table tennis, billiards, snooker and darts were played by all ranks in the respective games rooms. The games competitions had concluded.

JUNE

287 Squadron moved in during the month with Airspeed Oxfords, Bristol Beaufighters and Lysanders in an AA and fighter co-ordinator role.

1–2 JUNE
Normal routine duties.

3 JUNE
The Southend 'Salute the Soldier' week commenced today and a contingent of the RAF and the WAAF from the station took part in the procession.

Instructions were received on the posting of Pilot Officer A. Nelson, gas and fire officer to RAF Detling. No replacement was expected.

4 JUNE
The Southend Wing of the ATC was inspected by Air Marshal Sir Leslie Gossage, KCB, CVO, DSO, MC in the morning and in the afternoon there was a Drumhead Service followed by a march past of contingents of the different services including RAF and WAAF from the station.

5 JUNE
Normal routine duties.

6 JUNE
All RAF and naval personnel on the station were paraded with arms in accordance with the Station Defence Scheme when the station commander read the Order of the Day by General Dwight D. Eisenhower, Supreme Commander, Allied Expeditionary Force.

Lieutenant (E) R.N. Hawkes, Lt (A) R.N. Mears, Pay Sub-Lieutenant Weightill RNVR, naval liaison officers at Headquarters, ADGB, reported today for discussions in connection with the naval detachment at this station.

7–9 JUNE
Normal routine duties.

10 JUNE
Allied aircraft began operating from airfields built since D-Day in Normandy. Within the first three weeks of the Normandy campaign, no fewer than thirty-one Allied squadrons had been transferred to airfields in north-western France.

Normal routine duties were carried out on the station, and in the evening a dance was held in the Officers' Mess and included guests from the Royal Navy, Royal Marines and Army, and a number of local residents.

12 JUNE
Normal routine duties.

13 JUNE
Today the V1 Flying Bomb campaign opened. During the course of the day, Flakregiment 155(W) launched the first ten V1 flying bombs (code-named 'Divers' by the Allies) against Britain from launch sites in the Pas de Calais. The designated target for the missiles was Tower Bridge. However, due to technical failures only four weapons crossed the coast. Three exploded on open ground some distance from the centre of London and caused no casualties; the fourth fell at Bethnal Green, 2 miles from the aiming point, killing six people and injuring a further nine.

17 APC was still without a visiting squadron for armament practice. A Hurricane Mk IV (LE400) of the 287 Squadron Detachment from the station force-landed at Mersea Island. Extensive damage was caused to propellers, radiator, engine and fuselage. The pilot, Flight Sergeant Bowers, was uninjured. The aircraft was categorised 'B'.

14–15 JUNE
Normal routine duties.

16 JUNE
A total of 144 V1 flying bombs crossed the Channel today. Twenty-one were shot down by fighters or anti-aircraft fire, and seventy-three reached the London area. During the next ten days, an average of a hundred V1 flying bombs fell on England every twenty-four hours.

News was received from Headquarters, 11 Group, that 2702 Squadron RAF Regiment may be arriving in next few days.

17–18 JUNE
Normal routine duties.

19 JUNE
At 18.20hrs, two Flying Fortresses, 44-6133 captained by Lieutenant A.J. Ramacitti, and 42-97942, flown by Lieutenant L.L. Burns of 525 Squadron, Kimbolton, were returning from a raid on a rocket site in occupied France when they collided in mid-air over the Thames Estuary. Ramacitti's aircraft was seen to hit Burns' aircraft just behind the pilot's compartment; they locked together for an instant before falling away. The first aircraft (44-6133) was then seen to drop into a power dive at around 8,500ft before its wings were torn off by the stress and it went crashing into a minefield from where it could not be disturbed.

The second aircraft (42-97942) seemed to be under control although it was rapidly losing height; it was at this point that the pilot and seven of the crew were seen baling out and making a parachute descent. The aircraft was then seen to cross Canvey Point and make a left-hand turn and headed towards the foreshore between Southend Pier and Canvey Point as if the pilot was attempting to land the stricken aircraft on the mud. As the aircraft came down it took an angle of 45° and crashed nose first on to the mud and exploded. The pilot and three of the crew were taken to the Naval Hospital, Westcliff, and two to Southend General Hospital. Two of the other crew were picked up dead and a third was missing. The aircraft was a complete write-off.

A signal received from Headquarters, ADGB, that 2877 Squadron RAF Regiment, less 'B' Flight, were to move from RAF Horne to this station on 21 June.

20 JUNE
One officer, one senior NCO and sixteen other ranks of 2877 Squadron RAF Regiment reported at this station today as the advance party. A flying bomb landed and exploded 2 miles north of Rochford. There were no casualties.

21 JUNE
The main party of 2877 Squadron RAF Regiment arrived.

22 JUNE
A flying bomb landed and exploded at Hockley. No casualties were reported.

23 JUNE
2877 Squadron, RAF Regiment, had now settled down and all guns were in position. A flying bomb landed and exploded at Littlethorpe Farm. No casualties were reported.

24 JUNE
Normal routine duties.

25 JUNE
A flying bomb landed and exploded at Stambridge Farm. There were no casualties.

26 JUNE
Normal routine duties.

27 JUNE
Eight barrage balloons which had broken adrift due to stormy weather came down in this area.

28 JUNE
The monthly full-scale gas exercise was held at the station. During the last few days, the 287 Squadron Detachment at the station had been increased by the addition of three Oxford aircraft together with pilots and ground crew for night flying.

29 JUNE
A small detachment of 288 Squadron consisting of one officer, two senior NCOs, and two airmen arrived for AA co-operation.

30 JUNE
A flying bomb landed and exploded at Littlethorpe Farm. There were no casualties.

Physical training was carried out daily by 287 Squadron, 17 APC and Station Headquarters personnel.

Sports events for the month:

Parties of twenty a time were given swimming instruction from 10.00hrs–10.30hrs, Monday–Friday at the Westcliff Open-air Bath.
Tennis was played regularly on a hired PSI court. The station team was being formed for fixtures commencing in July.
Squash facilities were provided in Southend.
The Station Cricket XI played five matches, winning three and losing two.
Inter-section Cricket: three matches were played.
Tug-o-War: the station team was in regular training.
Table tennis, billiards, snooker and darts: the station team beat the National Fire Service team.

JULY

1 JULY
A Mustang (21066880) 'M' of 375 Squadron (USAAF) crashed 100 yards from the eastern perimeter of the aerodrome. The probable cause of the accident was structural failure of the port elevator. Damage was extensive and the aircraft was categorised 'E'. The pilot, Flying Officer J. Thomas, USAAF, was uninjured.

2 JULY
Air Chief Marshal Sir William Mitchell, KCB, CBE, DSO, MC, AFC, commandant, London Command ATC, visited the station and inspected the ATC.

3 JULY

A Spitfire Mk IXb (MK176) of 17 APC overshot on landing. Damage was caused to port and starboard main planes, undercarriage, propeller, engine and shock load test. The aircraft was categorised 'A/C'. The pilot, Squadron Leader J.R. Cock, was uninjured.

4–5 JULY

Normal routine duties.

6 JULY

Air Vice Marshal Sir Charles A. Longcroft, KCB, CMG, DSO, AFC, from the Air Ministry, visited the station today and inspected the ATC and their accommodation, and also the arrangements made for ATC summer camps at the aerodrome.

9 JULY

A second phase of the V1 campaign commenced with the firing of the first air-launched V1. The weapons were launched at night by specially modified Heinkel He 111 aircraft; these were operated initially by the third Gruppe of Kampfgeschwader 3 (KG 3), and subsequently by Kampfgeschwader 53 (KG 53).

7–10 JULY

Normal routine duties.

11 JULY

A signal was received from 84 Group advising that 127 Squadron and its Echelon would be arriving the next day for practice with 17 APC.

12 JULY

At 14.35hrs, 127 Squadron arrived with their Spitfire Mk IXs from RAF Tangmere; their ground crew arrived by road at 16.00hrs.

The Medway NAAFI closed the previous night and was continuing in use as a sub-bar. Every effort was made to make the camp NAAFI into a social centre for the camp and arrangements were in hand for a billiard room, reading and writing room, in addition to the present canteen facilities and recently opened games room.

13 JULY

Sixteen non-operational sorties were carried out today by 127 Squadron. A cycling club had been formed in the last few weeks which was becoming quite popular and had a large number of members. It was hoped the cycling club could be used as a basis to organise more outdoor activities.

14 JULY

127 Squadron flew numerous sorties over the next few days, with practice firing being carried out; twenty-seven non-operational sorties today, thirty-one on the 15th, thirty on the 16th, and thirty on the 17th (but with no firing).

Final arrangements made with the district superintendent, Group advisor and furniture inspector with regard to movement of furniture from Medway to camp NAAFI and the painting of tables and chairs at the sub-bar of Medway to match the surroundings.

Three officers and one sergeant of 32 Group, working directly under Balloon Command, arrived at the station requesting accommodation while they carried out a survey of the district.

16 JULY
An airman sustained slight injuries when a small fire occurred in the Piquet Post at the North Gate.

18 JULY
127 Squadron flew thirty non-operational sorties today for firing practice and 135 practice bombs were dropped.

The balloon personnel departed from the station. A visit was received from Wing Officer Smith of Headquarters, 11 Group, and from Lieutenant Commander Sandifer and Lieutenant (E) R.N. Hawkes (naval liaison officers) from Headquarters, ADGB, in connection with the naval detachment at this station. A visit was also received from Flight Lieutenant Brook, Headquarters, ADGB.

19 JULY
127 Squadron flew thirty-six non-operational sorties today during which 104 practice bombs were dropped. High-dive practice was also carried out.

Spitfire NH601 of 127 Squadron was damaged on returning to base; the bottom attachment of the tail oleo strut sheared off. Damage was also caused to the stern frame. The aircraft was categorised 'A/C'. The pilot, Flying Officer Vivian M. Jack (NZ), was uninjured.

20 JULY
127 Squadron flew thirty-six non-operational sorties today during which sixty-one practice bombs were dropped. High-dive practice and air-to-air firing practice was also carried out.

A visit was received from Group Captain Charlesworth, senior dental officer, of Headquarters, ADGB.

21–22 JULY
Normal routine duties.

23 JULY
At 09.30hrs, 127 Squadron left for RAF Tangmere, followed an hour later by their Servicing Echelon. Information was received that 17 APC was being increased by about ninety men on the servicing side and that the majority of them would arrive the next day.

24 JULY
74 Squadron arrived in the afternoon with eighteen Spitfires.

25 JULY
Information was received from sector that a number of RAF Regiment squadrons would shortly be deployed in this area, bringing with them 100 40mm guns and 272 20mm guns, and that this station would be responsible for feeding and administrating a large number of those squadrons.

Wing Commander Wiggin arrived to take over the duties of Wing Commander Sims as engineering officer.

26 JULY
Practice bombing was carried out today by Spitfires of 74 Squadron. The advance party of 2805 Squadron RAF Regiment arrived.

27 JULY
Gyro-sighting and low-level bombing practice was carried out by Spitfires of 74 Squadron.

Frequent signals were received today notifying the estimated time of arrival of the advance parties of eight RAF Regiments to be administered by this station. Lieutenant Colonel Howse, commander of RAF Regiment 'F' Wing, arrived in evening and proceeded straight to his Headquarters at 137 LAA Regiment, Rayleigh. Flying Officer Kirkland also reported here today, his duties being those of adjutant to Lieutenant Colonel Howse.

28 JULY
Air-to-air and air-to-ground firing was carried out 74 Squadron. Advance parties were arriving all day, some with rations for the next day, others without rations at all. Some squadrons had been two days on the road and had consumed their rations. None of them had brought tents, cooking utensils, and in some cases, cooks.

Immediate arrangements had to be made to feed, set up tents, and commence the issue of stores of five of the squadrons who were being completely equipped by the station.

The main party of 2805 Squadron, RAF Regiment, arrived and was met by an officer of the advance party who conducted them straight to their site.

The monthly full-scale gas exercise was held on the station.

29 JULY
Air-to-air firing practice was begun by 74 Squadron, but was quickly postponed owing to bad weather.

An officer of each advance party proceeded with Lieutenant Colonel Howse to Foulness to be shown where the squadrons were going to be deployed. In the meantime, the second in command of each advance party were being fitted out with the necessary remaining stores using 3-ton lorries loaned by 2805 RAF Regiment. All of the advance parties moved to their sites with sufficient rations for two days.

30 JULY
Air-to-air firing practice was carried out until 15.30hrs by 74 Squadron. Unfortunately, Flying Officer Bates made a heavy landing in Spitfire NH546, fracturing the stern frame. The aircraft was categorised 'A/C'. Six more squadrons arrived at the station.

31 JULY
Air-to-ground firing practice was carried out by 74 Squadron. Squadrons and various miscellaneous vehicles that had broken down en route yesterday were arriving as late as 02.00hrs this morning. 2761 Squadron, RAF Regiment, the last due at this station, arrived at 21.00hrs.

Physical training was carried out daily by 287 Squadron, 17 APC and Station Headquarters personnel.

Sports events for the month:

Parties of twenty a time were given swimming instruction from 10.00hrs–10.30hrs, Monday–Friday at the Westcliff Open-air Bath.
The Station Cricket XI played two matches, winning one and losing one.
Inter-section Cricket: three matches were played.
Tennis was played regularly on a hired PSI court; the station team won all five matches played this month.
The station tennis tournament was open to all ranks of the RAF and WAAF. All first round games played off.
Tug-o-War: the station team was in regular training.
The table tennis team was affiliated to the Southend Wartime Tennis League where they played and won all three matches.

AUGUST

1 AUGUST
No flying today owing to bad weather.

2 AUGUST
No flying again today. Information was received that 287 Squadron Detachment would be leaving next Friday or Saturday for RAF Gatwick.

3 AUGUST
During the morning, cine-gun attacks were carried out by 74 Squadron, and in the afternoon high-dive bombing practice. Information was received that 17 APC would be leaving in a few days' time.

4 AUGUST
Squadron bombing was carried out today with 74 Squadron making four sorties. Quite a high standard of bombing was observed.

5 AUGUST
Air-to-air firing was carried out today by all pilots of 74 Squadron. Owing to the squadron's move, scheduled for the next day, flying ceased at midday and all aircraft were put on the top line for the return to operations.

   There was plenty of administrative activity today with flying units of the station moving out, and the settling down of the RAF Regiments.

6 AUGUST
At 18.20hrs, 74 Squadron took off for RAF Tangmere. Also leaving was a small detachment of 288 Squadron that had been here for the past two months.

7 AUGUST
There was plenty of activity today with the 17 APC Servicing Party, consisting of approximately 100 airmen and one officer, departing for Fairwood Common.

8 AUGUST
The advance party of seventeen APC departed for RAF North Weald today. A convoy from 2 MT Company, consisting of twenty-five vehicles, reported at this station in the morning and the loading of the equipment of 17 APC commenced.

9 AUGUST
The main party of 17 APC departed for RAF North Weald today. Apart from the Station Headquarters Flight, this station was now without a flying unit.

10–13 AUGUST
Normal routine duties.

14 AUGUST
Notification was received that the RAF Regiment Band (thirty-two players) would be arriving on 22 August 1944, to play to the squadrons in 'F' Wing.

15–16 AUGUST
Normal routine duties.

17 AUGUST
A flying bomb fell and exploded near the main stores on the aerodrome today, but apart from a broken window and door latch there was no other damage.

18 AUGUST
A visit was received from Squadron Leader Dinsmore, Group education officer.

19–21 AUGUST
Normal routine duties.

22 AUGUST
The RAF Regiment Band, consisting of thirty-two players, arrived and gave a concert in the Medway Theatre for an hour from 20.30hrs. Instructions were received that the station would be reduced to a C&M (Care and Maintenance) basis w.e.f. 1 September.

23 AUGUST
Normal routine duties.

24 AUGUST
In the morning, a flying bomb fell behind a row of houses in Eastwood, killing nine people, including two children. A visit was received from Wing Commander Moule and Squadron Leader McIvor, from 11 Group.

25–28 AUGUST
Normal routine duties.

29 AUGUST

Squadron Leader Davies, commanding officer, RAF Hornchurch, and Flight Lieutenant Lach, administrative officer, visited to discuss the arrangements for the taking over of the various responsibilities by RAF Hornchurch.

The station commander, Squadron Leader B.P.A. Vallance, proceeded to RAF North Weald to act as station commander there in the absence of North Weald's station commander, and Flight Lieutenant N.E. Houghton took over the duties of officer commanding, RAF Southend, which was to become a satellite again w.e.f. 1 September and was to be administered by RAF Hornchurch.

30 AUGUST

A visit was received by Wing Commander Gadney, Org. Headquarters, ADGB. All RAF Regiment squadrons in 'F' Wing would be handed over to RAF Hornchurch for administration, although the catering would continue to be done from Southend.

31 AUGUST

Normal routine duties.

Physical training was carried out daily by RAF Regiment, and the ATC Squadron on weekly courses.

Sports events for the month:

Parties of twenty-five a time were given swimming instruction from 10.00hrs–10.30hrs, Monday–Friday at the Westcliff open-air bath.
Tennis was played regularly on a hired PSI court.
The station tennis tournament: the second and third rounds, semi-finals, and the final played off successfully during the month.
Inter-section Soccer: two matches were played.
RAF Regiment Inter-section League: three games were played. The station teams entered in Southend Wartime Football League.
Hockey and Rugby meetings were held and fixtures arranged for the season.
Squash facilities were provided in Southend.
Table tennis, billiards, snooker and darts were played by all ranks in the respective games rooms.

The strength of the station as at 31 August 1944 was:

	RAF	WAAF
Officers	79	2
Senior NCOs	140	6
Other Ranks	1,840	155

EPILOGUE

RAF Southend remained in the Hornchurch Sector until the Operations Room was closed down. In May 1946, the aerodrome was de-requisitioned and handed back to Southend Corporation for civil flying to be resumed, the licence for which was issued on 31 December. Gliding for ATC cadets was already taking place there.

On 1 January 1947, civil flying was returned to the aerodrome, but it was not until Saturday 9 August that it was officially opened. Although still furnished as a wartime airfield, it boasted a 1,500-yard take-off run in each direction and Mr Bernard F. Collins, the airport manager, was expecting full night-flying equipment to be installed.

The aerodrome enclosure was open to the public free of charge, and there was already a restaurant, limited residential accommodation and a swimming pool, and tennis courts were to be constructed. Many other amenities were to be provided to make the airport a centre of aviation in the area, and a general sports centre.

The LNER had purchased land on which the Southend–Romford–London railway line bordered the airfield with the intention of building a station for the airport – the task of which was finally under way in May 2009 and opened on 18 July 2011 as part of the airport expansion plans of the Stobart Group, which had purchased London-Southend Airport.

GLOSSARY

Ack: Under the old phonetic alphabet, 'Ack' stood for the letter 'A', thus 'ack-ack' was 'A-A' or anti-aircraft artillery.

AADC: Anti-Aircraft Defence Commander.

AC1: Aircraftman First Class.

AC2: Aircraftman Second Class.

Angels: A term used in airborne radio communications. One angel was 1,000ft, thus 'angels 13' was 13,000ft of altitude.

AOC: Air Officer Commanding.

ASR: Air-Sea Rescue.

Balbo: An air fighting tactic proposed during the Battle of Britain by 12 Group Commander Air Vice Marshal Trafford Leigh-Mallory and Acting Squadron Leader Douglas Bader. In essence, the tactic involved meeting incoming Luftwaffe bombing raids in strength with a wing-sized formation of three to five squadrons.

Bale or bail out: To leave an aircraft by jumping.

Bandit: Enemy aircraft.

CFS: Central Flying School.

Circuits and bumps: A pilot training exercise in landing an aircraft and immediately taking off again. Equivalent to the American term 'touch and go'.

Circus: A bombing attack by a light bomber escorted by a strong force of fighters. Designed to get the Luftwaffe fighters off the ground, it was, if anything, geared more to that than the damage that would be caused by bombing.

CO: Commanding Officer.

Coned: When one searchlight, often radar controlled, picked up an aircraft, all of the others in the target area would swing on to that aircraft, thus 'coning' it – then the flak would be 'poured into the cone'.

Debriefing: Where all crews met with the intelligence officer to share what had happened on the raid.

DFC: Distinguished Flying Cross – medal awarded to ranks of warrant officer and above for conspicuous bravery or long-term excellence while on active service in operation against the enemy.

DFM: Distinguished Flying Medal – same as a DFC, but for ranks of flight sergeant and lower.

DSO: Distinguished Service Order.

EFTS: Elementary Flying Training School.

ENSA: Entertainments National Service Association (or 'Every Night Something Awful', as often quipped by servicemen).

Flak: In reports 'heavy flak' did not refer to the concentration or degree of flak but to the calibre observed. 'Heavy flak' referred to anything of 88mm and up while 'light flak' consisted of quick-firing 20, 30 or 40mm guns. By extension flak came to mean any grief given to you by anyone else.

Flare path: A row of lights (either kerosene gooseneck flares, or, on a more permanent base, electric lights) that marked the boundary of the runway for taking off and landing.

Flight: A bomber squadron was often divided into two flights – 'A' and 'B' – consisting of six to eight aircraft and crews, and commanded by a squadron leader who was the flight commander or leader – 'A' Flight aircraft were lettered from A-N and 'B' Flight from M-Z.

Form 540: Pages of this form make up the Operations Record Books (ORB), which included columns for date, aircraft type and number, crew, duty, time up, time down, details of sortie or flight, plus references and summaries.

Fort or Fortress: Boeing B-17 bomber. Flown by the USAAF out of Amendola and Tortorella as part of the 15th Air Force, it was not used as a bomber in the Mediterranean theatre of operations by the RAF.

Fw: Focke-Wulf.

Gooseneck Flares: Gooseneck flares were shaped like a large coffee pot, the spout being shaped like a goose's neck. It was filled with paraffin and had a wick down the spout. After being ignited a round sheet metal cover about 3ft in diameter on short legs was positioned over the flares allowing the light to shine out on to the ground and the flares were not visible from height. When mechanics or riggers were detailed for night-flying duties you would often have to lay out the flare path with gooseneck flares. To give the pilot guidance about 2 miles from the airfield a bonfire was kept burning to indicate to the pilot where to turn in and line up.

Guinea Pig: After an incident where airmen were extremely badly burned, they would be sent to East Grinstead Hospital in the UK where some of the foremost plastic surgeons of the day performed cutting-edge surgery. The term was made up by the patients themselves. Many today proudly wear the maroon tie of the Guinea Pig Club.

He: Heinkel.

Ju: Junkers.

Mainplane: One of the principal supporting surfaces of an aircraft, especially either of the wings (both wings also considered together).

Me: Messerschmitt.

MTB: Motor Torpedo Boat.

MU: Maintenance Unit. An airfield where aircraft were taken to be repaired when the work could not be done on the squadron.

NAAFI: Navy, Army, Air Force Institutes (pronounced Naffy). An organisation which attempted to bring comforts to the crews (tea and buns, cigarettes etc.) to raise morale. It ran clubs, bars, shops, supermarkets, launderettes, restaurants, cafés and other facilities on most British military bases and also canteens on board Royal Navy ships.

NCO: Non-Commissioned Officer – in the RAF this meant sergeant or flight sergeant.

OTU: Operational Training Unit.

PAC: Parachute and Cable.

Port: The left side of an aircraft as seen from the pilot's seat.

Posted: Orders sending a crewman to another station or responsibility.

RAFVR: Royal Air Force Volunteer Reserve – members of the RAF for the duration of the hostilities.

Ramrod: Similar to a 'circus', but the emphasis was on the bombing operation rather than getting the enemy fighter squadrons into battle.

Rodeo: Fighter sweeps over enemy territory.

Roadstead: Dive-bombing and low-level attacks on enemy ships at sea or in harbour.

Rover: Armed reconnaissance flights with attacks on opportunity targets.

Rhubarb: Operations when sections of fighters or fighter-bombers, taking full advantage of low cloud and poor visibility, would cross the English Channel and then drop below cloud level to search for opportunity targets, such as railway locomotives and rolling stock, aircraft on the ground, enemy troops and vehicles on roads.

Round: One cartridge of .303 ammunition. Ammunition was measured in number of rounds carried.

Scramble: Mainly a fighter term – to get airborne as quickly as possible.

Sortie: One aircraft doing one trip to target and back.

Starboard: The right side of the aircraft as seen from the pilot's seat.

Ten-tenths: No visibility because of total cloud cover. Also 10/10ths flak – very heavy concentration.

Tracer: A type of machine-gun round which glowed as it moved, showing the way to the target and allowing for adjustments in sighting. Unfortunately, this also gave away the bomber's position. Usually every fourth round was a tracer.

Weaving: A gentle form of corkscrew. An evasive manoeuvre to allow gunners maximum view around aircraft.

Wing: A unit made up of two or sometimes three squadrons.

ZZ Landing: A blind landing system using R/T instructions from the ground.

Damaged aircraft were categorised as follows:

A – Repairable at front line/first line – Squadron Engineering.
B – Repairable at second line – Station Engineering.
C – Repairable at third line – MU (Maintenance Unit) – Strip-down & Rebuild.
D – Un-repairable – Useable parts recovered to service other aircraft.
E – Un-repairable – Aircraft 'struck off charge' – Scrap.

War Weapons weeks were different from other war charities, as no money was paid by people to a named cause. This scheme encouraged a town's residents to save their money in various government accounts, such as War Bonds, Savings Bonds, Defence Bonds and Savings Certificates. Cash would be paid into post offices or banks. It would coincide with a week of parades, exhibitions and other war paraphernalia.

INDEX

If you enjoyed this book, you may also be interested in …

Flying for Freedom: The Allied Air Forces in the RAF 1939–45

ALAN BROWN   £9.99

After the Dunkirk debacle in May 1940, Britain's primary weapon of defence was her air force. The exploits of the RAF featured almost nightly in the media; the men themselves were the objects of great admiration and respect. Yet, how many of these brave airmen were not British nationals? This book explores these courageous and often undervalued men who were caught up in a web of political argument.

978-0-7524-5998-1

Voices of Southend

FRANCES CLAMP   £12.99

This fascinating book brings together the personal memories of people who have lived and grown up in Southend-on-Sea during the last century. Reminiscences range from childhood games, working days and memories of the war years, to schools, churches and some of the local characters. The stories are complemented by over 120 photographs drawn from the private collections of the contributors.

978-0-7524-3215-1

To Scale the Skies: The Story of Group Captain J.C. 'Johnny' Wells DFC and Bar

PETER CORNWELL   £12.99

This well-researched account of one man's rise through the ranks of the Air Ministry is finely illustrated with contemporary images and is an excellent testimony of what was required of air pilots during the Second World War. Wells' story is both an inspiration and a gripping account of one man's journey through a service career spanning more than three turbulent decades.

978-0-7524-6353-7

Southend at War

DEE GORDON   £12.99

Illustrated with over ninety archive photographs and documents, *Southend at War* draws on the first-hand accounts of those who were present during the dangerous years of the First and Second World Wars and is sure to appeal to everyone interested in the history of Southend.

978-0-7524-5262-3

Visit our website and discover thousands of other History Press books.

www.thehistorypress.co.uk